THE BUSINESS OF BEING A WRITER

Novels by Stephen Goldin

A World Called Solitude
The Eternity Brigade
Assault on the Gods
And Not Make Dreams Your Master
Mindflight
Trek to Madworld
Herds
Caravan
Scavenger Hunt
Finish Line

and The Family d'Alembert series (created by E. E. "Doc" Smith)

Imperial Stars
Stranglers' Moon
The Clockwork Traitor
Getaway World
Appointment at Bloodstar
The Purity Plot
Planet of Treachery

Novels by Kathleen Sky

Death's Angel
Vulcan!
Birthright
Ice Prison

THE BUSINESS
OF BEING
A WRITER

Stephen Goldin and Kathleen Sky

1817

HARPER & ROW, PUBLISHERS, New York
Cambridge, Philadelphia, San Francisco,
London, Mexico City, São Paulo, Sydney

THE BUSINESS OF BEING A WRITER. Copyright © 1982 by Stephen Goldin and Kathleen Sky. All rights reserved. Printed in the United States of America. No part of this book may be used or reproduced in any manner whatsoever without written permission except in the case of brief quotations embodied in critical articles and reviews. For information address Harper & Row, Publishers, Inc., 10 East 53rd Street, New York, N.Y. 10022. Published simultaneously in Canada by Fitzhenry & Whiteside Limited, Toronto.

FIRST EDITION

Designer: Sidney Feinberg

Library of Congress Cataloging in Publication Data

Goldin, Stephen.
   The business of being a writer.
   Bibliography: p.
   Includes index.
   1. Authorship. 2. Authors and publishers. I. Sky,
Kathleen. II. Title.
PN151.G6   1982   808'.02   81–48035
ISBN 0-06-014977-9   AACR2

82 83 84 85 86   10 9 8 7 6 5 4 3 2 1

Dedicated to our agent

JOSEPH ELDER

in the fond hope
he'll become a multimillionaire
on his 10 percent

Contents

Acknowledgments

The authors would like to thank the following friends and colleagues for sharing their experiences, expertise, and information:

Joseph Elder, David Gerrold, D. C. Fontana, Jerry Pournelle, Robert Heinlein, Norman Spinrad, George Scithers, Frederik Pohl, L. Sprague de Camp, Catherine de Camp, Damon Knight, Merrill Miller, Lee Killough.

And a special thanks to Jane Fultz, who asked us to teach the courses that eventually led to this book.

Preface

This book came about as a result of our teaching a course in science-fiction writing at California State University, Northridge. We'd been instructing our students in the delicate art of writing and felt it would be cruel to send them out into the real world unprepared for the hardships they'd face there. We devoted one class session, near the end, to the business aspects of writing. When the three-hour session was over and we'd scarcely even begun, we knew this was a subject that needed further treatment.

We persuaded the university to let us teach a course exclusively on business practices—and found that even fifteen classroom hours weren't enough. When we learned that one of our students was regularly commuting to our class from San Diego (a round trip of over 250 miles one night a week), we realized how desperately this knowledge is needed. Since there are many more people who simply can't afford to take university extension classes, it seemed only logical to reach out to them by writing a book.

A few caveats are in order. We are both full-time professional writers, and we admit to being prejudiced in favor of writing to *sell,* rather than for personal amusement or artistic merit. We write primarily science fiction and fantasy novels, although we do have diverse backgrounds. In addition to writing novels, Stephen Goldin has also been, among other things, a technical writer, an editor of a weekly underground newspaper, editor of the *Bulletin of the Science Fiction Writers of America,* a short-story writer, and the editor of an anthology of original stories. Kathleen Sky has been a short-story writer, a reviewer, a writer of nonfiction articles, and an interviewer, in addition to being a novelist. Both of us have read slush-pile submissions for other editors. We can thus give a broad overview of writing, though our most specific examples will come from experiences in our own field.

A note on gender: Women are just as likely as men to be authors, agents, editors, and publishers. The English language, however, still has no acceptable third-person pronouns that imply this duality. Thus, while we have tried to avoid sexist terms wherever possible, there are places where style and good grammar force us to use the impersonal "he/him/his" when referring to a person of unspecified gender. The American publishing industry offers an outstanding example of male/female equality of opportunity, and it's not our intent to imply otherwise.

The Business of Being a Writer is for the freelancer working in the print media—primarily magazines and books. Survival in the dramatic media—theater, radio, TV, and movies—is a separate world altogether. We've caught enough glimpses of it to know that it merits a book of its own, but it's beyond the scope of this one.

Writing is a crazy profession, and every rule we state in this book is bound to have exceptions. The true professional, however, knows what the rules *are* before callously violating them and always has a specific reason for doing so. The rules became the rules, after all, because they work most of the time.

STEPHEN GOLDIN and KATHLEEN SKY

Sylmar, California

1

A Career in Writing

The general public has two conflicting images of what a "writer" is like. The first is Writer-as-Celebrity. This is the writer who wears expensive clothes, appears on TV talk shows, is invited to all those fabulous jet-set parties, is the soul of urbanity, smokes either a pipe or a cigarette in a long holder—and who works perhaps an hour or two a week, genteelly turning out a best-seller once every two or three years. Names like Truman Capote, Gore Vidal, and Joan Didion come to mind.

The second image is Writer-as-Artist. This is the writer who wears faded jeans and old sweat shirts, who sits hunched in a one-room apartment day after day behind a manual typewriter surrounded by stacks of paper, who drinks, smokes, or takes drugs to keep going and is totally oblivious to the material comforts of the outside world—and who works in artistic spurts, slave to the Muse and unconcerned with popular approval. (We can think of no current examples, since this type of writer seldom becomes famous while still alive.)

There may be some people who fit approximately into one or the other of these stereotypes. If you're one of them, you shouldn't bother reading any further. The writers at those extremes have no need for practical advice—the first because they're "above" it and the second because they scorn it. The people who think Art should not be tainted by commercial considerations are beyond anyone's help but their own.

The majority of writers that we know, however, are ordinary people with ordinary needs. They have to provide shelter, food, clothing, and other material benefits for themselves and their families. At the same time, they have ideas and thoughts they want to share with other people, and their method of sharing is to write and publish their concepts. Doing this takes time and effort; if their audience benefits from sharing these ideas, it seems only fair that the authors should benefit materially from creating them.

Writers who want to be paid for their work become business people. They are providing a product to the general public—in this case, the unique expression of their ideas—and they hope to interest enough people in buying their product to earn themselves some money. In this respect, writers are no different from shoemakers or tailors. There is no conflict between one's art and earning a living. A good shoemaker or tailor takes pride in his craftsmanship, but there's no reason why he shouldn't earn a satisfactory living at the same time.

Too often, we've seen writers of extraordinary talent just struggling along, while others of far inferior ability thrive. A large part of the explanation is business acumen. Without knowing how to deal with the business world, even the greatest writer of our day will earn but a moderate income; at best, all he'll do is make his publisher rich.

As a writer, what are the essentials of your business? You have a product to sell—your words. You must first sell your work to a publisher and then, ultimately, to the readers. (In this regard, you are like a shoe manufacturer, who must get a store to stock the finished shoes en route to the shoe-buying public.) In order to sell your product, you must learn effective marketing techniques. Like any business, you will also have expenses involved in creating your product, and you must learn to keep those within manageable limits. Even when you are selling regularly, there will be problems of cash flow that you must compensate for. You must learn the art of making successful deals and negotiating contracts with the purchasers of your merchandise. You must learn your legal rights and liabilities. Like any business person, you must learn to keep adequate records of costs and income and know how to deal with the income-tax people to best advantage. Finally, you must know how to promote your product, bring it to the attention of the public so that they will *want* to buy it.

There are scores of fine books on how to write, and hundreds—if not thousands—of courses in creative writing, taught at all levels from junior high school through college. Such courses almost invariably focus on the creative process: style, construction, content, plot, characterization, and so forth. Sometimes the class will be taught proper manuscript form—and, if the teacher's really sharp, some tips on marketing the work as well. But that's usually the end of it—and as we've shown in the preceding paragraph, there's a lot more to the writing business than just that.

In this book, we intend to cover what the others generally omit: the dirty, gritty realities of everyday existence for you, the writer, the things that should be happening when you're *not* busy putting your creative expressions on paper. We'll show you some methods for marketing your manuscripts and ways to deal with publishers, editors, and, eventually, agents. We'll explain rights, copyrights, and other legal factors. We'll talk about contracts and agreements, explaining what you should expect and how to bargain for a better deal. We'll explain how the income-tax laws affect writers, and how you should keep records for your own use as well as Uncle Sam's. We'll briefly discuss the world of self-publishing and show you how to promote yourself and your ideas to gain the widest possible audience.

Part Time vs. Full Time

Joshua Logan once remarked, "If anything can dissuade you from a career in the theater, let it." We generally like to apply that maxim to a career in writing as well. Writing is not for the faint of heart, the sensitive, the people who can't stand the thought of being rejected. It's a business very much guided by the principle of survival of the fittest; only those with tough hides and determined minds can hope to stick it out. As for the weaker ones, doomed to fall by the wayside, it's kinder to discourage them at the very beginning, rather than let them waste their hopes and efforts on a futile endeavor.

A sobering statistic: Of all the people in the United States who try to become writers, only about 10 percent will ever sell *anything* in their lives. Of that 10 percent, only a minute fraction will ever be successful enough to make a reasonable living exclusively from writing. Thus, starting from scratch, the odds are at least 99 to 1 against your making it.

More sobering statistics: In 1981 the Columbia University Center for the Social Sciences released the findings of a study it had done on behalf of the Authors Guild Foundation. Out of the 2,239 authors who responded to a questionnaire, less than half of them made more than $5,000 from their writing in 1979; in fact, 25 percent of the authors made less than $1,000 in that year. Nearly half stated that they had paid positions outside freelance writing, the largest percentage teaching at universities. Thus, for most people, freelance writing is no ticket to easy riches.

The life of a full-time freelance writer can be fraught with hazards. For one thing, you don't earn a steady paycheck; you have no assurance that every other Friday you can deposit a predictable sum in your bank account. Weeks or months may pass without any income at all. You are paid, instead, at the whim of your publisher—and despite anything to the contrary, even a written agreement with payment dates explicitly set, publishers pay when they're good and ready, and not a moment before. When the check does come, it may be for a very large sum indeed—thousands of dollars, perhaps, in the case of a book—but because it is usually later than you expected it, you have a stack of back bills waiting to be paid, as well as the knowledge that this check will have to last you for a number of months, until the *next* one comes in.

Most professional writers we know rely heavily on credit cards. As one very successful author told us, "I know that even if I don't have the money right now, the publisher's check will probably reach me by the time the charge account needs paying." *Getting* those credit cards, however, is another matter entirely. Credit evaluators look askance at someone without a definite employer and with uncertain income. One friend who was working as both a writer and an editor said he could get credit when he listed his profession as "editor," but not when he listed it as "writer"—despite the fact that he made far more money as a writer. It's not impossible for a writer to get credit, but you do have to live with the humiliating fact that someone working for minimum wage on an assembly line is considered a better credit risk than you are.

Being self-employed does have its advantages, of course. You're free to set your own hours; you can get up at noon and work till 3 A.M. if that fits your life-style better than 9-to-5. You have no boss looking over your shoulder, telling you what to do and how to do it (although you may have to take occasional orders from an editor). You don't have to commute to work unless you choose to rent an office away from home for your writing, and you don't have to maintain an expensive wardrobe to wear to work day after day. There are no office politics, no donations to the ever-present retirement fund for good old Joe who's leaving us next week.

But there are some serious disadvantages as well. You have

no employer to pay part of your pension and/or Social Security payments; you're responsible for all that yourself. There are no fringe benefits unless *you* provide for them. One of the chief disadvantages in these days of soaring medical costs is that you don't qualify for medical insurance plans at group rates; unless you're lucky enough to find some group that will include you, you'll have to pay the private rates, which tend to be astronomical. Some states do have state disability plans for self-employed people, but payments into this plan aren't automatically deducted from your paycheck; you have to make a deliberate effort to pay them or else face the risk of income loss if you become ill.

If you go for a long period without selling anything, you are not eligible for unemployment benefits—and trying to collect welfare when you have an irregular income is actually harder than if you had no income at all.

Then, too, unless you choose to rent an office elsewhere—and many writers do—you'll find you're at home a great deal of the time. If your spouse is also at home a lot, the long periods of enforced togetherness can put a strain on your relationship. And, because everyone knows you can make your own hours, you sometimes find yourself committed to running errands for family members or friends that they don't have time to run themselves.

But the hardest fact for some would-be writers to face is that they're totally on their own. Writing is basically a lonely job, conducted by you and your typewriter. There isn't anyone to gossip with or talk about last night's baseball game. There are no office parties, no social interchanges. If you're the gregarious sort, this line of endeavor may not be for you.

On the other hand, writing as a *part-time* occupation can be most rewarding indeed. If you have the income from a regular job, so that your financial situation isn't totally dependent on the vagaries of the publisher's accountant, and if your job provides a package of retirement and health-care benefits, then anything you earn from your writing is simply icing on the cake. Your writing becomes a lucrative second job, enabling you to make additional money while expressing yourself and gratifying your ego at the same time. The majority of writers, including a good many successful ones, are part-timers, and they enjoy the best of both worlds.

Part-time writers take no great risks. Their basic living income is secured; they write in their spare time, when people of other persuasions might be gardening or tinkering with their cars. Part-time writers write because they *enjoy* it, because they get a special thrill from setting their words and ideas on paper.

Part-time writers who manage to sell what they've written find they have supplemented their income in an enjoyable way. The money they earn can add to their basic living allowance, or it may allow them to buy some otherwise unaffordable luxuries. If the part-timers can continue to make a series of sales, they will have found a way to make their lives that much more comfortable.

It can be a tragedy, though, when a successful part-time writer decides to make the jump to full-time writing. The reasoning is very seductive: "If I can earn this amount of money working only one or two hours a day, I can easily earn five or six times as much working a full eight-hour day."

Unfortunately, real life has a way of invalidating those figures. For one thing, you run up against the law of diminishing returns. You simply cannot write eight times as much in eight hours as you do in one hour. The ratio may only be three to five times as much, if you're lucky. And while it's relatively easy to set aside a one-hour period each day that can be free from distractions, the longer the interval you try to set aside, the more distractions are bound to creep in.

For another thing, you run into a problem of diminishing markets. Suppose part-time writer Arthur Penman has been writing two articles or stories a month and has developed two or three markets for his work. He knows he's good enough to sell virtually everything he writes to those two or three editors. But suddenly, as a full-timer, he has to sell eight or ten pieces a month to earn his living. Those two or three editors he's got can't buy all those pieces; they have material coming in from other sources as well, and they have to spread the assignments around to give each issue of their publication some balance.

Penman suddenly finds he has a secure market for only a third of his output. He has to scramble around to find new markets for his work—and that scrambling will inevitably take time away from his actual writing. He'll find his output decreasing, which means he may have to look for higher-paying markets to get a larger income from a smaller number of sales. He may even discover that his original safe markets, which paid him adequately when he was a part-timer, are no longer rich enough to support him as a full-timer. Penman is now in a descending spiral where he has to work even harder just to stay afloat.

The solution most full-time writers find to this dilemma is to concentrate on writing book-length manuscripts. It actually takes almost the same time to plot out a short story or article as it does to plan a book—and while it may take months to write a book, as opposed to days or weeks to write a shorter piece, the pay scale is far greater. There is always the possibility of earning royalties on a book too, thus bringing in future income; most short works don't earn royalties, and the writer must depend on the chance of reprints for further income from the same piece.

This book is designed to help both part-time and full-time writers. Both types need to know how to conduct themselves in an organized fashion if they're going to be successful. The only difference is that while the information is important for a part-time writer, it's *crucial* for a full-timer. In either case, we assume the reader intends to sell more than one or two pieces and is aiming instead at a continuing series of sales. This is what will form either a full-time or a part-time career, and this is what separates the amateur from the true professional.

Deciding What to Write

Having made the decision to become a writer, whether part-time or full-time, you're now faced with the problem of deciding what you want to write. In some cases, this is no problem at all; you simply start writing one sort of thing before you consciously make the decision to become a writer. A doctor, for instance, might write an article on a medical topic for a general-circulation magazine, follow it up with another, and before he knows it he's got a career as a medical popularizer. Many writers have stumbled into their field this way, and there's little to do but shrug the shoulders and accept the inevitable.

There are others, however, who know they want to write but are interested in several fields. The question becomes whether they should generalize—that is, write on any subject that interests them—or whether they should concentrate in one particular field and become a specialist. There are arguments to be made on both sides, but we feel the specialist probably stands the best chance of success in the long run.

Particularly in the case of nonfiction, you are presumed to know more about your subject than the reader does. The more different areas you try to cover, the more widespread your knowledge has to be. It *is* possible to be versed in a number of different fields; Isaac Asimov, for instance, can write intelligently on virtually any subject, from science to Shakespeare to the Bible, and still have time left for fiction as well. But Asimov is a phenomenon unto himself, and there are few people who could hope to duplicate such feats.

Marketing is another problem that often confronts the

would-be generalist. Knowing the market is a must for every conscientious professional writer. The writer who tries to generalize must be familiar with a host of different markets. A magazine that would gladly print your article on child-rearing, for instance, might have no interest in your thoughtful essay on the history of classical music. You might well be an expert on both topics—but developing a marketing strategy for each takes twice as much time and effort, which in turn detracts from the time you can actually spend on writing.

We feel it's best—at least at the beginning of your career—to concentrate your work in one particular area. For one thing, it's easier to build up a reputation within one narrow field than in a number of diverse ones. As your career blossoms and your name becomes more established, you'll find it will be easier to branch out into other areas. You can still impress people with your versatility *after* you've built your reputation.

There is, of course, the danger of typecasting. Helen MacInnes has built her career on her fabulously successful suspense thrillers. If she were suddenly to write a nonfiction book on ornithology, her publisher might prefer that she use a pseudonym for it rather than confuse her regular readership, who have come to expect certain things from her.

Authors have been known to hate the pigeonholes they find themselves in. Sir Arthur Conan Doyle grew to resent Sherlock Holmes and tried to kill him off so he could write other things. His fans protested so strongly, however, that he was forced to resurrect his detective. Similarly, L. Frank Baum had no intention of writing a series of Oz books and tried several times to end the saga. Again, his readers (and probably his publisher) prevailed, and he continued doing the books until his death.

We suggest that you plan for such a contingency ahead of time. Give careful thought to the type of material you want to write. Make sure, first of all, that it's something you *enjoy;*

writing is a hard enough business as it is, and there's no point wasting your effort on something you don't even like. Make sure the field you've chosen as your specialty is a wide one, offering you plenty of latitude; otherwise you might find yourself rephrasing the same things over and over again. Make sure the field you choose is one you know something about; you might *like* to write sports articles, but if you're not well versed in sports, you'll never get anywhere. And finally, read widely in the field you've chosen, to keep abreast of it; if you choose to write mystery novels, you might waste a great deal of effort writing a Victorian cerebral detective story when the editors are all buying modern police procedurals. Even if you choose not to follow the herd within your field, you have to know where the herd is heading; otherwise you just end up looking silly.

Making a conscious decision about your chosen field can clear your mind considerably. It gives you a solid base to work from and an unambiguous goal to aim at. After you've established yourself as a writing talent, then you can broaden your base if you prefer.

Work Habits

It seems a simplistic thing to say, but the single most important thing a writer must do is *write.* Unless you produce copy that your editor can publish, all your knowledge, marketing skills, and negotiating abilities are completely wasted. And yet, this is a problem many writers do face at some point in their careers. Some face it every day.

An author sitting in front of the typewriter staring at a blank page doesn't seem to be working very hard, but creative endeavor is a particularly concentrated form. You can work creatively for three hours and come away as exhausted as if you'd spent a full day at hard manual labor. Most of the writers we know enjoy *having written;* they feel gratified by the growing pile of paper beside the typewriter at the end of the workday. But the actual act of writing is the price they must pay to attain that feeling.

Once again, part-time writers are in the best position. To them, writing is something to look forward to as they trudge through their regular job. If nothing else, writing is a relief from the monotony of their routine, and, like all hobbies, it can be approached with enthusiasm.

For full-time writers, though, writing is the job itself. Writing is more insidious than most jobs because there is no boss looking over your shoulder, forcing you to work whether you feel like it or not. Sometimes an editor may remind you of a deadline, but generally the push must come from within.

In writing, there is no substitute for applying the seat of the pants to the seat of a chair and putting down one word after another. Different writers have different methods of doing this. One writer may be able to write only when touched by the Muse and will then suddenly produce thirty pages in a single burst; another writer may faithfully set aside a certain number of hours each day during which he will stare at the typewriter until words form in his head; still another writer may set herself a goal of turning out so many pages per day; and yet another will jot down scraps of work in whatever spare moments come to hand.

The two authors of this book have very dissimilar work habits. Stephen Goldin sets himself the goal of writing a specified number of pages each day, sufficient to turn out between three and four books a year; part-time writers might achieve fewer pages per day because of other demands on their time.

Kathleen Sky is under her doctor's orders not to type because of an arthritic elbow. She has learned, instead, to dictate her work and pays a secretary to transcribe the dictations onto paper. Kathleen lies on a couch in her office, sets her portable tape recorder nearby, and begins telling her story. She has learned that she works best dictating in complete dramatic units, so she tries to do a chapter at a time, regardless of its length. Because her pace is more irregular, her output is lower than Stephen's, averaging only between one and two books per year.

No one method is preferred over any others, and comparisons between them are ludicrous. The only rule is to use the method that works best for you. This may take some experimentation at first, until you decide how you can make yourself most comfortable while turning out the optimum amount of material. Once you've found it, however, you should stick with it and make sure you *do* write. This is known as discipline.

Coming back to writing after a break or starting a new day's work is sometimes difficult, because there's a certain amount of mental inertia to overcome. Some writers have developed tricks to deal with this. One writer always ends one day's writing in the middle of a sentence; starting up the next day forces him to complete the thought and gets his mind back on track. Another writer starts her day by retyping the last page she did the day before; by the time that's done, her mind is back in the creative groove and all set to carry on from where she left off.

Where you write can sometimes be as important as what you write. Writers have been known to work in all sorts of strange places. Some merely clear a space on the kitchen table or set up a desk in the bedroom; others set aside an entire spare room and convert it into a writing den; still others rent a room or an office and make daily trips there to escape the hassles and distractions at home. Wherever you decide to write, it should be an environment as free from unnecessary distractions as you can arrange it.

All serious craftsmen choose their tools carefully, and a writer should be no exception. Your most important tool will be your typewriter. If you travel a lot while you're writing, you might prefer one that's portable. When you're just starting out, any cheap little manual will do, but as you sell more regularly our advice is to get the best model you can afford.

Names and Pseudonyms

One of the first decisions a writer must make is what name to write under. This may sound trivial, but it can actually be a decision of major importance to the writer's career, and it is not a choice to be made lightly.

Most people prefer to use their real names, but even this allows considerable variation. Take a hypothetical author named William Robert Smith. Without resorting to a pseudonym, he can legitimately use the variations: William Robert Smith, William Smith, William R. Smith, W. R. Smith, W. Robert Smith, Bill Smith, Bill R. Smith, Bill Robert Smith, or even, God help us, Billy Bob Smith.

The main point to keep in mind is that once you've chosen a name and it begins to appear on more and more bylines, you become stuck with it. Editors and readers alike will know you by that name, and you'll be expected to sign your autographs that way. If you give speeches anywhere, you'll be introduced by that name. At parties, people may point to you and call you by that name. Whatever you choose, make sure it's a name you'll be comfortable with for the rest of your life. (One point to be made about using two first initials: That makes it more difficult for casual acquaintances to get on a first-name basis with you. This may be an advantage or a disadvantage, depending on how sociable you are.)

There can be many reasons, however, why a person would use a name other than some form of her real one. Perhaps her real name is similar, or identical, to that of someone who's already famous. Perhaps it is the writer who is already famous in another field and doesn't want the publisher to capitalize unduly on that fame. Perhaps the writer is afraid of prejudice. (Until recently, for instance, many women authors went only by first initials, fearing they'd be treated unequally if a woman's name appeared on their work.) Perhaps the nature of the writing calls for it; publishers insist that Gothic novels, for instance, have women's bylines, whether they are written by women or men. Perhaps the writer has a reputation to protect; an elementary-school teacher who writes racy historical romances in her spare time would certainly not want to be personally associated with the product. Or perhaps a writer simply doesn't *like* her real name; someone named Jane Jones or Ludmilla K. Shchokorovikoff would certainly be within her rights to look for a more appealing byline.

Kathleen Sky is married to Stephen Goldin but doesn't use his last name professionally. She had begun writing as Kathleen Sky before their marriage and had enough goodwill invested in the name not to change it afterward. Socially, to avoid confusion, she goes by the name of Kathleen Sky-Goldin, and the names Sky and Goldin are both on the mailbox to prevent substitute letter carriers from becoming unduly perplexed.

Whatever the reasons for choosing a pseudonym, the same criteria apply to it as to variations on your real name. If your work were to become famous, and everyone in the country knew you by the name you'd picked, would you be happy with it? Could you smile and sign that autograph a hundred times in an hour without wincing? Make sure, at the very beginning, that the name feels right on you, because it will be hard, if not impossible, to change it later.

If you use a pseudonym you may face an additional problem. Sometimes checks will arrive made out to your pseudonym—or sometimes you may want to buy something under your pseudonym rather than your real name. The way around this problem is to speak to your banker. Most banks are quite willing to give you an AKA (also known as) account, in which you are listed under both your names. You can have separate checks printed up with your real name or your pseudonym, and you can deposit checks that come to either one. You are legally entitled to use whatever name you want in your business as long as you're not using it for purposes of fraud.

The writer who works under a pseudonym must, of necessity, lead a schizophrenic life. He is known to his readers and the world at large by one name and to his family and friends by another. In general, therefore, we feel that a writer should stick with his or her own real name unless there is a very good reason for changing it.

2

The Mechanics of Submission

Now you have decided to write. You know what you want to say, and you've done a rough draft or two so you know how you want to say it. The next step is finding someone who wants to publish your work—but before you even begin that arduous search, you have to know how to package your product.

Suppose you went into a supermarket and looked at two different brands of the same item at the same price side by side. In one instance, the can is shiny and smooth, with a colorfully printed label stating clearly what the contents are, perhaps with a mouth-watering picture of the product. In the other instance, the can is rusted and dented with no label; instead, someone has scrawled in crayon across the metal what is inside. Without knowing anything about the quality of the merchandise, which can would you be more likely to buy? Most people would choose the good-looking can, on the general assumption that the manufacturer who takes the trouble to package a product presentably has probably gone to some effort to make the quality of the product good as well.

The same is true in writing. Editors have a natural bias in favor of manuscripts that look neat and professionally done. This doesn't mean they'll automatically reject a brilliant work merely because it looks sloppy (although if it's bad enough, they might send it back and ask the writer to do it over). But the deck is heavily stacked against the beginning author as it is. First impressions count for a great deal. If you can convince an editor that you know what you're doing, that you truly are a professional—as opposed to all the thousands of amateurs out there who *think* they can write—then you are halfway toward making a sale. One of the best ways to appear professional is to turn in a professional-looking manuscript.

Virtually every book on writing explains proper manuscript format. Writing magazines repeat the advice at least once a year. Many writing courses spend a session or so telling their students how it should be done. There should by now be no excuse for anyone in the country not to know the proper way to present a manuscript to an editor.

Experience, however, dictates otherwise. Editors are constantly trying to top one another with horror stories about the manuscripts that come across their desks. Our own experience at reading the "slush pile" (that is, unsolicited manuscripts) also tells us that there are vast numbers of people who are totally ignorant of these basic rules. One editor we know has even gone so far as to print up his own two-page manuscript guide which he sends back along with his rejection notes.

So, tedious as the subject might be, we are going to repeat some of those rules for you now. Our discussion will cover only the most basic points; for a more detailed explanation, see one of the style guides listed in the Bibliography.

Manuscript Format

The first, most basic rule of all is that your manuscript (abbreviated MS; plural, MSS) *must* be typed; if you don't type yourself, then you must find someone to type your manuscripts for you. The typing must be double-spaced in dark black ink on one side of the page only. Use only standard-sized (that is, 8½-by-11-inch) *white* paper and try to leave at least a one-inch margin all the way around. Editors don't expect you to be a perfect typist; a few hand-printed corrections on a page are quite acceptable. Anything more than that should probably be retyped in the interests of neatness. Similarly, any pages that get damaged in the course of their journey should be redone.

Avoid "erasable" bond papers like the plague. Editors hate that kind of paper. Not only do the sheets stick to the fingers and to one another, but ink on them smudges very badly. Onionskin is also a bad idea for the same reasons. An editor who gets a submission on those types of paper will assume it's from an amateur and may be slightly prejudiced against you. Avoid sending carbon copies, too, because they tend to smear.

Somewhere on *each* page, usually at the top, you should have a word or two of identification as well as the page number. For instance, Arthur Penman might put at the top of the seventeenth page of his book *Growing Up in Wisconsin* the notation: penman/wisconsin/17. The reason for this is that most editors deal with many manuscripts at a time; if by some mischance Penman's manuscript should be knocked to the floor with several others, it will be easier to sort his pages out from the rest.

Your name and address should appear somewhere on the manuscript. In a book-length work, you might put it on a separate title page right at the front. In a shorter piece, title pages are optional; if you don't use one, put your name and address in one of the upper corners of the first page, then drop one third to halfway down the page, give your title and byline, and begin. You should also put your word count for the piece somewhere near your name and address. The word count may be obtained by counting the number of words on a few average pages and multiplying by the total number of pages in your manuscript (taking into account pages that are partially blank).

The Science Fiction Writers of America have defined a

short story as a work of fiction less than 7,500 words long; a novelette is fiction between 7,500 and 17,500 words long; a novella is between 17,500 and 40,000 words; and anything longer than 40,000 words long is considered a novel. These definitions are purely arbitrary, for award purposes only, but you may use them as general guidelines if you choose.

There are many other matters of format that are beyond the scope of this book. We refer you to such excellent works as the University of Chicago's *Manual of Style* and *Words into Type* by Skillin and Gay, both listed in the Bibliography. Learn the standard proofreader's symbols (given in Appendix A) and use them where needed.

We come now to one of the primary rules of submission: NEVER EVER, UNDER ANY CIRCUMSTANCES, SEND OUT YOUR ONLY COPY OF ANYTHING. Chisel that rule in stone and keep it on your desk in front of you. Sending out your only copy guarantees that *this* one, out of all your manuscripts, ends up lost or damaged. Carbon paper is the cheapest and easiest way to make copies, but carbon copies tend to smudge and are sometimes difficult to read. We prefer to type just one clean original and have it photocopied on a Xerox or other brand of copier; we send out the photocopy, leaving the original in our files in case of accident. This is a more expensive method than making carbon copies, but it guarantees that there will always be at least one good, readable copy available if we need it.

Many market reports state that the editors in question don't *want* to receive photocopies. This is not because there is something inherently objectionable about xerographic paper, nor are editors as a species allergic to the chemicals used for photocopy processing. Quite simply put, these editors are afraid that a photocopied manuscript is an indication that this is a simultaneous submission. We have yet to come across any editor, though, who objects to good-quality photocopied manuscripts once he's been assured that he is currently the only editor considering it. An explicit statement to that effect may be put in your cover letter, on the title page of your manuscript, or, to be on the safe side, in both places. (We're told that copy editors hate photocopies because the print smudges when erased and is hard to correct—but few manuscripts are done specifically to please the copy editor.)

If you have graphs, charts, maps, line drawings, or other illustrations that accompany your text, put them in a separate envelope at the back of the manuscript. Each illustration should be numbered, with notes written in the margin of the manuscript to show approximately where each illustration should be placed. Include a list of illustrations and captions, if necessary, in the envelope with the illustrations. If you have any photographs to include as well, put them in another separate envelope at the back of the manuscript, following the same procedure as before. Put your name and manuscript title on these individual envelopes, just in case they become separated from the rest of the work.

Submitting the Manuscript

There are two schools of thought on the matter of cover letters. We've heard some editors say that they never bother to read cover letters anyway, while others have said that they feel offended to be just handed a story without even a simple hello. It probably never hurts to enclose a cover letter, but keep it brief and to the point. Say that you are enclosing the following story or article for editorial consideration, briefly state its subject matter (if it's an article), and give the estimated word count. If there are any special circumstances about you or the piece—perhaps that you are a professional in this field of expertise, or that you have won some significant award for your writing—it's permissible to point these facts out briefly. What you should *not* do is bore the editor with the story of your life, or plead with him to buy the piece because your spouse and children are starving and you need the sale desperately. Above all, don't go into deep explanations of the symbolism in your story. If the story is any good, it will speak for itself—and if it isn't, the editor will reject it no matter how good a letter you've written. Close the cover letter by thanking the editor for taking the time and trouble to look over your work.

Never do anything that permanently fastens the manuscript together. Do not staple it, do not punch holes and put brass fasteners through it, do not have it bound. If the editor decides to publish it, the typesetter will have to work on it one page at a time, and disentangling the manuscript can be aggravating. On shorter works, a paper clip in the top left-hand corner is fine; for a book-length manuscript, stick it between two pieces of cardboard (the ones that come back with shirts from the laundry work beautifully) and wrap it with thick rubber bands across the length and width. That's all you need, honest.

As for mailing manuscripts, it again depends on the size. A very short piece of only two or three pages may be folded twice and mailed in a legal-sized No. 10 envelope. If the work is slightly longer, you may fold it in half and mail it in a 6-by-9-inch manila envelope. For manuscripts between 20 and 50 pages, a 9½-by-11 manila envelope works well enough, while for thicker manuscripts a larger manila envelope is recommended—say, 10 by 13.

For added protection, you may prefer some of the padded envelopes that are sold in stationery stores and some post offices. In the case of book-length manuscripts, it's sometimes best to put them in a box and wrap it with plain brown paper; the box that your typing paper came in (if you buy it in a box) or a box that held file folders will do nicely. The only real rule is that whatever you use to hold your manuscript should be large enough that the manuscript fits in it comfortably and sturdy enough to withstand the rigors the U.S. Postal Service is bound to subject it to. Do not, however, roll manuscripts into a cylinder and send them in a mailing tube; they're impossible to read that way.

Another primary rule of submission is that you *must* send along a self-addressed stamped envelope (SASE) if you expect to have the manuscript returned to you, or even acknowledged. Simply make up an envelope just like the one you're mailing the manuscript in, address it to yourself, affix enough postage to get it back to you, fold it in half, and slide it into the original envelope along with your manuscript and cover letter. The only exception is in the case of a book-length manuscript which you sent wrapped in a box. In that case, send loose stamps.

If you're submitting to a foreign market (which includes Canada), sending U.S. stamps is useless. In these cases, the Postal Service provides what are known as International Reply Coupons. Ask your postal clerk how many will be needed for a given manuscript. (For those of you with short memories, Hawaii is no longer a foreign country. Hawaiian editors complain about getting International Reply Coupons; use U.S. stamps there.)

On the important matter of postage, you have a choice. Manuscripts weighing less than twelve ounces may be sent first class, while heavier manuscripts may be mailed at what are called "priority mail rates." Realizing that many poor writers can't afford these exorbitant first-class rates, the Postal Service has designated a special rate for manuscripts. This rate is considerably cheaper, but it also moves much slower. *Only* manuscripts and books may be sent via this rate, and the postal authorities have the right to open your package if they get suspicious that you're sending any other material like cover letters.

To get around this obstacle, mark the envelope in large easy-to-read letters SPECIAL 4TH CLASS RATE: MANUSCRIPT and affix the proper postage. Then stick on a first-class stamp and make another notation: FIRST CLASS LETTER EN-CLOSED. It's also advisable to write RETURN POSTAGE GUARANTEED under your return address in case the manu-script is undeliverable; otherwise the Postal Service might just discard the package rather than go to the trouble of sending it back to you.

For overseas submissions you have a choice between sur-face mail and air mail. Surface rates are cheaper by far, but sending something via surface mail can sometimes mean a delay of up to two months before it's delivered. Sending your manuscript by air will get it to its destination within two weeks, but the rates are astronomical.

The only suggestion we can make for saving money is that, if you're submitting an unsolicited manuscript to a foreign publisher, you should send a photocopy and explain in your cover letter that if the editor doesn't accept your piece he is simply to throw the manuscript away and send you a rejec-tion letter. You can then get by with sending just enough International Reply Coupons for an airmail letter.

How can you tell whether your manuscript has actually reached its intended destination? One trick we've heard of is to enclose a postcard with your submission. Address the front side to yourself; on the back, you can write a simple state-ment to the effect that "I acknowledge having received the designated manuscript on the date indicated." Type in the manuscript's title, leave a space for a date and a signature. In your cover letter, ask the editor to date and sign the postcard and send it back to you.

What about insuring manuscripts or sending them by reg-istered mail? The cost of these services is not outrageously high, and if it soothes your mind to spend a little extra money, it certainly won't hurt. (But be warned: The mere fact that a manuscript arrives by registered mail doesn't im-press an editor in the slightest.) In our opinion, though, the only thing that will really ensure the safety of your manuscript is to have a good copy in your own files.

To close with two horror stories: A writer of our acquaintance mailed a manuscript to a publisher. The envelope arrived safely, but it was empty. The manuscript was lost—and to make matters worse, the writer had no other copy of her final draft. To repeat our warning: ALWAYS KEEP A COPY.

Another writer mailed a novel to a publisher. A few days later, she received an anonymous phone call. The caller claimed to have her manuscript and tried to extort a large sum of money for its return; otherwise, he said, he'd submit it himself. The writer refused to pay; instead, she immediately contacted her postmaster and wrote letters to the major publishers telling them to be on the lookout for her manuscript. Nothing ever came of it—but the very thought of such a "kidnaping" is a chilling one!

Following these rules doesn't guarantee that your writing will be instantly accepted, just as violating them doesn't mean automatic rejection. The quality of your writing will ultimately determine that. But because there are so many would-be writers who don't know or don't care about these procedures, following them means your manuscript will stand apart from run-of-the-mill submissions. The editor will begin reading with a favorable frame of mind, simply because you've known enough about what you're doing to present your work properly. Anything that will get an editor into a good mood is to be encouraged; and while outstanding pieces are usually bought and dreadful ones are usually rejected no matter how they're presented, a professional appearance may make the difference for a work that falls between those two extremes.

3

Marketing Your Work

While there are definite guidelines on *how* to submit your manuscript, there are no solid rules on *where* to submit it. Each article, each story, each book is a phenomenon unique unto itself, and each must be marketed to take advantage of its uniqueness. Marketing is most definitely an art rather than a science. The experienced professional develops a feel for which manuscripts should be sent where and eventually can work by instinct alone. Beginners, however, are faced with a bewildering array of places where they *might* send a freshly finished masterpiece; how can they possibly choose among them?

One answer is to have an agent handle it for you; we'll discuss this possibility in Chapter 9. What we'll do in *this* chapter is outline a strategy you can use to find and evaluate the proper markets on your own. No battle plan can guarantee you a sale to the first market on your list, but a well-thought-out campaign can shorten the time between completion of the manuscript and its acceptance by a publisher.

Narrowing the Choices

The first thing you have to do is rule out the majority of places that wouldn't be interested in your work. Much of this is obvious. You wouldn't send a short story to *Popular Mechanics* or an article on tree surgery to *Vogue.* You wouldn't try to sell a sports book about officiating in the National Football League to a small publishing house that specializes in religious subjects. It's particularly easy with magazines to see the general topics they're interested in—and thus you can eliminate 98 percent of all possible markets immediately as inappropriate for your work. But dismissing all the inappropriate places doesn't tell you where you *should* be sending your work.

For short fiction and articles, you'll have to concentrate on the magazine field. There used to be a great number of so-called general circulation magazines which would print fiction and nonfiction on a wide variety of subjects, but in recent years the number of these magazines has decreased dramatically. Today's magazines appeal to specialized audiences, and you have to be able to slant your writing accordingly.

Go to your local library and to several large newsstands with the broadest range of magazines. Look at which magazines publish articles that are even remotely like what you want to write. Buy the latest copies and study them thoroughly; if possible—and this is where libraries can be very helpful—study a backlog of the magazines for the past six months or a year.

You will be looking for several things. First, what is the intended audience of the magazine? Is it for men, women, or both? Is it for singles or families, or doesn't it matter? Is it for young people, old people, or those in their middle years? Is it for intellectuals or the general public? Is it for people of high or middle-income levels?

One way of evaluating these factors, quite apart from the copy in the magazine, is to look at the ads and see who they're intended for. Advertisers are very careful about where they spend their dollars; they try to pinpoint a market specifically. If a magazine carries a lot of ads for stereo equipment and video cassette recorders, it's probably aimed at an adult middle-to-high-income bracket. If a magazine carries a lot of ads for rock albums, it's probably aimed at young adults and teenagers. If a magazine carries a lot of ads for hair care products and perfumes, it's probably aimed at women. By asking yourself, "Whom are these advertisers trying to reach?" you'll probably identify the magazine's audience pretty closely.

Second, what slant do the magazine's editors take? Do they prefer fiction, nonfiction, or both? If fiction, do they like their stories upbeat, downbeat, serious, comical, realistic, fanciful, written in elegant style, or told in straightforward language? Do they have any taboos about subject matter or profanity and obscenity? Do they prefer longer stories or shorter ones? Do they have a preference for protagonists of one sex or the other, or doesn't it matter?

If they publish nonfiction, do they want articles of fact, or opinion, or a combination of both? Do they want articles simple and generalized or full of carefully researched detail, complete with bibliographies? Do they consistently favor one point of view over another, or do they insist on balanced reporting? Do they have certain themes or topics that recur in issue after issue? Do they prefer an objective third-person omniscient viewpoint, or do they let their authors write subjectively in first person? Do they take a cautious approach to issues, or are they inclined to be muckrakers?

Third, how is the material presented? Do the editors run lots of photos and illustrations, or do they prefer straight text? If they do run pictures, does the magazine supply them or do you have to provide your own? Is the layout straightforward and conservative, or does it go in for screaming headlines, lurid photos, and outrageous graphics? Does the magazine feature authors' names prominently, perhaps with small biographical sketches, or are authors considered less important than what they have to say?

Another factor you must take into account when you analyze a potential market is the time lag between acceptance and publication. Most general magazines need several months to get an issue put together, printed, and distributed; the material you see in the current issue was actually bought anywhere from three months to a year ago. Not only does this mean you have to sell Christmas stories in summer and Halloween articles in spring, it also means you should be careful about following trends. If a magazine has run two good articles on abortion, for instance, it might seem the perfect market for your own article on the subject. But what you don't know is that the editor already has three more articles in stock awaiting publication and is by now heartily sick of the subject; what he really wants is a good article on something else entirely. This is why you should avoid current events or book or movie reviews unless you've checked with the editor first. It saves you from wasting your time on something that isn't needed.

By studying all the magazines in your field with regard to these various factors, you can soon get to know each publication almost as well as its own editors do. This is essential if you intend to aim your work at the proper markets.

A cynic in our fiction writing class asked whether we were thus recommending he tailor his stories to a particular market, rather than writing what he truly feels. In fiction writing particularly, you must ultimately create the story the way it feels best to you, though keeping an eye on the potential markets is never a bad idea. *After* the story is written, use your marketing knowledge to determine which markets are more likely to prefer this kind of story.

No matter how large a newsstand you go to, however, there are bound to be some publications they don't carry. Some reference volumes in your local library may help you locate further markets. *The Editor and Publisher International Yearbook* lists newspapers and syndication services in the United States and around the world. *The Standard Peri-*

odical Directory lists over 65,000 publications in a wide variety of fields. If you can't find those, there's always the *Reader's Guide to Periodical Literature;* you can check under the subject headings that interest you to find markets you may have missed. For fiction and poetry there are many small so-called literary magazines that have no general distribution. Many of these are listed in *The International Directory of Little Magazines and Small Presses;* your local college library may also carry them. These smaller markets frequently only pay their contributors in complimentary copies—but once you've had your work published, it's sometimes easier to use it for a collection of your stories or sell reprint rights to an anthology.

The same marketing principle applies to books. If you want to market a book-length manuscript, go to the largest bookstores in your area and make a list of all the companies publishing works in your field of interest. You can also check the subject index of *Books in Print,* which most bookstores and libraries carry for reference. Publishers' lines differ considerably from one another. One publisher may print nothing but coffee-table art books, another nothing but volumes on religion; still another publisher may have a varied line of nonfiction but no fiction, while a large company may have departments that publish in many different categories. With an estimated 40,000 books appearing each year, there are bound to be some publishers interested in your field of specialization.

As an adjunct to—but *not* a substitute for—these procedures, you may want to check some of the annual volumes such as *Writer's Market* and *The Writer's Handbook.* Again, these books may list some sources you missed, but we advise taking their information with a great deal of caution. They are compiled anywhere from six months to a year before the date they cover, and much of their information tends to be outdated. The publisher may have moved, been sold to another company, or even gone out of business entirely. There may have been a complete change of editors, or merely a shift in editorial policy, so that they no longer want the material that's listed. These volumes are useful for getting addresses of various publishers—but for detailed information about what the market is *really* like, you have to roll up your sleeves and do the actual research we've described.

Another source to be wary of is the market reports in writers' magazines. These are more up-to-date than those in the yearbooks, but the mere fact that they're published so widely means that the editors are immediately inundated with manuscripts and proposals—particularly if they say they accept fiction or poetry. The quality of these submissions is so universally awful that some major publishers try to avoid being mentioned; it's usually the smaller publishers, either just starting up or desperate for material, who seek these listings—and while they may indeed need what you have to offer, you'll be wading through a quagmire of competition.

The R. R. Bowker Company publishes the most comprehensive information about the publishing industry. (See address in Appendix C.) *Books in Print,* to which we've already referred, is an annual Bowker publication; as its title implies, it is a list of every book regarded as being "in print" by the major publishers in America. (Actually there are three lists, because each book is listed by title, by author, and by subject.)

Another Bowker publication is *Literary Market Place* (often abbreviated LMP). This is an annual volume containing the addresses and principal editorial staff of most American magazine and book publishers. LMP also lists many agents, writers' organizations, book manufacturers, public-relations services, writing conferences, and awards. Most public libraries keep a copy on hand in the reference section, and it's well worth your while to look through it. Depending on how prolific and wide-ranging your subjects are, it may even be worth your while to buy a copy.

Still another Bowker publication which we have found useful in dealing with book publishers is the magazine *Publishers Weekly*. It's expensive as magazine subscriptions go (and again, most libraries subscribe if you don't want to go to the expense yourself), but it is chock full of information about the industry: news of the perpetually shifting editorial positions, articles about different phases of the book-publishing business, reviews of many new books, tales of who has sold rights and permissions, news events that can affect writers as well as publishers.

For those who can't find success with the major publishers, lists of lesser markets are also available. *Small Press Record of Books in Print* and *Directory of Small Magazine/Press Editors and Publishers* are both adjuncts to the previously mentioned *International Directory of Little Magazines and Small Presses;* all three volumes are published annually by Dustbooks. The markets they list won't pay much, if at all, in advance, but sometimes a small press can offer you a more satisfactory deal on royalties and/or on the way your work is presented.

The Submission List

By following the preceding advice, you can narrow down the field of possible markets to a manageable number—anywhere from one to a couple of dozen, depending on how general your topic is. Now you'll have to decide what order to try them in. This is often a subjective procedure because there are various factors you must weigh and compare.

One of the prime considerations, of course, is money. Most writers like to be paid as much as they can get for their work, and the higher-paying markets should definitely be at the top of any list. But the *amount* of money is only one consideration. If you need the money quickly, for instance, you might actually prefer a market that pays a little less, but pays it on acceptance rather than on publication, which can sometimes be months—or even years—later. Or you may have learned from experience that a high-paying market has to be nagged several times before it gets around to paying you, while a lower-paying one is prompt; you might prefer to try the lower-paying market first just to reduce your aggravation.

Another prime consideration is the company's policy of buying rights to the material it publishes. The amount of rights the publisher takes limits the further use you yourself can make of your material. A magazine that buys only first rights to a story or article gives you the opportunity to resell the piece to someone else after it has appeared in that magazine. A magazine that buys all rights means that you no longer have control of that particular piece, and the magazine can do what it wants with it from that time forward. And there are, of course, all gradations between those two extremes. (See chapters 5 and 7 for a more complete discussion of these matters.)

Resales of older work can be a good source of profit, since you get paid again for something without having to do any additional writing. Some of our own short stories have earned more through resales than they earned when we sold them the first time. From this standpoint, it is definitely worthwhile to submit your works to markets that let you keep as many rights as you can. Sometimes, though, this can be a trade-off. Some of the slick magazines—*Playboy,* for example—have a policy of buying all rights to the works they publish . . . but they offer large sums of money for the privilege. In a case like this, you'd have to decide whether potential resales—which can *never* be counted on as a sure thing— would offset the larger amount you would get now for an all-rights sale. It's a gamble either way.

Then there are the publishers who pay low rates and demand a lot of rights. We recommend you put them low on your priority list. And the ones who pay low rates, take all rights, and pay after publication (if at all) should be dead last.

Although money and rights are the two prime considerations in making your submission list, there are other factors which can be classed under the general heading of "author satisfaction." Perhaps one magazine has a larger circulation and therefore more potential readers of your piece. Perhaps you like one editor more than another, or one editor gives you star billing. Perhaps one market responds to your submissions in two weeks, while another, which might be better in other regards, takes months to give you a decision. Perhaps you feel that one book publisher will keep your book in print longer and promote it better than another company will. These and a myriad other considerations have been known to influence an author's choice of where to submit a manuscript.

All these factors must be weighed according to your own personal wants and needs. If rapport with an editor is more important to you than the amount of money he pays, by all means put the friendliest editor at the top of your list. If you're young, with an outside income and no immediate need of cash, you might prefer selling a book to a company offering a lower advance but a higher royalty rate that promises to earn you more money in the long run. Each decision is a calculated gamble—but then, so is every decision in any business.

If you deal with only a few potential markets or if you're very experienced, you may be able to keep all this information in your head. The beginner, however, might find it useful to write down all these data in a notebook or, better yet, on a set of 3-by-5 cards—one card for each market. On the card you'd write such information as the publisher's address and phone number, the editor's name, the rate and time of payment, rights bought, and any other relevant information.

When you finish a manuscript and are ready to send it out, use these cards as a guide to your priorities and list the order in which you wish to try the different markets. Since each article and story is unique, each piece you write may list the markets in a slightly different order. Keeping these cards up to date is a continuing activity; old markets fade away, new markets are born, editors move to new publishing houses, editorial policies change, etc.

Once you've made your list, send your piece to the market at the top. If that place rejects it, send it to place number two, then number three, four, and so on. Work your way steadily down the list until you come across one that will buy it.

If rejection discourages you, you'd best quit now, while you're ahead. *Every* professional writer, even the best, gets rejection slips. Don't ever take them personally, because they're seldom meant that way.

Never argue with editors about rejections, because it shows you up as an amateur. Editors are paid to exercise their judgment, and that's what they're doing. Even if you know an editor is totally wrong, even if the rejection note shows complete unawareness of the point you were making, it's a waste of postage to say so. If the editor didn't like your submission, your arguing the point won't improve matters. Above all, don't call editors names or insult their taste; that's a way to guarantee you'll never sell to them.

Save your rejection slips; turn them into a learning experience. If you're lucky enough to get a note of explanation, analyze its advice. You don't have to agree with it, but editors have been known to be right on occasion—and if a number of different editors mention the same thing, you might consider making a change. Kathleen Sky once lost out on a sale because she refused to change a story's ending the way the editor wanted it; sometimes she looks back wistfully and wishes she'd made the change after all.

Rejection doesn't always mean your piece is bad. An editor may have many reasons for turning down a story that have nothing to do with its quality. It may be on a theme the editor thinks has been overdone, or there may be a similar piece already in the works. It may be entirely the wrong length, or

it may be perfect in every detail but the editor is so back-
logged with material that he couldn't print it for months and
feels it unfair to hang onto the manuscript when he knows
you might be able to sell it elsewhere. (If he tells you this,
make a note to try him again in a few months if the piece is
still unsold.)

The point is, you can't allow yourself to be discouraged
after a manuscript has been rejected one or two times—or
even fourteen or fifteen. We've each had works sell after that
many rejections, and the editors who bought them were quite
enthusiastic about them. Tastes differ, and sometimes all a
work needs is to connect with the editor who appreciates it
properly. The more experience you gain in marketing your
work, the more familiar you'll become with editorial tastes,
and the number of rejections should decrease markedly.

Even if a piece remains unsold after being sent to every
market on your list, don't throw it away (unless it's an item
that will become dated quickly). Put it aside and wait. The
publishing world is an ever-changing one. A new magazine
may start up that needs material just like yours, or one of the
old markets on your list may change its editor and/or its editorial policy. An editor's backlog may evaporate. Times
change, and editors' needs change with them. If your topic or
your writing style was "out" when you originally marketed
the work, it may come back "in" at any moment. We've had
stories sell after lying fallow for years; you simply never know
when a piece you've written may become viable again. It's
best to be prepared.

We mentioned choosing markets on the basis of the
amount of money they pay and the rights they buy—but how
do you find out that kind of information? Sometimes it's presented as part of a market report in one of the sources we've
already mentioned. The report might say, "Buys first North
American serial rights, pays 3–5¢ per word." If you're a beginning writer, don't expect to receive the top rate right

away; that's usually reserved for the magazine's more important writers.

More often, you can't find the information listed anywhere. In that case, there's a very simple solution: Write to the editor and ask him what his policies are. What is his rate of pay, and when does he pay it? Does he send complimentary copies to the author, and, if so, how many? What rights does he buy, and does he print individual copyright notices? (We'll explain the importance of these factors in Chapter 5.) Does he accept unsolicited manuscripts, or does he prefer seeing a query letter first? Will he read a simultaneous submission?

None of this material is top secret, and any reasonable editor is willing to divulge his policies—particularly if you've enclosed a SASE with the letter of inquiry. An editor is a busy person and it may take a while before he gets around to answering your questions, but most editors will do so eventually. Some of them have already gone to the trouble of printing up information sheets answering all the standard questions and can just pop one in your SASE and send it out in the return mail.

When submitting a work, it's always best if you can target it to a specific editor. The person to whom the manuscript is addressed may not be the first person to actually read it—editors at the larger publishing companies usually have first readers who sift through the mountains of unsolicited manuscripts and reject the obviously unsuitable ones—but putting a specific name on the envelope helps move it in the right direction faster. If you have a proposal for a cookbook, for instance, and you merely sent it to a company that publishes general nonfiction, the manuscript might bounce around from desk to desk until it reached the person who can make an official decision; it would receive more prompt attention if you sent it directly to the editor in charge of cookbooks.

How do you know which editor is the right one? With

magazines, the best idea is to look at the masthead, a listing of the staff explaining who does what. The masthead is usually found at the front of the magazine, near the table of contents. A small magazine may have only one editor who handles all material, while a large magazine will have different editors in charge of different departments, all listed neatly for you on the masthead. Decide which department is most likely to be interested in your piece, and address the manuscript to that particular editor.

The problem is harder in the book-publishing field, because individual editors are not usually named and a large company may have dozens of editors on its staff. *Literary Market Place* lists major editors at most publishing companies, but the information may be outdated by the time you read it. A telephone call to the publishing company can net you a specific name to put on the envelope. If the company published a book on your subject, ask at the switchboard for the editor who handled that particular book; if you have no definite leads, just ask the company's switchboard operator who handles the department you have in mind. (Of course, there'll be times when the switchboard operators don't know this information, either.) Telephone calls can cost money, of course, particularly if they're long distance; you have to decide whether the information gained will justify the expense.

Simultaneous Submissions

Waiting is the hardest part of a writer's life. While you're working on a manuscript, you have complete control over it and can regulate how quickly or slowly it progresses. The instant you drop that manuscript into the mailbox, however, its fate—and yours—are out of your hands. You're first at the mercy of the Postal Service, never knowing how quickly they'll make their appointed rounds. But more importantly, you're at the mercy of an editor, or sometimes an entire editorial department—and they can be notoriously slow.

We have known some editors who are extremely conscientious and who will reply on all manuscripts within one or two weeks of receiving them. We've known other editors with similar good intentions who were so pressed for time that reading submissions received low priority; these editors could take several months before replying.

Some beginners have been known to write frantic letters to an editor if they haven't gotten a report within a week. As more time goes by, these panicky neophytes become progressively more shrill, making themselves reputations as "troublemakers" in the process.

Give an editor some time. If two months pass without a report, it's okay to send a polite letter mentioning that you mailed a submission on such-and-such a date; was it received and, if so, what has become of it? If this doesn't produce a reply within another month or so, write again—asking for a report soon. After four months, if the editor hasn't given you any satisfactory explanation, you're probably justified in asking for your manuscript back; write a note formally withdrawing the piece from consideration. It's a shame the process sometimes takes this long for such sorry results, but that's how the business is.

Even with the most considerate editor, the time during which the manuscript is out of your hands seems like an eternity—and if he returns it, for whatever reason, it's an eternity that's been wasted. All those bitten fingernails have been in vain, and now you have to submit yourself to the process all over again—never knowing whether this time will be wasted too.

Some writers try to short-circuit this lengthy process by sending copies of a manuscript to several editors at the same time—hence the term "simultaneous submission." From the writer's point of view this is a perfectly understandable and efficient procedure; it cuts down on the waiting time and may even allow him to choose from among several offers if a number of editors decide they want to publish it.

Most editors, though, dislike simultaneous submissions unless they come from an agent, and a look at the situation from their side of the desk will explain why. Editors are very busy people, and reading incoming manuscripts is only a small part of their job. Frequently there isn't enough time during official working hours to get around to it. Most editors take manuscripts home to read in their "spare time." Imagine how upset an editor will be if he spends an hour or two reading your manuscript and deciding he likes it, and then he finds that someone else has beat him to it and he can't buy it anyway. That hour or two could have been spent reading something he *could* buy—or maybe he would have used the time to relax and enjoy himself. He may very well feel you've cheated him out of a valuable commodity, his time. There's not much he can do to you now—but he'll watch for your name in the future, and you may have trouble selling to him. It's never wise to antagonize a possible future market.

Some editors, knowing the pressure writers are under, will consider simultaneous submissions. When you find editors who are willing to do this, treat it as a favor they're doing for you and thank them accordingly. If you're not sure whether an editor will accept a simultaneous submission, write and ask. Even if the answer is no, you're no worse off than you were before.

And by all means, when you're submitting a manuscript simultaneously to several publishers, be sure to *tell* them you're doing so. Even editors who normally accept simultaneous submissions like to know about it at the time. Springing it on them as a surprise is not a technique calculated to win their favor.

Unsolicited Manuscripts

In the February 12, 1979, issue of *New West* magazine, writer Chuck Ross reported the results of an experiment he conducted to see how receptive publishers were to submissions of unsolicited manuscripts. He typed up the manuscript of Jerzy Kosinski's novel *Steps,* which had originally been published by Random House in 1968 and had won the National Book Award for Fiction in 1969. He then submitted the work to a number of publishers using an assumed name (and being careful never to say that he had actually written it). Every publisher he sent it to rejected it. Some said they didn't accept unsolicited manuscripts, some just sent printed form rejection slips, and others said that, while it had promise, they didn't think they could publish it successfully. (Random House and Kosinski's more recent publisher, Houghton Mifflin, were among the rejectors.) Not one of the editors recognized the book despite its success. Ross used these rejections to point out his claim that publishing companies don't pay much attention to unsolicited manuscripts.

We don't dispute the fact that it's difficult for a beginner to break into print, but Ross's much-publicized experiment and conclusions were too downbeat, in our opinion. Publishers of nonfiction are generally receptive to new writers if they've got fresh approaches to topics of proven interest. In genre fiction—mysteries, suspense, Westerns, science fiction, Gothics, romances, etc.—beginners can receive a fair trial because the editors know that a genre book has its own built-in market; a certain minimum number of readers can be counted on to buy the book whether it's any good or not.

Mainstream fiction, though, is a total gamble. The typical mainstream novel that can't be categorized lasts through one printing and then is gone forever. If it doesn't catch on quickly, it's a failure and the publisher may lose a lot of money.

Moreover, there's no way of knowing which books will catch on. Every publishing company has its history of books that were just tossed off and went on to be enormous sellers, and of others that the editors thought would be dynamite but the public refused to buy. With so much risk involved, it's little wonder editors are often unwilling to gamble on a mainstream novel, even by an established writer. A manuscript out of the slush pile has very little chance at all. (This is why we advocate starting in one of the genres if you want to write fiction; once you've built up a reliable reputation it's a little easier to move into the main stream.)

Publishers are inundated with manuscripts all the time. The bigger the publisher, the more submissions he receives. It's not unusual for some of the bigger magazine and book publishers to receive a thousand or more unsolicited manuscripts in a single week. These come from all sorts of people: students fresh out of school eager to make their mark on the world, housewives hoping to become the next Erma Bombeck, English professors writing the Great American Novel, little old ladies trying their hand at a Gothic romance, and many others.

The editor knows that the majority of these submissions will be unusable. Even if *all* of them were well written—and, alas, most aren't—the yearly budget isn't large enough to publish them all anyway. He has to do something to winnow through this pile and separate the wheat from the chaff.

A small publishing house may have only one editor who does a wide variety of things—and reading unsolicited manuscripts is one of them. Much as the editor would like to give detailed literary criticism to each prospective writer, there simply isn't enough time. If a brief glance at a manuscript reveals it's not suitable—and an editor can usually tell just from reading the first few pages, with a quick glimpse at the middle and end to be sure he's not missing something—he'll simply slip the manuscript into its return envelope with a printed rejection form and send it back to you. If your technique shows promise, he may include a personal comment or two—and if he thinks the piece can be salvaged, he may include some suggestions on how he'd like to see it done.

At a bigger publishing office, there may be a junior editor or a first reader assigned to read through the slush pile. This person is empowered to reject but not to buy; a piece that is remotely suitable for the company is set aside for someone else to evaluate, while the reader carries on the dismal task of rejecting more manuscripts.

This is why we tell beginners that their work *will* be noticed if it's any good at all. Unsolicited manuscripts are generally so terrible that something with the slightest claim to literary merit stands out from the crowd. First readers want to justify their salaries. The publisher won't need to pay them if *everything* coming in is rejected; these readers *want* to find manuscripts they can pass along.

A growing number of publishers, critically eyeing the waste of manpower and money used to handle unsolicited manuscripts, have solved the problem by eliminating the job altogether. They have made it a policy not to read unsolicited manuscripts; they return them to authors unread. These publishers will deal only with manuscripts they have asked to see, or manuscripts submitted by a recognized agent. This presents a barrier to the unagented freelancer—but fortunately it's not an insurmountable one.

The solution is known as the query letter. This would include a brief description of your article, story, or book, and a discreet inquiry as to whether the editor would be interested in seeing it. If the editor replies positively, you're in; the very fact that he's asked to see it means that the manuscript is no longer unsolicited. If he answers negatively or, more probably, doesn't answer at all, then you've saved yourself the time and postage of shipping off your entire manuscript.

The mere fact that an editor asks to see your work does *not* mean he intends to buy it. Only proven professionals with established reputations can expect an editor to buy something sight unseen. The editor has moved you one step up the ladder by promising to read your work, but he still reserves the right to reject it if it disappoints him.

While the simultaneous submission of a manuscript may be frowned on, no one would object if you sent query letters to a number of publishers simultaneously. You haven't wasted the editor's time by forcing him to read a manuscript, and you haven't even offered him a chance to buy something; you've merely asked if he's *interested* in seeing your work. It's not unheard of for a writer to send out twenty or so query letters at a time and then make up his submission list depending on the degree of interest the various editors expressed. As a matter of politeness, though, you should type up a fresh copy of the query letter for each publisher rather than simply sending around a photocopy of the original letter. (Editors can get away with sending printed forms to writers, but not the other way around. Life is manifestly unfair.)

How do you write a good query letter? When one writer we know was starting out, she wrote letters to editors saying, "Dear Sir, I have written a novel. Would you care to see it?" Not surprisingly, the answer always came back, "No." The query letter may be your only chance to present this idea to this editor, so you'd better make it your best shot.

First of all, be brief. If you ramble on for pages and pages describing your idea, what was the point of writing the letter at all? You might as well have submitted the manuscript and be done with it. One paragraph should be sufficient to describe a short story or article; a full page—two at most—can adequately describe a book. If you can't describe your basic concepts that succinctly, you have no business being a writer in the first place.

Second, make it interesting. Every theme, every story has been done before in one way or another, and an experienced editor has seen plenty of variations. You must prove to him that *your* expression of this idea will be unique and interesting. If you've aimed your piece at a particular group of readers, say so, and explain why you think this approach is valuable.

Third, be polite. The same considerations apply as for the cover letter. Don't bore the editor with your life story. If the details are germane to your presentation, fine; if you've been a country doctor for twenty years and this book is a collection of anecdotes from your experience, by all means mention that. If you have significant writing credits, you can use them to impress the editor with your professional background. Having been a staff writer for two years on your college newspaper, or having written a weekly column in a local magazine, might be impressive; at least it shows you've produced satisfactory results for other editors over a period of time. But if your only credentials are that you helped put together your high school yearbook or you're president of the local writing club, don't bother listing them. Don't drag in biographical details that have no bearing whatsoever on your ability to write the piece in question. Ask yourself whether *you'd* be impressed by those credentials if you heard them from someone else.

Query letters are also helpful in learning whether there's a market for a given piece before you write it. An idea may occur to you that sounds interesting but would involve more research than you'd care to invest without some guarantee of sale ahead of time. In this case, your query would determine whether there's enough interest to go ahead with the project. Most editors will be noncommittal to an author they haven't worked with before, but once you've established a reputation at a given market they may listen more closely and be more candid with their advice. There is even the chance that your query will turn into a definite assignment, if the editor likes it enough.

In the book-publishing field, a proposal is a step up from a query letter. A proposal contains a *detailed* outline of the book—usually between ten and twenty pages, depending on how complex your project is. If the editor is familiar with your work, this may be all he needs to make a decision; more often, however, you'll need to submit a sample of your writing as well. This may be one or several chapters, or an excerpt from an important part of the book. (In selling *The Business of Being a Writer,* we used our chapters on contracts as part of the proposal.) Fifty pages should usually be enough to prove whether you've got the talent or not.

An editor who buys a book on the basis of a proposal is gambling that the writer can finish the book to the editor's satisfaction. This is why editors sometimes refuse to consider proposals from beginners and insist on complete manuscripts instead. The more published credits to your name, the more editors will be willing to trust you. Successful writers shouldn't have to write anything completely on speculation unless they want to.

4

Dealing with Editors

To the writer, editors seem to have it made. They get a salary for sitting in an office and reading. They only have to move occasionally to reject a manuscript or, on rare occasions, to accept one. They have plenty of time to ponder the fate of the writers whose lives they affect, giving their divine blessing to one while dooming another to despair and rejection.

This image, while picturesque, is nowhere near the truth. Writers prefer to think that the people who sit in judgment on them are calm, dispassionate people who can devote their full attention to the manuscript before them. Unfortunately, most editors are underpaid and overworked, with a minimum of three different things constantly demanding their immediate attention. An editor deals with many writers, sometimes on a very personal level, and usually knows what a writer's problems are. The reverse is not always true. We think it helps a writer's perspective if he knows some of the problems an editor faces. Magazine editors have different needs and responsibilities than book editors, so we'll discuss each in turn.

Magazine Editors

A magazine editor is someone who puts together jigsaw puzzles while racing against the clock. The typical magazine is published on a rigid schedule and contains a fixed number of pages. Of these pages, a certain number will be taken by advertising and a few others will contain miscellaneous matter like a cover illustration, a masthead, a table of contents, etc. The rest of the magazine must be filled with articles or stories that will interest the reader. The number of pages may vary slightly from issue to issue, depending on the amount of ads in stock.

Some publications are totally staff-written, meaning that the editor gets all the material from writers who are on salary to the magazine. The editor directs their efforts by telling them what subjects to cover and how long their articles should be. Unless you're interested in a job as a staff writer—which is a very good way for beginners to learn their craft—you needn't worry about this situation.

Most editors do accept outside submissions. Even in these cases, a magazine will usually have *some* staff-written features, like book or movie reviews, editorials, advice columns, etc. The editor therefore knows he can count on filling another set amount of his pages each issue. For the rest, he has to gamble on receiving the proper outside submissions.

An editor will be looking for what is called "balance." For a fiction magazine, this usually means a number of short pieces and maybe one or two longer ones (one of which may be a serial); for a general magazine, it may be all short articles of approximately the same length. The editor tries, whenever possible, to buy material at a constant rate, but the slush pile is unpredictable. Sometimes a long interval may go by without any acceptable short works and lots of long ones that are spectacular. If the budget is flexible enough, an editor may try to buy all the good long ones and stockpile them against the inevitable drought, but sometimes he may regretfully have to reject a piece that he otherwise would have bought with delight, simply because he's already got too many other things of that length in his inventory.

On the other hand, sometimes a hole can develop at the last minute, and an editor needs a 2,000-word piece in a hurry. There have been times when such editors, in desperation, have accepted a story or article that's not up to their usual standards, merely because it was the right length.

This is why editors like to build up a stable of freelancers they know they can count on. If there's a writer who's written for the magazine before, an editor would prefer to go to that writer again and say, "Can you write me a 2,000-word piece by next Thursday?" This is a position a freelancer would like to be in; that's why we feel you should develop a reputation for dependability. Make it a practice to turn in quality work and, if given a deadline, try hard to meet it. Once an editor starts depending on you, your success at that market is assured.

Magazine editors have plenty of duties other than reading manuscripts. Good editors try to schedule several issues in advance, in order to juggle pieces if any last-minute hitches occur. Editors plan the covers and the cover headlines. They work with the art department on the question of layout. They set the tone for each issue and develop ideas to build future issues around. They keep up with sales figures and reader reactions, to see what was popular in previous issues and what can be dropped. They copy-edit manuscripts and proofread the typeset copy, then approve the overall layout once the art department is finished with it. If a piece of writing comes in that's not quite right, they have to know how to change it to make it better. (And that includes knowing how to pad an article or delete material if something comes out just a little too short or long.) And editors have to know how to compensate for the inevitable foul-ups that will occur at one stage or another.

Depending on the size and frequency of the publication, all these functions could be handled by different people or by one very harried individual. But as you can see, the editor is someone in a hurry. He has little time for long, friendly letters or chatty phone calls to or from his writers. What you may detect as rudeness on an editor's part may only have been an untactfully brief comment brought on by deadline pressure. Try to be understanding, and don't snarl back.

Book Editors

Book editors have a slightly different set of problems. They, too, have schedules to meet—but in this case they must fill a list of individual books rather than a specified number of pages. A small publisher may print only a few titles a year, while a large one may print dozens each month. The length of each book is not of such crucial concern as it is for the magazine editor, although it *is* an economic issue discussed at editorial meetings.

A book editor's career depends in large measure on the success of the books he's chosen. If his "line" makes money for the publisher, he thrives; if his books fail consistently, he'll have to look for a new job. It's to his advantage to have the books he buys do as well as possible; not only does he try to acquire books that will sell but also to package and promote them in an effective manner. His job seldom depends on a single title; your book, while important, is usually only one of a number he's currently nursing.

This identification of an editor with his line can work well, but it also has its disadvantages. If the editor who bought your book leaves this position, your book is suddenly an orphan. The new editor is frequently less than enthusiastic. For one thing, he'll want to establish his own line, his own tastes.

For another, he knows he won't get proper credit in the matter; if your book succeeds, the original editor will get the praise for it. The new editor might as well let the book go its way without undue effort, and if it fails—well, blame the original editor who bought it.

A book editor must devote more time to each individual manuscript's publication than a magazine editor does. In the latter case, the manuscript is only part of a larger whole, while in the book business the manuscript is transformed into the final product. The editor must first acquire the property, on terms that make it economically feasible for his company to print it. This may involve a number of conferences with other executives in the firm for detailed analyses of a book's sales potential, manufacturing costs, and so on.

Once the book is acquired, the publishing process depends on the size of the company involved. In a small company, a single editor may be responsible for copy-editing, approving format and artwork, typesetting, layout, writing blurbs, printing, binding, distribution, returns, publicity, and sales of subsidiary rights. In a larger company, each of these functions may be handled by different people: a manufacturing department, sales director, publicity director, subsidiary rights director, and so forth. Even in a large company, though, an editor still has to guide each project through succeeding stages, which means constant liaison with all the departments—especially since an editor will have a number of works moving through the system simultaneously at various stages of development.

In addition to these duties, an editor must attend staff meetings, handle correspondence, and have lunch with agents to hear about new writers and new books and to exchange publishing news and gossip. Occasionally an editor is even called upon to take a visiting author out for a meal or a drink. All these things are in *addition* to reading submissions, which many editors have to do at home (for which they get no extra pay). They should be forgiven, therefore, if they are not kindly disposed toward writers who don't follow proper submission procedures, or writers who do nothing but whine and complain about the way they're treated.

Author-Editor Relations

The editor is usually the only person at a publishing house with whom the writer has any contact. He reads the author's submissions and notifies the author of acceptance or rejection. If there is acceptance, he negotiates the terms of the deal. If changes are required in the manuscript, he is the one to notify the author. If the author has any questions during the production process, they naturally are handled by the editor. After publication, it's the editor who receives the compliments or complaints.

In many cases, though, the editor is not the person responsible. The publisher's needs and resources, with input from his accountants, dictate the payment policy; the publisher's lawyers have considerable influence on the acceptable contract terms; the art, sales, or marketing departments usually have final say over the layout and artwork (although the editor is supposed to make final checks to see that everything is acceptable); and the publicity and subsidiary rights departments of a book publisher handle their own fields. Nevertheless, the editor is the only one the author generally knows, so the editor is the one who catches hell if anything goes wrong.

Most editors make their careers in the publishing field because they genuinely enjoy writing and publishing. Many editors either are or have hopes of being writers themselves, so they can sympathize with a writer's problems. But the editor is in the awkward position of being a buffer between author and publisher and is caught in the middle of any dispute.

On the one hand, an editor wants to keep writers happy. As we've said, a good writer is a valuable commodity. If a writer is upset over not being paid enough, or not getting enough recognition, or over bad manuscript editing or unappealing artwork—if any of these factors, or a hundred others, are bothering the writer, he naturally turns to the editor for redress.

On the other hand, the editor is an employee of the publisher and, in the final analysis, has to represent the publisher's position to the author. Sometimes, if the complaint is a minor one like the size of the author's byline, the editor can take action independently. But on substantive issues like pay and contracts, an editor must act according to the publisher's demands.

An editor is usually a reasonable person and tries to steer a course of compromise whenever disputes arise. As the author's intermediary, he'll go to the publisher with complaints and argue the author's case as best he can. But it's the publisher who makes the final decision. The editor must then go back to the author and explain that decision. If it isn't quite what the author wanted, the editor must try to convince him that was the best deal he could get and make him accept it, knowing that the author may go elsewhere if he's still not satisfied.

Like most peacemakers, editors are frequently in trouble with both sides in a dispute. If they toe the publisher's line too strongly, their writers will think they don't care enough about them. If they stand up to the publisher too often, they run the risk of being fired. We've heard of some courageous editors who quit rather than ask their authors to accept impossible deals, but such situations are rare indeed.

What does all this have to do with you, the writer? Just this: Realizing the pressures an editor is under can help you deal with him more effectively. If you behave in a professional manner you will simplify the editor's life and he will have that much more respect for you. The editor is *not* your enemy. Working together to overcome any problems will usually turn the editor into a valuable partner in your effort to get your work before the general public.

We've already discussed the matter of cover letters and query letters. In general, because of an editor's busy schedule, all correspondence should be kept basic and straightforward. If you have a question, go ahead and ask it; if you have a complaint (or, better yet, a compliment; editors seldom get enough of those), voice it in as polite and diplomatic a way as you can.

This is not to say you should be as humble as Uriah Heep, begging for favors. An editor will listen to a legitimate grudge, forcefully presented. But don't waste time with trivialities, and avoid name calling at all costs. The editor is just doing a job, after all, and any mistakes were probably unintentional. If you feel that a particular editor really is treating you in an incompetent or malicious manner, deal with it as best you can for the time being and submit your work elsewhere in the future.

A curious pavane is being danced in publishing circles. Editors jump from one publisher to another with astonishing frequency. There are a number of reasons for this, most of them having to do with career advancement. Publishers, like many other employers, tend to undervalue their own employees while looking at outsiders with envious eyes. They'll frequently hire an editor away from a competitor at a larger salary, rather than promote from within their own company. As a result, editors who want to get ahead may have to change companies to get the respect they feel they deserve.

(This is not the only reason for job-switching, of course. Sometimes an editor feels unable to get certain programs through at one publisher—or may simply not get along with coworkers. Whatever the reason, be assured that the game of "musical editors" is prevalent all through the publishing industry.)

This instability makes it vital that you avoid making enemies among editors. You may have a very cozy relationship with the editor at Publisher A, while the editor at Publisher B gives you nothing but trouble. So your tell the second edi-

tor to get lost, and you take all your business over to Publisher A. What happens next? Well, A's editor retires, or leaves
to seek greener pastures, and A hires the editor from Publisher B as a replacement. Suddenly all your work is committed
to this person you've insulted. If the treatment you received
was bad before, just imagine what it will be like now. *Moral:*
If you don't get along with a certain editor, try to avoid con-
frontations or use passive resistance—but don't be deliberately antagonistic, because in this uncertain business you never
know when you may be forced to work with that editor again.

A good author-editor relationship can be a wonderful
thing. The friendly editor can provide you with a ready market for your work, can promote your career by featuring your
name prominently, can give you choice assignments that occasionally come up, can fight harder for you in the publisher's office, and can sometimes even expedite matters through
the bureaucratic machinery if an emergency arises and you
need promised money in a hurry. Conversely, the bad editor
can foil you on all those levels without even doing anything
deliberately malicious. He can take longer to report on your
submissions (with the justifiable claim that he was too busy
to get to them sooner); he can bury your work in among other
people's; he can stick to the publisher's line and not try to get
you anything extra; and, if an emergency should come up, he
can shrug his shoulders and tell you he's sorry, but there's
nothing he can do to help.

Building a good rapport with an editor, then, is a positive
step in your career. Author-editor relationships have at times
evolved into deep friendships and have been known to last for
many years, to the benefit of both.

Negotiating

The magic day comes at last, and an editor writes to you or
calls you, offering a deal on your manuscript. There's always
an initial surge of elation when you learn an editor likes your

work—but the true professional has to temper that elation with practical considerations. The deal an editor offers is one that will be good for the publisher—but if it's not a good deal for you, you'll have to ask for a better one.

Beginning writers are hampered by ignorance. They don't know which terms are standard in the industry, which are to their advantage, and which are out-and-out power grabs by the publisher. They're also a little afraid that if they refuse the deal exactly as it's offered, the editor will withdraw the offer completely and they'll lose the sale. In this state of mind, they're easy prey for anyone who wants to take advantage of them.

It's possible to lose out on a sale by being too obnoxious or pushy, but you'd have to make an effort. The editor liked your material enough to offer you the deal in the first place; you're not suddenly a bad writer if you make polite inquiries about how firm the bargaining stance is. In the book-publishing field, nearly every contract is negotiable to some extent, and bargaining is an accepted procedure. In magazine publishing, offers are much less flexible; magazines usually have firmly established policies regarding pay rates and rights bought, and getting them to vary in a beginner's case is difficult.

If you knew the rules when you started, of course, you have no basis for argument whatsoever. For instance, suppose you query an editor before submitting your work and are told that the rate is 3 cents a word for world English-language serial rights; if you send something in anyway and are offered that deal, you can hardly complain. Even if an editor says the payment rate varies between 3 and 6 cents per word, you shouldn't argue if you're offered the lower rate on your first few sales. In such cases, payment is at the editor's discretion. Higher rates may go for exceptional pieces or to regular writers, but newcomers can expect only basic minimum. If you sell several pieces and continue to receive minimum rates, you might be justified in writing a polite note asking whether you haven't graduated to a higher level by now. If the answer is no, you have to decide whether to stay with an editor who won't raise your rates or try to find someone new.

Sometimes the rights an editor asks for are subject to negotiation. One editor we know says the publisher asks for all rights, but is perfectly willing to change that to first world serial rights the instant anyone complains. If you don't ask, you won't receive—but be sure to ask politely. If you think an editor is demanding too much, write and ask if he'd accept less. If he says no, you're no worse off than you were before.

In book publishing, negotiation is a more wide-open business. The editor may call or write to you expressing interest in your book and offering to publish it. At this stage, editors generally mention only two aspects of the contract: the amount of the advance and the royalty rate. If you think the offer on either is too low, say so and make a counter offer. Be prepared to haggle a little—politely. (Notice how often we use the word "polite"? We've found it works a lot better to get a reputation for reasonableness than to be known as a troublemaker. You don't have to let people walk all over you; it's possible to be *firm* and polite at the same time. Just don't forget the polite.) When you've gotten up to the highest offer you can and agree to a deal, the editor will then have one of the company's standard contracts drawn up and sent to you.

Each publisher has what is called a "boilerplate" contract, the basic agreement. Keep in mind that it was written by lawyers who were paid by the publisher; they're naturally going to slant it in his favor. Some companies' contracts are good, some are worse, some are positively awful. Your job will be to persuade the company to change as many of the bad parts as possible and maybe add some good ones along the way. The meanings of the individual clauses will be explained in detail in Chapter 8; the rest of this chapter is devoted to techniques of negotiation.

An editor who agrees to issue a contract usually has to send an order down to the publisher's legal department to have one made. This can be a formal or informal procedure, depending on the company. We've seen some cases where the legal department will take weeks to "cut" a contract, as they say, even though the forms are already printed up and all they have to do is fill in the amounts you've already agreed to. Finally, the contract will be sent to the editor, who in turn sends it to you for your signature.

We've seen book contracts that were as short as one page, and we've heard of some that ran well over twenty pages of small printed type. Most of them look terribly official, as though daring you to alter even a comma. Despite their intimidating appearance, you'll have to learn to examine them closely and question every clause.

Suppose you've gone through the contract and found six changes you'd like to make in it. Don't just write the changes in and send the contract back to the editor, because if some of your changes are unacceptable, the legal department will have to cut a new contract, and that can delay matters interminably.

Instead, make a list of the changes you want on a separate piece of paper. Say, "In Clause 2, I'd like the second sentence deleted. In Clause 4, I'd like the words 'English-language' inserted between 'world' and 'rights.' I'd like Clause 7 stricken entirely and replaced by the following new clause." And so on. When you've outlined all your changes explicitly, send the list to the editor. Hold on to the contracts yourself until the negotiations are finally settled; the publisher already knows what they say, and getting them back from him once the deal is finalized could only waste more time. Keep a copy of the list for yourself. In fact, it's a good idea to keep copies of all your correspondence with editors, particularly dealing with contractual matters; you never know when you'll have to refer to them.

In due time you'll hear back from the editor. "We can accept your first two changes. We can't budge on number three or five. On four and six, we'd like to alter your wording as follows." You may feel that these agreements make the contract satisfactory enough for you to sign, in which case do so. If not, you may want a few more rounds of negotiation back and forth. Eventually there'll come a point when further dickering is obviously useless. At that time, you'll have to decide whether to take the contract as amended or shop around for another deal.

Once all the changes have been agreed to by both sides, it's time to make the changes on the document itself. Changes should either be typed or made in permanent ink—and be sure to make the same changes on *all* copies of the contract. The simplest change is a deletion; just take a ruler and draw a line through the offending word or phrase. If you want to add a few words or substitute a short phrase for one that was deleted, put a slash mark (/) where the insertion should be and type or print the addition either between the lines (if there's room) or in the margin next to the line where the addition should appear. If the addition is a little longer than can comfortably fit in the margin, put in a footnote sign (*,+, etc.) and put the correction in the space between that paragraph and the next, or at the top or bottom of the page, wherever there's sufficient room.

If you're deleting an entire section, you can run a giant X from the beginning of the section to the end. If you're adding clauses that were omitted in the publisher's version, there is sometimes blank space left at the end of the contract for just such contingencies. If the printed contract ends with Clause 23, you can add Clause 24, 25, etc. If there isn't room you can add one or more additional pages, making a note on the original that the additional pages are part of the same agreement. If you're putting substitute wording into one of the earlier clauses and the new wording is more than a short sen-

tence, type the new wording on a separate slip of paper and
staple it to the contract in the appropriate place, making a
note on the contract referring to the attached sheet. We've
had contracts with extra pieces of paper fluttering all over
the place. It looks terribly messy—but then, the courts don't
often give awards for neatness. It's the wording of the contract that matters, not how tidy it looks. As long as all the
changes are legible, that's what really counts.

Once the changes are made on *all* copies of the contract,
put your initials in the margin beside each change, sign all
the copies, and send them back for the publisher's signature
and initialing to indicate that they accept all the changes.
There will be at least two copies of the contract, one for you
and one for the publisher; your agent, if you have one, will
need a copy too. Sometimes a publisher wants several copies:
for the editorial file, for the various departments, and one to
record at the Copyright Office. When a copy is sent back to
you, properly initialed and signed by the publisher, the deal is
official.

Sometimes during negotiations an editor may try to undermine your position by saying, "Well, I promise you I'll take
care of that; no need to put it in the contract." He may even
be telling the truth. You may have found, from previous dealings, that he's the nicest person in the world. But it's still wise
to get as much of the deal as you can in writing—to prevent
future misunderstandings, if nothing else.

Sometimes the editor will be even more blunt: "What's the
matter, don't you trust me?" This is a particularly nasty ploy.
If you say you do, you've half admitted that you don't really
need that wording in the contract, and weakened your bargaining position; if you say you don't, you've insulted him
and possibly damaged your future relationship with him. (Although we've noticed that an editor who resorts to this tactic
frequently *isn't* trustworthy.)

You can make an equally sneaky countermove against this

ploy. Simply say, "Oh, I trust *you* perfectly—but the contract isn't with you, it's with the publisher. What if some other publisher recognizes your true worth and hires you away for more money and a higher position, and then someone else takes over handling my contract? The new person might not be as good as you are. That's why I'd prefer to have this promise in writing."

This is an argument any editor should understand. With editors changing jobs so frequently, and with publishing houses being bought by heartless conglomerates, continuity is a legitimate fear to many authors—and even to editors themselves. If an editor presses the argument beyond this point, start looking for the cards he's got up his sleeve.

Sometimes publishers will put clauses in their contracts that are outright grabs but will back off instantly if you know enough to call them on it. Stephen Goldin once received a contract from a publisher that contained no clause to revert the book to him if it went out of print. When he pointed out the omission, the editor immediately sent him a mimeographed attachment to add to the contract. This amendment had already been printed up and was ready to be shipped to any writer who spotted the problem. It was the publisher's way of saying, "Well, I guess you caught me this time." But if Stephen hadn't asked, the change would never have been made, and there would be no reversion clause.

(The importance of this matter was borne out a few years later, when the book *did* go out of print. Stephen was able to use the new clause to revert the rights to him, and subsequently sold the book to another publisher for additional money. This is money he would have lost if the original clause had been in effect.)

Don't expect to get all the changes you ask for in your first contract—but on the other hand, most boilerplate contracts we've seen are so heavily slanted toward the publisher that you'd have to be a fool to sign them as written. Don't be afraid to ask for changes before you sign, if you think they're reasonable, because you certainly won't get them if you don't ask. Once a change has been accepted on this contract, it will be considered standard on your subsequent ones, so you can use each succeeding contract as a step up, a new position from which to bargain even more effectively until you come close to getting everything you ask for. Just remember that patience, politeness, and a firm knowledge of what you want will see you through even the most convoluted negotiations.

5

Rights and Copyrights

Beginning writers are often paranoid. We've been asked on more than one occasion, "How can I protect my ideas? How do I know an editor won't steal them and either write about them himself or give them to one of his pet writers?"

Bluntly speaking, there *are* no new ideas. Everything you're likely to think of has been done many, many times before and is part of the common background we all share. What the writer really means is, "How do I protect my particular expression and combination of elements from being stolen?" It's only the way old ideas are uniquely expressed that gives your work its originality.

We're told that theft is a fairly routine occurrence in the movie and TV industry. Two writers of our acquaintance, Harlan Ellison and Ben Bova, successfully sued a producer and a film studio for appropriating their concept. But such theft is very hard to prove, simply because ideas are so common. Theatrical movies are a *director's* medium; the director is the person who finally shapes what is seen on the screen. Different directors can take the same script and make two vastly different movies. Consequently, the writer's words and ideas aren't highly valued because it's the director whose expression makes the work unique. (If you don't believe us, try listing the writers of Hitchcock's or De Mille's movies.) The producer and director feel they can get a writer anywhere to come up with a script; the director is the superstar.

Television, by contrast, is a *producer's* medium, particularly episodic TV. On a regular series, the show may have a different writer and director every week; it's the producer who has the overall vision to maintain quality and consistency. Unless you're in the industry you probably can't name many writers or directors, but most people have heard of Norman Lear and Quinn Martin. Again, the writer's ideas aren't highly valued; it's the producer who ultimately shapes them into the form that can be expressed in his TV show.

But in magazines and books, the *writer* is the star. An editor may suggest a project to a writer and may fine-tune some of the wording when it comes in, but it's the writer who controls the combination of ideas and the expression of them. That's why theft of a writer's ideas is remarkably rare in the print media.

Suppose you submit a really dynamite idea and the editor wants to steal it. If your idea was only submitted to him in proposal form, he's got an immediate problem. He'll have to get *somebody* to write it. Maybe he'd try it himself, but that would take time—something editors have little of. Or he might give it to another writer he knows. But he'd have to pay that other writer something too, wouldn't he? And while that other writer is working away, you might sell your proposal elsewhere and publish your version first—in which case he'd be out of luck.

On top of that, there is a universal loathing for plagiarists and thieves in the publishing business. Any editor with substantiated charges against him would be fired by a reputable house—and word gets around quickly in the publishing industry. He would have a hard time getting a job anywhere in an established company and he'd either have to give up his career completely or go to work for some small, out-of-the-way firm that never heard of him or was too crooked to care (there are a few of those, but not many).

If your idea is for a short story or article, the editor would be cheating you out of, at most, a few hundred dollars; for a book, that might be a few thousand. For these small sums of money, he'd be risking his entire future career. We don't know many people who'd care to take that risk, and we doubt you do, either.

Since the editor has to have the piece written by somebody, why shouldn't it be the person who thought it up? If he likes the idea but feels your writing style needs improvement, he may try to edit it himself once you've handed in the completed work. If he finds your writing style so abominable that it would take too much of his time to edit correctly, he might recommend that you collaborate with another writer—and perhaps suggest a few he knows. But if you insist on doing it your way and you still can't please him, he'll shake his head sadly, return your manuscript, and wish you better luck somewhere else. Editors receive so many submissions that the loss of one project, no matter how potentially exciting, is not going to make or break them. They are more concerned with their entire *line* than with any single portion of it.

There's an old wives' tale that you can protect your work by mailing yourself, via certified mail, a sealed copy of your manuscript and storing it away unopened. Then, so the advice goes, if there is any question of authorship, you can show the postmark date on the envelope and have its contents notarized.

This circuitous method may even work, for all we know. We've never heard of a case where it came to court, but it's possible such evidence might sway a judge or jury. But why go to such Machiavellian extremes when, for a bit more money, you can obtain full protection that will hold up in any court in the land?

Subsidiary Rights

The U.S. government—and the governments of most civilized countries—recognize that authors have the right to benefit from their creations and have established a form of protection called the copyright. This is a shield that protects authors from having their unique expression of ideas used without their consent. The copyright is a legal statement of ownership, much like a deed to a piece of land.

Beginning writers sometimes confuse the "rights" to a work with the "copyright." This is natural, since both terms contain some of the same letters in the same order and both are used to describe the way your work can be utilized. There is a subtle but very real distinction between the terms, and we'll try as best we can to explain it.

The deed to a piece of land means you legally own it and can do anything you want with it (or at least anything the zoning laws will allow). The government has a certain right to make sure you don't use it for illegal or hazardous purposes. But within broad limits, the land is yours.

Suppose there's a house on your property, but you prefer to live somewhere else. You can rent the house to someone else and collect money for the privilege. If there happens to be oil under your land, you can lease out the mineral rights and authorize someone to drill for it on your behalf. The driller would want a large share of the profits to reimburse him for his drilling expenses, but you're still entitled to a share because it *is* your land.

Some people like to live on the land themselves; they'll even build their own house and farm the land as best they can. But whether they use the land themselves or never set foot on it, it's theirs. They can give other people the right to use the land for certain purposes without losing their ownership. Or they can sell the deed and thereby lose ownership—

but if they do that, they might never get ownership back again.

Copyright is the deed to the work you created. It *includes* within it rights to develop the literary property in various ways, but the whole in this case is more than the sum of its parts. You can transfer *all* rights to a work and still own the copyright, just as you can let other people do whatever they want with your land and yet still own the deed.

The Copyright Act of 1976 gives the owner of a copyright the exclusive right to do (or to authorize others to do) the following things: (1) to reproduce the copyrighted work in copies or phonorecords; (2) to prepare derivative works based on the copyrighted work; (3) to distribute copies or phono-records of the copyrighted work to the public by sale or other transfer of ownership, or by rental, lease, or lending; (4) to perform the copyrighted work publicly; and (5) to display the copyrighted work publicly. The fifth right applies largely to art, sculpture, choreography, movies, etc., but all five can have some importance to writers in the print media.

The first and third rights are pretty obvious. A writer wants his work to be published and distributed so a lot of people can read it. The Copyright Act gives you the exclusive right to do this for your work. If you don't own your own printing press and newsstand, however, you might find it a little difficult. Most writers authorize someone else to do this task for them: the publisher. In return for performing this service, the publisher asks to be allowed to profit from your work as well—which is only reasonable, since the publisher's using his money to print and distribute it. The publisher pays you for the right to publish the work and then tries to make that money back. Publishers are speculators in the thoughts of others.

Because there are various ways a work can be published, there are different subsidiary rights a publisher can buy. If he wants to print it in a magazine, he buys "serial rights."

(For some reason dating back to the Dawn of Man, publishers use the word "serial" when they mean "magazine," whether the piece appears in one installment or many.) Serial rights are further subdivided. If a publisher wants the right to publish the work in a magazine before anyone else has used it, he buys "first" serial rights; that means no one else can publish it before he does. A publisher who doesn't mind whether the piece appeared somewhere else first can settle for "second" serial rights. (Presumably there are also third, fourth, etc., serial rights, but most publishers use the term "second serial rights" to mean anything after the first serial rights.)

A magazine publisher who wants to publish a long work in several parts will ask for "serialization" rights; or he may want to shorten it to run in one issue, so he'd ask for "condensation" or "abridgement" rights. Editors of a textbook or a collection may want to publish a group of articles or stories, including one of yours, in book form; they may refer to these as "anthology" rights or, more loosely, "reprint" rights.

A book-length manuscript can be published in a number of different forms. It can be published in a hardcover, or "trade," edition; in small paperback editions (known variously as "cheap," "reprint," or "mass-market" editions); or in an intermediate form that is just starting to become popular, the large-sized quality paperback, usually referred to as a "trade paperback" edition. A book can be published in a special large-type edition for the visually impaired; it can be published in Braille or spoken onto records and tapes for the blind. Each of these different methods of publication has its own rights associated with it.

Rights can also be made to cover specific geographic areas in which publication may occur. When you give permission to (or "license") a publisher to publish a work, you may specify that it can only be published in the United States, or Canada, or the British Commonwealth, or any other limited area; or you can give "world" rights, which covers everything. Rights may also be limited in time or duration. You may grant the publisher the right to use your work only for a year, or two years, or ten years, or until some other specified conditions are met. For instance, the publisher may only have the right to publish and distribute the work as long as it is kept in print; if it is allowed to go out of print, the rights revert to you.

The second exclusive right granted by the Copyright Act is the right to prepare derivative works based on the copyrighted work. Derivative works come in all forms. Translation into another language is technically a derivative work, since it is a change from the original copyrighted work that was done in English. You, as the author, have the right to license French translation rights, German translation rights, etc., ad infinitum—and each individual language is considered a separate entity.

You may also license someone to adapt your work into audiovisual form by granting "dramatic" rights, "radio" rights, "motion picture" rights, or "television" rights. In general, any medium that currently exists or may exist at some future time is covered by its own set of rights.

Perhaps you've come up with a great slogan in your writing, and someone wants to make it into a poster and sell it. Or maybe you've created a character who becomes popular and some company wants to market a doll based on it. These, too, could be considered "derivative works" based on your original, and there would be separate rights for them. In general, you'll find them listed under a catch-all term like "merchandising" or "commercial" rights.

Rights may be "exclusive" or "nonexclusive." When you created a copyrighted work, the Copyright Act gave you all rights exclusively, meaning no one but you can do anything with them. If you transfer one of your rights to someone else, you can also do it on an exclusive basis, which means no one but that person—not even *you*—can use that right as long as that person possesses it. It's also possible to transfer the right nonexclusively; this means the person you give it to may use your work for that purpose, but you also have the option to let other people—or yourself—use that same right. (The use of the word "first," as in "first North American serial rights," implies a certain exclusivity, because you've agreed that no one else can use the work until after the owner of the first right has used it.)

You can also sell "options" on certain rights; this means you promise to consider that person's offer if you ever choose to sell that particular right. Options may also be exclusive or nonexclusive and may be of fixed duration. If you sell an exclusive option it's wise to limit it in some way, such as for a fixed period of time only; otherwise, while the person holding the exclusive option can't force you to sell to him, no one else will ever be allowed to make an offer until the option holder relinquishes his option (or his exclusivity).

Each right you have is another way of selling your work and thus another potential source of income. It's not to your advantage to give them away haphazardly to people who don't need them or can't use them. If a magazine publisher isn't also a movie producer, why should he be allowed to control the movie rights to your short story? He won't be able to use them himself; at best he could only sell them to someone else, and then he'd get the money for them rather than you. Writers therefore try to sell as few rights as possible to each purchaser, and to limit the sales in other ways by imposing conditions of nonexclusivity, time limits, author approval, and other conditions on the way the rights can be used.

Publishers, in turn, want to get the most value for their money by buying as many rights as possible, exclusively and without any encumbrances: ideally, they'd like all rights forever.

Somewhere between these two extremes, a bargain is

struck. The publisher may demand to handle some rights, even though he's not equipped to use them directly, as the price you must pay in exchange for his money. You give up the rights because you know the publisher won't buy the ones you're willing to sell without the total package. A large portion of any publishing agreement spells out in detail which rights belong to which party. As you become more successful, you'll find more pathways opening for you to sell your work, and you'll be able to keep more of your rights to sell yourself.

What Can Be Copyrighted

Copyright is granted for "original works of authorship" when they become fixed in a tangible form of expression (even if you need a machine or device to perceive that expression, as with a phonograph or a movie projector). Since this book is primarily intended for writers using the print media, we'll assume that means copyright can be given for books, articles, stories, pamphlets, poems, letters, and other written materials and adaptations of them.

A work that is not protected by copyright is referred to as being "in the public domain," meaning anyone has the right to use it for whatever purpose he chooses. A large body of work is so old it was never copyrighted—Homer's *Iliad,* for instance, or the works of Shakespeare—or else any copyright a work may have had at one time has now expired, such as Hawthorne's *The Scarlet Letter.* If you wanted to print your own edition of *Hamlet* or *The Scarlet Letter,* no one could legally stop you; the only factor you'd have to consider was whether you could sell enough copies of your edition to make money.

You might have a bit more trouble, though, if you tried to publish your own edition of the *Iliad.* As long as you published it in the original Greek, you'd be perfectly safe, because that version is definitely in the public domain. The market for classical Greek-language versions within the United States is limited, however. For more success, you'd want an English translation, and *there* would be your problem, because translations can be copyrighted in and of themselves.

If you prepared your own translation of the work from scratch, you'd still be okay; in fact, you could even copyright your translation because it's your own unique expression of a work. No one else could use your translation without your permission. You also have the option of using one of the older English translations that have lapsed into the public domain. But if you intend to use a modern translation, you'd have to seek the permission of the person who owns the copyright on that translation.

Translations in general provide a problem because of their dual nature. If you want to publish a French novel in English, you must get permission from both the novelist and the translator (or at least the person who owns the rights to the translation). If the novelist agrees and the translator doesn't, you'll have to decide whether it's worth having a new translation made. If the original author denies permission, then you can't do it no matter what the translator says.

Not just translations but *all* derivative works are copyrightable apart from the original. That includes plays, scripts, abridgements, songs, etc. They all complicate the copyright picture by increasing the number of permissions that must be obtained before a work can be used.

There are certain things which cannot be copyrighted. We mentioned at the beginning of this chapter that there are no new ideas, and so an idea by itself can't be copyrighted. Take the following story line: The tale takes place during a war and immediately afterward. (It doesn't matter which war you choose: the War of the Roses, the Revolutionary War, World War I or II, Korea, or Vietnam—all work equally well.) There are two married couples, A and B. The wife of couple

A is hopelessly infatuated with the husband of couple B and throws herself at him every chance she gets—much to the dismay of her own husband. Not until wife B dies does wife A realize she's loved her own husband all along—but now it may be too late.

There's nothing particularly unique in that idea, and it isn't copyrightable. We could hand that outline to ten different writers, and the end result would be ten entirely different and unique stories—*each* of which would be copyrightable. (One version, Margaret Mitchell's *Gone with the Wind,* has already enjoyed some success.)

The same principle applies to facts, which are the common heritage of people who want to use them. The Declaration of Independence was proclaimed in Philadelphia on July 4, 1776. That someone else may have used that fact in a story or article doesn't prevent you from using it also. All a copyright protects is your unique way of expressing a fact, not the fact itself. (If this weren't the case, it would be impossible to do research, since the person who wrote the original article would have a copyright on the facts.)

Works that haven't been put in tangible form also aren't subject to copyright. If you give an extemporaneous speech to a group of librarians, that speech is not copyrighted. If you tape-record it, however, the recording could be copyrighted. If you go home after the speech and write down what you said, that could also be copyrighted.

Confusion has sometimes arisen over the fact that titles can't be copyrighted. While going through used bookstores one afternoon, Stephen Goldin found four separate novels entitled *The Wanderer,* all by different authors and published at different times. Each author had a perfect right to use that title; so do you, if you care to do so.

What, then, is to prevent you from calling your book *Gone with the Wind* or *Shōgun* and cashing in on the fame of those two best-sellers? While it's true those titles aren't copyrighted, there is a legal principle called "unfair competition." When titles like those become so famous that the general public associates them with one particular thing, someone who takes advantage of that identification is presumed to be trying to mislead the public. Even if the famous work is in the public domain, such as Dickens's *Tale of Two Cities,* the publishers of the original could make a case against you if you tried to publish a book of your own with that title.

The question of whether something is famous enough to be vulnerable to unfair competition is a matter of judgment, and only a court can decide the matter definitively. Harlequin Books brought suit against Simon & Schuster/Pocket Books, charging that the latter company's line of Silhouette Romances unfairly competed with Harlequin's own immensely successful books. In that case, Harlequin asserted that Pocket Books was stealing not the titles of the individual books but the layout and overall marketing design that Harlequin pioneered and made famous. The case was settled out of court late in 1981, so we may never have a clearcut ruling on where the line may be drawn.

You may have to rely on your publisher's legal staff in this matter. If they feel your title is too easily identified with another work, they may ask you to change it.

The Old Copyright Law

If you were publishing work before January 1, 1978, it was subject to the provisions of the old copyright law, which was enacted in 1909; works published from 1978 on are covered by new regulations. Even if you're brand new to writing, it pays you to know what the old law was like—if only so you can see how much better off you are now. Before discussing the law as it is today, we'll show you how it used to be.

Under the old law, a manuscript had what was known as "common-law" copyright as soon as it was created. This protection lasted until the work was published. It could sit around in your files for years without harm, or you could make a few copies to show to editors without worrying. You couldn't register an unpublished work, but as long as it wasn't publicly distributed you were safe.

Common-law copyright ended as soon as the work was published. The definition of "publication" was never made clear; it could be reading your work aloud in public or circulating photocopies of it without restriction on the use people could put them to. The law was *very* specific on one point, however: When you published your work, you *had* to print with it (in one of several very specific places) a proper copyright notice. If you followed the steps as required, your work gained "statutory" copyright, protected by the law. If you published your work *without* the proper copyright notice, however, it instantly fell into the public domain and you could never have any protection for it again. Anyone could use it without your permission, and you'd have no recourse. This made publication of the proper notice a crucial factor.

Statutory copyright lasted for a period of 28 years. During that twenty-eighth year—not one day sooner or later—you could apply to renew that protection for a second term of 28 years. (For example, if a work was originally published on July 1, 1920, the Copyright Office wouldn't accept your renewal application before July 1, 1947. After that, you had a year to get the application in. If your renewal application didn't reach the Copyright Office until July 2, 1948, you were out of luck; the copyright had expired and that work was now in the public domain.)

After the second term of copyright, the work could not be renewed any further and automatically lapsed into the public domain. Thus, the most protection a copyrighted work could have in the United States was 56 years. This could be unfair and embarrasing to a long-lived author. Suppose Arthur Penman sold his first novel at age twenty and then went on to have a long, distinguished career as America's foremost novelist. Suddenly, when he's seventy-six and at the height of his glory, his first novel lapses into public domain and anyone can print it, cashing in on his fame.

It becomes grossly unfair to have a living writer's work in the public domain, and yet that situation has happened any number of times—either because the writer has outlived the two terms or, more frequently, because he didn't observe the renewal procedure correctly. (Sometimes writers forgot about it completely until it was too late; after all, something you wrote 28 years ago is not constantly in your thoughts.)

Each copyrighted work had to be renewed separately, and a fee was paid each time. If Arthur Penman was a prolific short-story writer and had fifteen published in one year, 28 years later he would have to pay fifteen different fees for fifteen renewals—again, an unfair and costly procedure.

The 1909 copyright law also had a protectionist clause for the U.S. printing industry. Books had to meet certain manufacturing conditions within the United States; if manufactured outside the United States and brought into this country, there was a chance they could lose copyright protection and fall into the public domain.

The old copyright law was not clear about the division of rights that make up the copyright; in fact, the concept of divisible rights was not firmly established until well after the law was passed. If a magazine bought a piece, printed it, and had the copyright notice in its name, and no agreement was made about which rights had been bought, there could be a long heated argument over who owned which rights to the work.

In short, the old copyright law offered protection but forced writers to walk a tightrope. If they published without the proper notice, they were out of luck. If they didn't renew properly, they were out of luck. If their published work wasn't manufactured according to proper criteria, they were out of luck. If they lived too long, they were out of luck. If they didn't make proper rights agreements, they were out of luck.

Publication and Registration

The new copyright law does away completely with the concept of common-law copyright. Statutory copyright—that is, full copyright under the law—is in effect as soon as the creative work is fixed in tangible form. For writers, that usually means the instant the last page of final draft rolls out of the typewriter. Your work is then fully copyrighted, and all the exclusive rights we mentioned earlier belong to you.

Since publication is no longer required for a work to obtain statutory copyright, this now means that unpublished works can have their copyrights registered with the Copyright Office. This is the protection we mentioned at the beginning of this chapter, and it's available to anyone. The fee, as of this writing, is $10, and only one form need be filled out. Most writers would use Form TX, which covers published and unpublished nondramatic literary works. It's a comparatively simple form, as government forms go, and it comes with complete instructions. (Appendix B gives the address of the Copyright Office and a list of the forms and informational pamphlets they have available, all absolutely free.)

Since copyright is automatically invested in an unpublished manuscript, a copyright notice is not necessary for it. Once the manuscript *is* published, however, the law does require that the notice be placed. Under the old law, failure to publish the proper notice doomed the work to fall into the public domain, with no chance of ever getting it back again. Under the new law, publication without the proper notice is undesirable but hardly fatal. If the work was registered before publication, the copyright is safe. Even if it wasn't preregistered, you can still register it within five years of publication. The law also says that you and/or the publisher have to make a reasonable effort to add the notice to all copies distributed to the public after the omission has been discovered.

What is the proper notice like? The copyright notice contains three basic elements: (1) the symbol © or the word "Copyright" or the abbreviation "Copr."; (2) the year of the work's first publication; and (3) the name of the copyright owner. Any of the following would be acceptable:

© Arthur Penman 1982
Copyright 1982 by Arthur Penman
Copr. 1982 Arthur Penman
Copyright © 1982 by Arthur Penman

If an older work has been renewed, both the original and renewal dates should be mentioned. If the copyright was originally made by a magazine and renewed by the author, the notice should state that too. For example:

Copyright 1952 by Jones Publishing Corporation
Copyright renewed 1980 by Arthur Penman

The notice should be placed in such a way as to "give reasonable notice of the claim of copyright." In a book, this is usually on the page following the title page. In magazines, it is usually found near the masthead or the table of contents.

It had been standard practice, under the old law, for a magazine, anthology, or other collective work (called "compilations" in copyright jargon) to copyright the entire compilation under one notice; for instance, © 1969 by Real Good Stories. Thus, even if *Real Good Stories* only bought first serial rights and you owned all the rest, the copyright was still technically in their name. To get the copyright back, you either had to ask them to complete a transfer notice, which you could then file with the Copyright Office, or else you could wait until the first term was ending and renew the copyright in your name. (Even under the old law, only the author or the author's heirs were allowed to renew the copyright no matter who held the original, except under very rigidly defined special conditions.) Most publishers were very accommodating about transferring the copyright if you asked them, but it was an annoying bureaucratic mess nonetheless.

Under the new law, even if the entire magazine or compilation is copyrighted in the publisher's name, each individual contribution is considered to be copyrighted in the name of its own author (unless it was a work for hire, a term we'll explain shortly). Technically, therefore, a magazine should publish a number of copyright notices: one in its own name, to cover the publication as a whole, and one for each contribution to it in the name of each individual author. The additional notices could be under the publisher's notice at the front, or they could accompany the individual articles throughout the magazine. They could be put under the title, or on the bottom of the first page of the article, or at the end of the article—someplace that would give "reasonable notice."

Old habits die hard, however, and many magazine publishers still only publish the one overall notice. This doesn't invalidate your ownership of the copyright, but it can cost you a bit of money when you register the works, as we'll show you shortly. You really should insist that the magazine run a separate copyright notice for your work. It's very little trouble or expense for the publisher, and it can save you some of both.

The new law doesn't require you to *ever* register your work; your manuscript is protected by copyright and you still own all the exclusive rights mentioned earlier even if you never send a notice to the Copyright Office. However—and it's a big however—there are strong advantages for you if you do register. For one thing, the courts won't bother with an infringement case on an unregistered work; if someone reprints your piece without permission and you want to sue, it *has* to be registered. Moreover, the sooner you register, the better off you are. If registration is made within three months after the work's publication, you get full copyright protection; that way, if someone infringes on your work, you can collect statutory damages and attorney's fees as well as actual damages. Or if registration is made any time later than that, but still before an infringement occurs, you can collect all that's coming to you. If you wait until *after* someone has infringed, though, and then register the work so you can file suit, all you're allowed to collect are the actual damages and profits he made on the work—something that's very hard to prove in any case. You'd have to pay your own attorney's fees, and you wouldn't be able to collect statutory damages, which can be the most sizable part of an infringement settlement. As you can see, it is very much to your benefit to register a work as soon after publication as you can. (If you register your work before it's published, it's already covered and you don't have to register it again afterward. It doesn't hurt, though, to register a particular edition after it's been published, just in case.)

As we mentioned earlier, registration is a simple procedure. You fill out an application on Form TX, pay a set fee (currently $10), and make a deposit of the work being registered. The nature of the deposit depends on the circumstances. If you're registering an unpublished work, you only have to send one complete copy of it along with the application. If you're registering a published work, include two copies of a complete edition. If your piece was a contribution to a collective work like a magazine or anthology, you only need to send one complete copy of the edition.

If you've sold a book, the publisher will normally handle these registration formalities on your behalf; the expense and the trouble are minimal in this case. But the situation is very different for collective works. While the publisher will generally register a collective work as a whole, it's rare that he will register the individual contributions in the authors' names.

For one thing, the only people allowed to register a work are the author or a duly authorized agent, a person who owns the copyright (if an author has given it away), or a person who owns some exclusive right to the work. A book publisher normally falls into this last category because typical book contracts grant the exclusive right to print and distribute the work in the United States. Unless you've sold some exclusive right to a magazine or anthology, its publisher legally *can't* register the work for you.

For another thing, registering the work for each contributor would be financially prohibitive. Even if the publisher bought some exclusive rights, there would be a separate registration procedure for each author. Ten different authors in the magazine would mean $100 in fees in addition to the $10 to register the magazine as a whole. Magazine publishers, therefore, usually leave this chore to the individual writers.

The natural question becomes, How can a poor writer afford all these fees? If he writes books, there's no problem; even if the publisher won't register them, they're still only $10 apiece. But how does a prolific magazine writer who turns out one or two dozen stories a year avoid bankruptcy from paying $10 for each registration?

The Copyright Office has taken this into account too; they now have a procedure for "group registration," where you can register a number of published works for one fee. There are some conditions, however. All the works must have been contributions published within the same twelve-month period, they must all have been by the same author, and they must all have been published with individual copyright notices. (*This* is why you should insist that a magazine or anthology publisher give you a separate notice; if he doesn't, you can't take advantage of group registration.)

The procedure would then work as follows: You fill out one copy of Form TX and one copy of Form GR/CP (for group registrations) as an adjunct to it, pay one registration fee, and include one copy of each publication that contains your work. All the material should be sent together in one envelope; otherwise the Copyright Office might not accept it.

This group registration will cover all contributions published within a twelve-month period. However, as we explained earlier, maximum copyright protection occurs when a work is registered within *three* months of publication. If you're prolific enough to have articles published throughout the year, you might prefer to do a group registration every three months rather than every year. It will cost you an extra $30 a year, but you might find the peace of mind it brings worth the price.

Group registration is only applicable for *published* work. If you want to register a number of unpublished short stories, poems, or articles, you would technically have to register each one separately. There is a way around this, however, and that is to make up your own unpublished anthology and register that as a single work. The registration would apply to the collection as a whole rather than to the individual pieces, and each piece should be registered again when it's published, but it does provide reasonable protection for the truly paranoid among us.

Recordation

Under the new copyright law, the copyright owner cannot transfer exclusive rights to anyone else unless the transfer is made in writing. Verbal agreements simply aren't good enough. This is another form of protection for a writer, since a publisher can't claim you transferred some exclusive right without producing evidence—but it does have some paperwork attendant on it.

If you submit a story or an article to a magazine and the editor accepts it with just a check and no contract, the new law presumes he has bought exactly two rights, both nonexclusive: (1) the right to publish that piece in his magazine; and (2) the right to publish that piece in future editions or issues of that same magazine. For instance, if you sold an article to *Omni* magazine without a contract, the publisher would have the right to print that article in every issue of *Omni* from then on—but never in *Penthouse*, even though both magazines are published by the same company, and he couldn't prevent you from selling it elsewhere. (*Omni* does have contracts, by the way.) If you don't want the publisher to be able to keep printing your work in his magazine, make sure you have a contract giving only one-time printing rights.

It's to the publisher's advantage, too, to get a contract in writing, because he can't claim any exclusive rights to your work unless he does. If he wants legal protection for the exclusive rights he's bought, he must record the transferral with the Copyright Office. The government calls this procedure "recordation," a particularly ugly example of bureaucratic jargon.

Again, the new law says this recordation is not mandatory; the publisher could buy these rights from you and never bother to notify the Copyright Office. But if any question of ownership comes up, the transfer can't be proved in court unless it is recorded.

Because it's to the publisher's advantage to have a legal record of the exclusive rights he's bought—if he doesn't, after all, you could sell nonexclusive rights to someone else and compete with him—he's usually the one to file recordation. Surprisingly, there is no form to be filled out. The recorder merely pays a fee (currently $10 for the first six pages and 50¢ for each additional page), which is *in addition to* any registration fee, and submits a statement describing which rights were transferred. This statement may be in one of three forms: an original copy of the contract signed by the writer, a notarized copy of the contract, or a summary of the transfer clauses in the contract, signed by the writer.

The ordinary book contract contains a lot of clauses the Copyright Office doesn't care about—warranties, indemnities, royalties, etc. All that matters to the Copyright Office are the rights that were transferred. Sometimes a publisher will draw up a summary along with the contract, outlining which rights he's buying, and send that to you for signature so it can be properly recorded. He is basically doing you a favor by saving you the recordation fee. Before signing it, however, make sure he's not doing you too good a favor; make sure the summary accurately reflects what's in the contract. It should grant to the publisher *only* the rights that the contract itself grants, and it should also describe out-of-print clauses, approval clauses, and any other limitations of these rights; if the contract specifically says that certain rights are reserved by the author, then so should the summary. The summary should also state that it's subject to all the terms of the full contract between you and the publisher, dated as of the date of the contract.

There are times when it will be in *your* best interest to record a transfer of rights—particularly if some rights you had previously granted to a publisher have now reverted to you. The publisher might be a little reluctant to record that, so you'll have to do it. Send a copy of the transfer document, along with the recordation fee, to the Copyright Office; it's that simple. (Remember, if it's a matter of rights reverting to you, the document you send should be signed by the person or company doing the transferring, or be a notarized copy of it.) The Copyright Office will make its own copy and return the original to you, along with a certificate of recordation.

Duration of Copyright

Any work that was in the public domain as of January 1, 1978, remains that way forever. The new law doesn't have the power to raise such works from the dead, as it were. Anything that was still under copyright protection on that date, however, gets a new lease on life, in the form of at least 19 additional years, possibly more.

If a work was already in its second term under the old law as of that date—that is, if it had been properly renewed after 1950—it automatically gains an additional 19 years of protection. The author doesn't have to do anything to get this gift, just sit back and enjoy it. This extends copyright protection to a term of 75 years. It's unlikely many authors will outlive that term, so fewer copyrights will expire during the author's lifetime. Seventy-six years after its first publication, the work enters the public domain.

If a work was in its *first* term under the old law as of that date—that is, if it was first published between 1950 and 1977—it will have to be renewed if you want its protection to extend past the twenty-eighth year. There have been improvements, however, to make the process better and easier.

The best improvement is that the second term will be for 47 years rather than 28—again bringing the total copyright life up to 75 years rather than 56. After the second term is over, the work goes into the public domain.

The second improvement is in the period during which renewal may take place. Under the old law, a work could only be renewed between the twenty-seventh and twenty-eighth anniversary of its first publication. If you didn't know the exact publication date, you could make a crucial error and miss out on your renewal. The new law depends only on the calendar year of publication and the calendar year of renewal. A work published on June 22, 1960, for example, would be eligible for renewal at any time from January 1, 1988 to December 31, 1988. The date, by the way, is the date the Copyright Office *receives* the renewal application, not the date on the application itself or the postmark. The earlier in the year you file for renewal, the better; don't wait until late December, when you have to compete with the Christmas mail.

The third improvement is that some renewals can now be handled as a group, the same as new registrations. Under the old law, each renewal had to be handled separately with its own separate fee. Even under the new law, novels, plays, and other items that are individual units must be renewed separately—but contributions to periodicals may all be covered by a single fee (currently $6). The conditions for group registration are: (1) All the works must be by the same author, who is or was an individual (not an employer of work for hire); (2) all the works must have been contributions to periodicals, including newspapers, and were copyrighted on their first publication; (3) the person renewing the copyright, and the basis for doing so, must be the same for all the works; (4) all the works must be eligible for renewal in the same calendar year; and (5) the renewal application (Form RE) must identify each work separately, including the name of the original periodical and the date of first publication.

In general, there are strict limits on who is allowed to claim the copyright renewal. If the author is alive, he or she is the only one allowed to claim it (unless it was done as a work for hire, in which case the employer does it); if the author is dead, a widow, widower, or child of the author may claim copyright; if there's no surviving spouse or child and the author left a will, the author's executors may claim copyright; and if there's no will, the next of kin may claim it. If a work was first published after the author's death, whoever possessed the initial copyright may claim the renewal.

The Copyright Office can only renew registrations if the work was registered the first time. It's been known to happen that a magazine publisher, to save a little money, didn't send in the magazine's registration when it was published. The copyright will still be valid if the correct notice was printed in the original issue . . . but someone will have to *register* that issue before you can renew your contribution. Your first step is to notify the publisher and inform him of that fact. If the company is out of business or can't be located, your only other option is to register the magazine yourself. (You'll have to submit two copies of that issue, and sometimes it's hard to find them after 28 years.) As long as all the necessary fees, copies, and applications are received in the Copyright Office before the end of the first copyright term, you're permitted to make simultaneous original and renewal applications. This is another reason why you should send in your renewal applications early in the year; if any snags like this come up, you'll have more time to deal with them.

We come now to the best category of all: works copyrighted on or after January 1, 1978. From now on, new works don't have to worry about renewal deadlines. All copyrights issued since the new law went into effect last for the length of the author's life, plus 50 years more (to give his heirs some use of the material), and then lapse into the public domain all at once. If there was more than one author, the copyright continues for 50 years after the death of the last surviving collaborator. This makes it virtually impossible for a work to be in the public domain during an author's lifetime, avoiding all sorts of embarrassing situations. Furthermore, it simplifies the job of finding out whether a work is in the public domain or not; just find the year of the author's death and add fifty more to it. There'll be an awkward transition period while renewals of old copyrights run their course (or fail to be properly renewed, as the case may be), but things will be much easier after that.

Let's give a complex example. Suppose Arthur Penman began his writing career in 1970 with six magazine articles. In 1973 his first novel was published, and his second came along in 1976. From 1978 until his death on July 7, 2002, he published ten more novels. What is the status of his works?

The six magazine articles came up for renewal together in 1998, and Penman renewed them as a group. In 2001 his first novel needed renewing, and he did so properly. He was dead in 2004 when his second novel needed renewing, and his widow carelessly forgot to do so. The rest of his novels were published after the new law went into effect, so they didn't have to be renewed.

Here's the picture, then. The six magazine articles are protected by copyright until December 31, 2045 (47 years after their renewal, 75 years after publication). Penman's first novel is protected until December 31, 2048. All his novels published after 1977 are protected until December 31, 2052. But that second novel lapsed into the public domain when renewal was not made; anyone could publish it after December 31, 2004. His widow becomes very annoyed to see all these unauthorized editions of her late husband's book popping up, but there's nothing she can do.

If you wrote something before 1978 but it wasn't published, it was covered under common-law copyright according to the old law. That category was abolished with the new law, and every unpublished creation gained full statutory copyright. For legal purposes, it's as though that work was created on January 1, 1978, and is subject to all the benefits and provisions of the new law, including the life-plus-50-years term of copyright.

There are some exceptional circumstances. An anonymous work is protected for a period of 100 years after its creation or 75 years after its first publication, whichever term is shorter. There's an exception even to this, however, in that the law has a 25-year grace period; no work of this type created but unpublished before 1978 can expire before 2002. If, for example, you found an old diary in your attic written by some anonymous soldier who'd served with Washington at Valley Forge, you could still protect it by copyright even though more than 100 years had elapsed since its creation. In fact, if you publish it before the end of 2002, you may even be able to get an additional 25 years of protection, through the end of 2027.

Works published under a pseudonym are given the same 75/100 year term as anonymous works, since the date of death won't be known if the author's true identity isn't known. If you let the Copyright Office know you're the real author of your work, however, they'll record the fact and change the term to the usual life-plus-50-years. There is the same grace period on these works as on anonymous ones that were unpublished before 1978.

Work for Hire

The author of a work is usually the owner of its copyright unless he or she chooses to sell it. The copyright owner owns a vast store of subsidiary rights. But there is one major category where the writer doesn't hold these rights, and that's in the case of "work for hire."

A reporter or staff writer on a periodical is the obvious example of a writer doing work for hire. According to the copyright law, anything you write as part of your job, for which you get a regular salary, is considered work for hire—unless you and your employer have a specific agreement to the contrary. In a work for hire, the *employer,* rather than the writer, is considered the creator—and the *employer* is the one who holds the copyright and all the goodies that entails. A reporter's news articles or a journalist's columns would thus be copyrighted in the name of the publisher, and the writer would have no further say about their use.

A work can also be considered made for hire if there is a contract saying it is. This practice is quite common in the publishing industry. If you're hired to do the novelization of a movie script, for instance, you'll be asked to sign a work-for-hire contract, because the film studio owns the rights to the work and is merely hiring you to put it into book form. If you're asked to continue a series of novels that was started by someone else, or to make updates on someone else's older work, you'll probably get a work-for-hire contract because the original creator owns the rights to the original work on which yours is based.

When you write for hire, you forfeit all claim to the work; your employer has full authority over its fate once it leaves your hands. If it's a work of fiction, for instance, the publisher can change your plot, characters, and writing style and even put another name on it (unless it specifically states in your contract that you have control over any of these factors). Because your employer is considered the creator of the work, any minor or subsidiary characters you created to further your story now belong to *him;* you're not even allowed to use them in future works of your own without permission.

Why does anyone do work for hire if it robs them of such basic rights? The best answer is that it's usually easy money. The characters, backgrounds, situations, sometimes even the story and the dialogue, are provided; all you have to do is put them into book form. The size of the advance is usually enough to compensate a writer for his time—but the lack of further interest in the book usually means it's done hastily and without concern for the final product. (If you've ever wondered why novelizations of film or TV scripts seemed of low quality, now you know.)

Because the owner of the copyright in a work-for-hire situation is usually a company and doesn't "die" in the usual sense, the life-plus-50-years term of normal copyrights doesn't apply. Works for hire created after 1978 have the same 75/100 year duration as anonymous and pseudonymous works; works for hire published before 1978 follow the same rules as anything else, except that only the copyright owner can register for renewal.

If you're ever offered a work-for-hire contract, think about it carefully. Realize that you will never have any control over what you've written, and ask yourself whether the money you're getting is ample consideration. Remember, too, there is nothing about work for hire that *prevents* a publisher from paying you royalties. You're entitled to ask for a share of any money earned by selling the work or any rights to it. Some movie novelizations, for instance, have become best-sellers; how would you feel if a book you wrote lasted for weeks on the best-seller lists and you didn't receive another cent? Try to get as much as you can, because you'll need it. It's very hard on the ego to be only a passive partner, seeing your work go out into the public marketplace and knowing you have no say in its destiny.

Termination of Transfers

The new copyright law contains a provision which allows for the termination of transfers after 35 years. That is, if you transferred one of your rights to someone who abused it and refused to let you have it back, you can take it away from him after 35 years. Admittedly that's a long time, but it does give you a chance to correct earlier mistakes; this is particularly true for writers who have matured in their craft and learned from past follies.

The 35 years is dated from the time you transferred the right to the other person—or, if one of the rights you transferred was the right of publication, the time is either 40 years from the date of transfer or 35 years from the date of first publication, whichever is shorter. Once that time has started, you have a 5-year period during which to force the rights to revert to you. If you don't take advantage of the chance then, you've lost it forever.

According to the procedures laid out by the Copyright Office, you have to give the person who currently owns the right between 2 and 10 years' notice that you intend to take them back. You can send that letter as early as 25 years or as late as 38 years after publication or transferral of the rights. The letter should describe which work you mean, which rights you want to revert, and the exact date on which you want them to revert. The wording of this letter may be tricky, so your best advice is to hire an attorney who's knowledgeable in the copyright field to write it for you. A copy of the letter is sent to the current owner of the rights (preferably by certified mail, return receipt requested, so you know it's been received), and you should record a copy with the Copyright Office as well. Then, on the date mentioned in your letter, the rights automatically revert to you.

Please note, however, that the person who had the rights before is entitled to profit from any derivative works he licensed before the rights reverted. If, for instance, the publisher in question had the right to license translations of the work and did so, the publisher can still collect a share of the royalties on those translations even after the right reverts to you.

Please note, also, that this clause doesn't help you if you wrote a work for hire. Only the copyright *owner* may cause such rights to revert—and in work for hire, the owner is the person who hired you. This is yet another reason to be careful about doing work for hire.

Let's look at an example to see how the principle works. Suppose young Arthur Penman sells his first novel, *Slimepit,* in 1979, and it's published in 1980. He was so excited about the sale that he didn't look closely at the contract; he ended up giving Sleazy Publishing Company all rights to the book in perpetuity, with no reversion clause, and in return he was to get royalties of 2 percent on all American copies sold and no share of any subsidiary money. *Slimepit* goes on to be an enormous hit; Sleazy sells the film rights, and the movie wins an Oscar. Overseas translations do well too. But all poor Penman gets is 2 percent royalties on the books sold in the United States; Sleazy keeps all the rest of the money.

Penman realizes he's been shafted, but there's little he can do except bide his time. His reputation for having written *Slimepit* soars, and he writes other books that do well (for other publishers; he certainly doesn't want to deal with Sleazy again), but the thought of Sleazy getting rich on *Slimepit* galls him.

On January 2, 2006 (after 25 years in publication), he writes the reversion letter to Sleazy, being careful to send it certified and to get a return receipt. In the letter he demands that all rights to *Slimepit* revert to him on January 1, 2016 (the day after the thirty-fifth year from publication). Penman makes sure to record a copy of the letter at the Copyright Office.

Ten more years pass, while Sleazy goes on its merry way making money off *Slimepit*. In December 2015, Sleazy prints a large number of copies and sends them out for a final distribution. Finally on January 1, 2016, without any fanfare, the rights revert to Penman. It's not a great victory; Sleazy can still earn money off the residual profits on the movie and the translations it licensed before it lost the rights. But at least Penman knows *Slimepit* belongs to him again, and he can benefit from any future deals. (The fact that Sleazy bought the rights "in perpetuity" means nothing; this reversion clause in the copyright law takes precedence.)

For older works that were under statutory copyright before 1978, there is a reversion benefit as well. There is the same 5-year grace period during which the termination may be made, and there is the same need for giving between 2 and 10 years' notice. In these cases, the 5-year grace period begins either on January 1, 1978, or after the fifty-sixth year of statutory protection (when the old copyright would have expired), whichever is later.

Infringement

When someone prints your work or adapts it in some other form without your permission, that is an infringement on your rights, just as if someone trespassed on your land and began digging holes without your permission. If you learn that someone has infringed on your work, you're entitled to sue—within certain limits, of course.

As with most crimes, there is a statute of limitations. You must file suit within three years of the infringement, or your case will be dismissed and the infringer will get off free.

If you registered your work within three months after its first publication (or at least before the infringement occurred), the law provides for statutory damages, actual damages, court costs, and attorney's fees, as well as empowering you to stop the infringer from distributing his copies, to seize the copies and even sell them yourself. If you registered your work late—more than three months after publication and after the infringement occurred—you can't collect the statutory damages or attorney's fees; you have to show that the infringing copies hurt the legitimate sales of your work, and you can only collect for the amount of damage. As you can imagine, that's often difficult to prove with any certainty.

Unless the infringer is an out-and-out thief and doesn't care, he'll try to claim that the infringement was done in "good faith," that he didn't know the work was registered. In order for this defense to hold up, he had to have based his infringing work on a copy of your piece with a defective copyright notice. If the name or date was missing, or if the notice was omitted entirely, his defense is good—as long as he stops the infringement the instant he's notified that you registered your work. This defense will also hold if the date in the copyright notice is more than one year later than the date publication actually occurred.

The defense is weakened, however, if the only error in the copyright notice is that the wrong person is named as copyright holder. (This could occur, say, in a magazine that had an overall notice but not separate notices for the individual articles.) If you didn't register your copyright before the infringement and the infringer made a deal with the magazine, he or she could be judged innocent of the infringement. Even in that case you wouldn't be totally without recourse, though, because the person who falsely gave permission can be held legally accountable to you for all the monies he derived from the sale. (While we're not lawyers, we suspect a good case could also be made against him for fraud and misrepresentation.)

But if you did register your work properly with the Copyright Office, the infringer can't plead ignorance just because the wrong name was on the published notice. The law assumes that people will check with the Copyright Office to find out who the real owner is before going ahead with plans to use your work.

As you can see, your basis for a successful suit against an infringer rests chiefly on three points: (1) a proper copyright notice being printed when the work was published; (2) registration of the work within three months after it was published, or at least before the infringement occurred; and (3) recordation of which rights were transferred and which were retained. None of these three is absolutely necessary, and you might win a case without any of them—but with all of them together, your case becomes ironclad.

You can take care of the second two points yourself, but what about the first? Unless you're publishing your own work, how can you guarantee the publisher won't slip up and neglect your proper notice?

The law provides that the publisher is liable if he made an agreement with the writer to publish a proper copyright notice and failed to do so. Writers must stop taking matters of copyright for granted. They will have to insist that a clause be put into every agreement and contract that the publisher is responsible for printing a proper copyright notice in the author's name in each copy of the work published. That way, if an infringer gets off the hook because of a faulty copyright notice, you have legal grounds to go after the publisher instead.

Other Provisions

The Library of Congress has a section known as the Division for the Blind and Physically Handicapped, or the DBPH. Under the new copyright law, registration Form TX has a space where you can grant the DBPH a nonexclusive license to reproduce and distribute copies of your work in Braille or on recordings for the blind and physically handicapped. Under the old law the DBPH had to write to each copyright holder separately for permission; it's hoped this new provision will simplify their paperwork.

This assignment is totally voluntary; it won't hurt your copyright registration at all if you refuse to go along with it. The license requested is nonexclusive, so you'd be free to grant these rights to other people as well as long as you do it in a way that doesn't interfere with the DBPH. You can also revoke this license whenever you want by sending the DBPH a termination letter; the license will terminate ninety days after they receive your letter (or at any later date you specify). Otherwise the license lasts as long as the copyright.

The market for Braille and phonorecordings is limited at best, and you probably won't be losing much money if you agree to the license. It all depends on how you feel about the matter, of course, but we personally think this is a worthwhile cause to support, and it requires very little effort on your part.

The new law also contains a special provision to benefit public broadcasting by making published musical and graphic works subject to compulsory licensing. This is somewhat similar to the right of eminent domain, where if the government needs your land for some important public purpose—to build a highway on it, for instance—the government can take the land but must pay you a fair price for it.

Under the new copyright law, public broadcasters in radio and television have the right to license your work for their purposes even without your permission, as long as the broadcast is noncommercial. They do, however, have to pay you a fair price. If the offer they make is not what *you* consider adequate, you may appeal the matter to the Copyright Royalty Tribunal, a panel created by the new law to oversee, in certain cases, whether royalty rates are fair. The Copyright Royalty Tribunal has the final say in the matter, and you'll have to take what they decide to give you.

The old copyright law had a provision known as a manufacturing clause, which as a piece of protectionist legislation intended to guard the American printing industry against foreign competition. Putting such a clause in the copyright law was grossly unfair to writers. If you couldn't find a publisher in this country and had to get your work published abroad, you couldn't bring very many copies into the United States without losing your copyright. If your publisher, without your knowledge, had your work printed outside the United States and brought into the country it was you, rather than the publisher, who was penalized by having the work lapse into the public domain. Few, if any, other countries have similar provisions in their own copyright laws.

Our new law liberalizes the restrictions on the number of foreign copies that may be brought into this country, eases the burden on foreign writers and on American writers who live or are published abroad, and considers manufacture in Canada equivalent to manufacture in the United States. The manufacturing clause is scheduled to terminate altogether as of July 1, 1982, eliminating all restrictions on foreign editions. American printers are currently fighting this change, and we can't be sure at this writing how the battle will turn out.

There is no such thing as an international copyright that

applies identically in all nations under all circumstances, but there have been several treaties to protect authors' rights on an international level.

The United States is signatory to the Buenos Aires Convention, as are a number of Latin-American nations. A work copyrighted in one signatory nation is considered copyrighted in all of them. The only formality is that there must be some indication that all rights have been reserved. This is usually done by printing the phrase "All Rights Reserved" or "Derechos Reservados" on the copyright notice.

The United States is also signatory to the Universal Copyright Convention, as are most of the world's civilized nations. This treaty requires that works published in a signatory country (or by a citizen of a signatory country) be protected by another signatory country to the extent that country would protect works by its own citizens.

As of this writing the United States is *not* signatory to the Berne Convention, which called for the life-plus-50-years duration, although the new copyright act brings us more in line with the terms of that treaty and makes it likely that we may join it eventually. Since Canada *is* a signatory, many book publishers will publish an edition simultaneously in Canada and the United States, gaining a writer protection that way.

The Berne Convention contains an interesting provision for what are called the author's "moral rights," which are explained as follows: "Independently of the author's economic rights, and even after the transfer of the said rights, the author shall have the right to claim authorship of the work and to object to any distortion, mutilation, or other modification of, or derogatory action in relation to, the said work, which would be prejudicial to his honor or reputation."

In a country like France, where moral rights are well established by law, this means that a publisher can't force you to use a pseudonym or put someone else's name on your work without your consent; if the publisher puts out a version of your work that you don't like, you have the right to recall it (although you might have to pay the publisher's expenses); and if your work is put to a use that you disapprove of, you can withdraw it.

Moral rights cover a broader base than those delineated by the new copyright law, which are mostly concerned with economic and physical matters. The Berne Convention provides that each signatory nation may legislatively protect these moral rights in its own way—so even if the United States does join the Berne Convention, it will still be up to Congress to decide what the limits of "moral rights" protection will be.

6

Legal Matters

By the very nature of their business, writers stand apart from the general throng of humanity. The verb *to publish* means "to make public," and that's what writers do—they make their thoughts, opinions, and emotions public for other people to see and comment on. Unlike the ordinary person who communicates only to relatives and acquaintances, the writer stands up and speaks to everyone who'll listen.

When you call special attention to yourself, you create special problems. For one thing, you become an easier target and you need protection. For another, since you're deviating from the norm, society needs to protect its members from *you*. Your voice, as a published author, is louder than that of the ordinary person; therefore, society has an interest in seeing that what you say is not harmful. It demands that you use your special status more responsibly.

Chapter 5 dealt with society's attempt to protect you through the mechanism of copyright. By using that tool correctly, you can guard your work against unscrupulous people who might otherwise steal your public utterances and try to pass them off as their own. Copyright law is far from perfect, and many injustices can still occur, but society has done what it can to give you the protection you need when you stand up and shout.

But society also has a stake in protecting itself from unscrupulous writers, and that's what we'll discuss in this chapter. In addition, we'll discuss a matter that is ignored by the overwhelming majority of writers: how to set up a literary estate for your heirs.

Fair Use

As important as copyright protection is, to apply it uniformly all the time under every circumstance would be ridiculous. A news broadcaster may want to emphasize his point by quoting from a magazine commentary. A teacher may want to illustrate a principle of literature by quoting a couple of lines from a contemporary poem. A public speaker may want to punch up a speech with a timely political quote. If these people had to apply for permission from the original author each time they did this, the world would become bogged down in paperwork and authors would be so busy writing permission letters they'd have no time for their own work.

Society therefore has a clear interest in allowing people to use some copyrighted material without permission. On the other hand, it would be wrong to allow a broadcaster to read a complete column over the air, or for a teacher to photocopy entire poems for the whole class, because that would violate the spirit of copyright protection. Somewhere between the two extremes is a vague boundary line known as "fair use."

Until the new copyright law came into existence, there was no official definition of fair use. It was merely a common-law concept that people should be able to use short excerpts from copyrighted work for educational or critical purposes. The new law gave formal recognition to the idea for the first time. It said that copying copyrighted material "for purposes such as criticism, comment, news reporting, teaching (including multiple copies for classroom use), scholarship, or research is not an infringement of copyright."

Even so, the borderline between fair use and infringement

is very ill-defined. How much copying can be done before fair use turns to infringement? The law states four principles to use in judging each particular case: (1) How much of the work is being quoted? (2) What kind of work is it? (3) How are the copies going to be used? (4) To what extent will the copies be competing financially with the original?

In most cases, the last criterion is the most important. If the copying is for noncommercial purposes, like news reporting or scholarly criticism, an awful lot can be excused. Even so, if a substantial amount of the work is to be excerpted, permission should be obtained from the copyright holder if possible. Quoting two lines out of a very long poem might be perfectly acceptable for a teacher, but quoting two lines from a four-line humorous verse could be considered expropriating a major portion of the work. Above all, common sense should be the guiding spirit in the matter.

Infringement may inadvertently come out of research. Alex Haley, the author of *Roots,* was sued by another author who claimed that sections of *Roots* were lifted from his own earlier book. Haley ended up paying a settlement, admitting that the sections were similar; he had done so much research from so many different sources that he'd lost track of what was his own wording and what was someone else's. Needless to say, you'll be better off if you get permission from the author when you quote a research source at length.

Be careful, too, about quoting lines from dramatic works. Just because you hear a song over the air all the time doesn't give you the right to quote it at will. The music industry has very stiff regulations about that and has established official channels such as the American Society of Composers, Authors, and Publishers (ASCAP) for clearing permissions.

Photocopying was a matter of major concern that kept Congress wrangling for a decade over the new copyright law before it was finally passed. In these days of cheap photocopying technology, there had to be some guidelines for when a work could be copied without violating copyright. Teachers and librarians wanted to be able to make copies for their purposes, while authors and publishers wanted them to buy new volumes of the works. After a lot of bitter feuding, a compromise was reached.

Teachers are now allowed to make copies of material if the need for it arises spontaneously (that is, if they decide in midterm that some material might be needed), if the work isn't in print and reasonably available, and if the students aren't charged more than the photocopying costs. The copying can't be repeated during the next term, because it's assumed the teacher could order regularly printed copies by then. This law recognizes the spontaneity of teaching but doesn't make photocopies a long-term substitute for buying the original work.

Librarians working for institutions whose volumes are available to the public are also permitted to make some photocopies under restricted circumstances. They can make a copy of shorter works if the copy contains the proper copyright notice. They can make copies of works in their own collections to replace ones that have been stolen or destroyed, provided the work isn't readily available. Again, photocopies are supposed to be for spontaneous or emergency use, not a substitute for buying the work.

There may come a time when you need to quote from someone else's work in your own writing, or when you're editing a textbook or anthology and want to reprint a selection. In that case, you may find yourself on the other side of the fence, with the possibility of infringing on someone else's copyright. Treat other people the way you'd want to be treated yourself in such a case. If your use of that excerpt doesn't fit within the fair-use guidelines, you should try to track down the copyright holder and ask permission to use the selection.

Finding the copyright holder is much easier said than done. The first step is to go to the source where you originally saw the material you want to copy and check the copyright notice. Write to the publisher's permissions department and explain your situation. Ask for permission to reprint the excerpt. If the publisher doesn't have the authority to grant that permission, either ask for the author's address or ask that your request be forwarded. Publishers are usually willing to help, but sometimes even they don't know a writer's current address—particularly if the piece you're interested in was published some time ago. The writer may have moved or died in the interim, and no one knows where to find him or his estate.

There are other places you can turn. Some of the writers' organizations listed in Appendix C keep tabs on their members and are willing to forward mail to them. As a final resort, check with the Copyright Office. They have a Search Service that will check the files on the work and let you know who owns the rights you're requesting (as of the most recent recordation) and where they can be contacted. The Copyright Office charges for this service: the current rate is $10 per hour or fraction thereof, but they're usually well enough organized that an hour or two is all you need. Even the Copyright Office isn't infallible, however, particularly if the author or the author's estate doesn't keep them informed of transfers or address changes. (The Copyright Office might also find out who, other than the author, owns the rights you want to use if they've been transferred to someone else.)

When you finally contact the person who owns the rights, you will want him to sign a letter giving you permission to quote from his work. If you write the letter yourself, so that all he needs to do is sign it, it may simplify things. In the letter, mention *your* work by title and publisher and specify exactly which portion of his work you want to use. Ask for permission to use his work in all editions and translations of your own work. Figure 1 shows a sample of a permission letter you might send. (Don't forget to send a second copy for the writer's own files.)

Dear Jane Prolix:

I am editing an anthology entitled 100 STRANGE RECIPES for Gastronominous Press, and I would like permission to quote from your article "How to Barbecue a Warthog" as published in Disgusting Magazine of January, 1980 (Vol. 3, No. 1). I would like the quote to begin from page 16, line 3, and go through page 17, line 6, from the phrase "Cleaning a warthog is easier than finding one" through "Make sure you've removed the tusks." The total wordage of the quote is 1,413 words.

I would like permission to use this quote in my book, and in all future editions and revisions thereof, including nonexclusive world rights in all languages. This permission will in no way restrict you or others authorized by you from republishing this material. If you don't control these rights, could you please tell me how I may get in touch with the person who does?

I intend to use the following credit line unless you instruct me otherwise: "The warthog recipe is from the article 'How to Barbecue a Warthog,' copyright 1980 by Jane Prolix, and is reprinted by permission of the author."

If you agree to this permission, please sign in the indicated space below. Thank you very much for your cooperation.

Sincerely,

Arthur Penman

I hereby grant permission for the use requested above.

(signature) _____

(date) _____

Figure 1. Sample letter for permission to quote an excerpt.

Depending on the length of the quote and the generosity of the writer, you may be asked to pay for the permission. This money usually comes out of your pocket, not your publisher's. If you and the writer can't agree on a price you can afford—or if, as is often the case, you can't track the writer down at all—you'll have to make the decision about how important the quote is to your work. You may have to leave it out altogether, or else refer to it indirectly and paraphrase what it says.

If you do get permission for the quote, you should also publish a copyright notice on behalf of the author. The notice should give the title of the piece (or a description if it's just an excerpt), the copyright information, and the name of the person or organization who gave you permission to reprint it. If you're given specific wording for the permission notice, be sure to follow it exactly. The notice should preferably go on your own copyright page, or it may be printed as a footnote on the page with the excerpt.

Obscenity

We live in a society with strangely skewed values. As an author, you can write about hatred, murder, torture, mayhem, riots, brutality, and dismemberment with all the graphic detail you choose; but if you describe the actions of two people who love one another, you risk being charged with writing obscene material.

Censorship is society's method of protecting itself from things it finds disturbing. The debate over censorship is probably as old as the written word, if not the spoken word. Most authors feel they have the right to voice their ideas, whatever they are, while most censors feel that right should be limited in some way. We won't take any position here on this always controversial issue, but we do want to point out some facts about the law as it now stands.

Before 1973, the crucial factor determining whether a work was obscene was whether it was "utterly without redeeming social value." We've known of occasions where pornographers commissioned dry, scholarly articles on sexual matters and published them illustrated with lurid photos. The work as a whole could then be said to have some redeeming social value, even if the purchasers never bothered to read the dull prose. Similarly, a racy novel could be considered acceptable if the protagonist repented of his or her wild actions at the end, showing that virtue triumphs at last.

But on June 21, 1973, the Supreme Court handed down a decision that changed the scope of obscenity significantly. There is now a threefold set of guidelines to be used in judging whether a work is obscene: "(a) whether 'the average person, applying contemporary community standards' would find that the work, taken as a whole, appeals to the prurient interest . . . ; (b) whether the work depicts or describes, in a patently offensive way, sexual conduct specifically defined by the applicable state law; and (c) whether the work, taken as a whole, lacks serious literary, artistic, political, or scientific value."

These new guidelines present a minefield for authors, artists, and publishers, because they're so generalized that no one knows precisely what they mean. The most devastating part of the ruling was the phrase "contemporary community standards." What exactly is the community? It could be a few-square-block neighborhood, a whole town, a county, a state, or even a large region like the Midwest. Most magazines and books are distributed on a national basis—but how can a publisher be sure that what is acceptable by New York standards won't be judged obscene in Alabama or Kansas? The publisher who wants to play it safe must aim at the lowest common denominator and hope for the best—and there are many who doubt that this development can lead to an improvement of literature.

The word "contemporary" makes the guidelines a double-edged weapon. Times change, and people's tastes change with them. If the country undergoes a strong puritanical swing, you could find yourself charged with writing pornography years after your work was published. There is a time bomb ticking, and no one can be sure when it will go off.

The vast majority of published books and articles have nothing to do with sex and face little threat from the sexual censors. But if you feel there's a chance your work might be construed as obscene by the average citizen in some community, you'd better check with a lawyer. Even now, nearly a decade after that decision, no one really knows what obscenity is—and yet most publishers want *you* to take the blame if a jury rules against you. Make sure you know what you're doing before taking any risks.

Libel and Invasion of Privacy

Censorship is society's method of protecting the general public from harmful material. Laws against libel and invasion of privacy were designed to protect specific individuals from the harmful things writers can do. These grievances are a little better defined than obscenity, but there's still a vast shady area you must tiptoe through very carefully.

Libel is the act of defaming someone through the written word. Because a writer publishes a work generally, many people see it—and many of them believe anything they read because "they wouldn't print it if it wasn't true." A writer could easily make an offhand statement—or a deliberate insult—and hurt innocent people. Fear of libel suits keeps writers in line.

In order to sue for libel, a plaintiff must prove that your statement caused his or her reputation to suffer. Depending on whether the plaintiff is a private citizen or a public figure, it may also be necessary to prove that you made your statement with knowing or reckless falsity.

Often, the best defense against a libel suit—particularly if the plaintiff is a public official or public figure—is that the statements made are true. But you'd better be able to *prove* they're true, because the burden of proof could lie with you. If you publish the fact that Ollie Badwater is a philanderer, you'd better have something to back that up—preferably photos of Ollie in bed with some woman other than his wife or a sworn deposition from Ollie's mistress. The court would then assume you hadn't damaged Ollie's reputation by publishing the fact; Ollie had damaged his own reputation by engaging in socially disapproved fashion, and you merely brought the fact to public attention. A minority of states allow truth as a defense, however, only if the writer had good motives and justifiable ends in publishing the truth.

If Ollie Badwater is a public figure or official—that is, a government officeholder, film star, sports celebrity, or anyone who has assumed a role of special prominence in the affairs of society or has thrust himself into a particular public controversy—you might not even have to prove your charges conclusively. A plaintiff who is a public figure or public official has the burden of pleading and proving falsity and of establishing falsity with convincing clarity. Like writers, public figures stand out from the crowd and lose some of their rights because of it. In order to win a libel case, a public figure not only must prove that the statements made were false but that you made them with actual malice—legally defined in this sense as a "reckless disregard for the truth or knowledge that the offending statement is false or probably false." If Ollie is your city councilman and you spot him going into a motel three times a week with different women, you could be excused your conclusions even if they turned out to be false, as long as your published statements touched on

Ollie's fitness to hold office. If you had a grudge against Ollie and just wanted to make something up that would hurt him, however, you'd be in serious trouble; courts have ruled that a reporter's thoughts and state of mind at the time of writing an article do have a bearing on a libel case.

If Ollie is only a private person, your defense becomes shakier. If your defamatory remark was made about a matter of public interest—say, associating him with known gangsters—then he'd only have to show that you made the false remark negligently (knowing that the statement was false or could give a false impression), rather than with malice, in most jurisdictions. If your statement was on a matter that wasn't public, like Ollie's sex life, he doesn't even have to prove that much; if you can't back up what you said with hard proof, you've lost.

Times are getting hard for writers. Courts are ruling more and more often in favor of the plaintiff in cases like these. Writers are often targets of nuisance suits, where a plaintiff will go to court on the slightest pretext in hope of getting *something* out of the deal. If you discover that you've inadvertently libeled someone, printing a retraction may help a bit, but it won't completely absolve you of guilt.

If you write nonfiction and mention the names of living people, be careful. Make sure you can verify in court everything you say. Remember, too, that repeating someone else's defamatory statement can also be judged defamatory, even if you're only making a direct quote of the original source—and even if you say that you personally don't believe it. Even using the word "alleged," so popular with the news media these days, is no surefire protection. Stating that something is your own opinion is a little better, but there are some conditions under which even that won't work.

Even in fiction, the water is very muddied these days. You've probably seen the statement in the front of books or in movies that all the characters described are fictitious and that any resemblance to real people is purely coincidental. But that statement is no defense against a libel suit. We all know there's the type of book known as a *roman à clef,* in which real people are slightly fictionalized. Any number of these novels have been best-sellers, usually by depicting the bizarre antics of movie stars, rock singers, Greek shipping magnates, and other newsworthy personalities. One recent libel case has thrown the entire publishing industry into a tizzy, and no one is precisely sure what the ultimate effects will be on the future of literature.

In that case a psychologist, Paul Bindrim, sued author Gwen Davis Mitchell and her publisher, Doubleday, concerning Ms. Mitchell's novel, *Touching.* Ms. Mitchell had attended an encounter group led by Bindrim and signed an agreement with him that she would not use any incidents from the sessions in her book. She then wrote a novel about some women who take part in an encounter group similar to Bindrim's.

Bindrim sued both Mitchell and Doubleday for libel. Three people who knew Bindrim testified that they could recognize him as the model for the psychologist in the book. Bindrim contended that the psychologist was depicted in a way that would damage his professional reputation. Mitchell and Doubleday held to the argument that the work was fiction, that the character was not meant to portray Bindrim, and that he had no cause for complaint.

The court ruled that Bindrim had indeed been defamed, and that Doubleday had acted with malice, not only in publishing the book but in licensing a paperback edition of it after knowing a libel suit had been filed. This ruling has been upheld by the U.S. Supreme Court and is a precedent for libel cases throughout the country.

Whether this will have a dampening effect on the publishing industry remains to be seen. It could be argued that this was a special case because of Mitchell's signed agreement with Bindrim *not* to depict what had happened. It's hard to say how much effect that fact had in the decision, but one thing *is* certain: Publishers will take a long, careful look at anything that has even the possibility of being libelous before they publish it.

What can you do about the situation? The obvious thing is to avoid writing anything that could be construed as depicting actual people, but that's not always possible—or desirable. The next best thing, if you intend to do a fictionalized portrayal of someone, is to get permission in writing that the person understands you will be using a similar character and agrees not to sue you. The person may want something in return for this, of course. If it's a friend of yours, a copy of the book and an acknowledgment may be enough. Someone else might ask for the right to approve the book before it's published, to make sure of being treated fairly. Another person might ask for all of those plus cold hard cash. The ultimate decision of how much it's worth is up to you—but remember, if you don't come to terms you may have to drop the project completely. The very fact that you approached this person and asked permission to portray a similar character is an indication that you intended to do so; if the person later sues for libel, that point will weigh very heavily against you.

Invasion of privacy is similar to libel in that it can cause harm to an individual, but it differs in several respects. One is that even public figures are entitled to their privacy, and their protection is not nearly as diminished as it is in libel cases. A second difference is that the truth of your statement is no defense; disclosing real things about someone's private life is grounds for a suit. A third difference is that invasion of privacy doesn't have to be derogatory; you can say *nice* things about a person's private life and still be found guilty of invasion of privacy.

There are four basic ways that a person's privacy can be

invaded. You can use someone's name or likeness for some business or commercial purpose without his consent, such as by saying he uses or endorses a certain product. You can physically invade someone's home or place of seclusion, or eavesdrop, such as by wiretapping to get material for a story. You can put the person in a false light by making up things and printing them as truth; even if the things you make up are complimentary, they still misrepresent the person and can lead to misunderstandings. Finally, you can reveal to the public personal facts about the subject that may be damaging or embarrassing; even if you printed the truth, so the person can't sue you for libel, you may still be charged with invasion of privacy for printing things the public didn't need to know.

Libel and invasion of privacy are both very tricky subjects, open to many interpretations. If your work deals with real people and you feel you may be liable to a suit on these grounds, we strongly suggest you discuss the matter with a lawyer familiar with these topics. It's better to spend a few dollars now to be safe than to rush into print and have to pay a hefty settlement later.

Wills and Estates

No one likes to think about death, particularly his own, but writers who don't give some thought to that inevitable future are only creating problems—and possible financial hardship—for people they love who live on after them. Intestate problems are bad enough when an ordinary person dies, one who only owned tangible property like stocks, bank accounts, jewelry, houses, land, etc. The situation becomes far more complex when there is intangible property, like copyrights, involved.

If a writer dies without a will, the copyrights go automatically to the surviving spouse. If there's no spouse, the copyrights go to the writer's children. And if there are no children, they go to the next of kin as determined by a court.

Think about it for a minute. Maybe you're an experienced writer and know how to handle all aspects of your business. Can you say the same about the person who stands to inherit your estate? Does your heir know how to record copyrights? Does your heir know how and when to apply for renewals of copyrights granted their first term before 1978? Does your heir know how to negotiate a contract for a reissue of your work? Could he or she be suckered into accepting a ridiculously cheap deal for all rights? Is your heir someone you'd trust to carry out *your* wishes with respect to your work? Does your heir even know what those wishes are?

If you're not happy with the answers to any of those questions, you ought to think seriously about making a will. That's the only way you can be sure your wishes will be carried out. Maybe you think you're not famous enough, and that your literary estate isn't worth bothering about, but history has a funny way of discovering artists after their deaths, and it's always best to be prepared.

There are two types of people named in a will. There are *beneficiaries,* people or institutions who benefit from the assets you leave behind. Then there are the *executors,* the people or institutions who manage the estate and follow your instructions as best they can. An executor may or may not be a beneficiary, depending on circumstances. There can also be more than one executor, sharing the duties according to your wishes or their abilities.

It's vital for a writer to have an executor who knows the publishing business. If you feel that one of your beneficiaries is competent, you may want to name him as literary executor. If not, you might consider some other writer you know, or your agent, or even an editor. You should, of course, ask first whether that person wants the honor and responsibility before naming him in your will. An executor generally gets a fee out of the estate for managing it; depending on circumstances this might only cover expenses, or there might be a bit of profit to be made.

Consider your executor's age, too, as you make your decision. If an executor is so old he'll die a year after you do, he won't be much help in the long run. Many people turn to banks and other institutions to serve as executors because they provide continuity even if individual officers die. This is fine for most financial matters, but few bank officers really know the ins and outs of the publishing world, and they could make serious mistakes in handling your work. One solution is to divide the responsibility for your estate among several executors—one who handles the artistic end and one who deals with money matters. Even this can cause problems, as the sale of rights involves both monetary and artistic considerations. The more explicit you make the instructions in your will, the less bickering there's likely to be later.

Tad Crawford, in *The Writer's Legal Guide,* gives some guidelines you should use when you're drawing up instructions. Are there any of your previous works you *don't* want reprinted? What about unpublished works—should they be destroyed or published after your death? May they be edited and, if so, by whom? What about your incomplete works, notes, outlines, etc? Does the estate have the right to hire someone to complete them for you and, if so, whom? How should the byline appear in that case? Do you want to license derivative works like films, plays, TV shows, or merchandise? What about your private correspondence—do you want to give someone the right to publish the letters you wrote or received? Who should have access to your file material? Do you want to appoint an official biographer? How should the estate deal with inquiries about your life and work?

Once you've made these decisions, don't just write them into your will and forget about them; make sure your loved ones know what the provisions are. A will is often not read until a week or two after the person's death, and by that time some actions may have been taken that can't be undone. The widow of Sir Richard Burton, the nineteenth-century adventurer/explorer and translator of the *Arabian Nights,* burned many of his unpublished papers immediately after his death; even if he'd left a will with instructions to preserve the papers, it wouldn't have done any good. Also, don't lock your only copy of a will in a safety deposit box; there are sometimes legal problems getting a box opened in time after your death.

There are other matters to be considered as well, not the least of which are financial. Estate taxes must be paid when you die, and these come out of the money that would otherwise go to your beneficiaries. There are steps you can take while you're still alive to minimize these taxes, such as giving copyrights away to people you'd want to inherit them anyway; they may still have to pay a gift tax, but there's an exclusion on some of the value.

Because everyone's will and estate is different, and because laws vary from state to state, it's beyond the scope of this book to give a detailed breakdown of the situation. You may want to consult several different sources: a lawyer, an accountant, a life-insurance broker, a banker, or other financial consultant. Any or all of them can help you draw up a plan best suited to your situation. But we *do* urge you to consult someone knowledgeable. Your survivors will grieve enough at your death; don't give them any additional grief with your literary estate.

Public Lending Rights

There's a new development in the world that writers should be aware of. In a number of European countries and Australia, the governments have passed laws giving authors royalties on books that are checked out of libraries. Think about it for a moment: A library may buy one copy of your book and let hundreds of people read it instead of buying their own copies. After the initial royalty on the one copy the library bought, you haven't gotten another cent for all the use your book has received. You may even have lost money, because someone who read your book in the library might not care to buy his own copy later. The concept of public lending rights is intended to rectify the situation.

The immediate question is, Who pays for this? The concept of free public libraries is almost sacred in Western society; it would be unthinkable to force library patrons to pay a fee for checking books out. (Although it's not nearly as unthinkable as it once was. The Los Angeles Public Library, for one, sometimes charges fees if you want to borrow current best-sellers.) Librarians, faced with inflation and horrible budget cuts, pale at the thought of losing any more money from their minuscule allowances.

The answer is that the money should come from the government, meaning the taxpayers as a whole. If you accept the principle of public libraries at all, you accept the fact that society profits by having the knowledge stored there available to the people. If society profits, it should pay for what it's getting. A special fund should be set aside (*apart* from the normal library budget) to reimburse the authors who contribute their thoughts to the enrichment of society.

The second question is, How do you decide who gets paid? Some popular books are continually checked out, while others sit on the shelves gathering dust. How can a system be devised that will fairly reward authors? Again, librarians shudder at the thought of the additional record keeping they'd need to count the number of times each volume was checked out.

Different systems have been devised to deal with the problem. The Netherlands pays a special fee for each book bought at the time of purchase by a library, regardless of how many times the book is eventually borrowed, thus evening out the statistics. Denmark uses an inventory system; since librarians must take periodic inventory of their collections anyway, the Danes have arranged that every time a book shows up in the inventory, the writer gets another royalty payment. (This system makes no distinction between books that stay on the shelves and books that are frequently borrowed. It also leans heavily on the side of the more prolific authors.) Sweden and Britain use a system like the TV ratings, where a few representative libraries are monitored; national borrowing patterns are established from that, and royalties are paid depending on a book's popularity. Most countries limit the maximum payment to an author in any given year, to prevent best-sellers from hogging all the money and leaving none for less popular writers.

At the moment, all this is irrelevant to writers in the United States. The system has just started up in Britain, and authors there had to fight for twenty-five years to get it adopted. The fight has barely even begun here, and Congress is unlikely to adopt the concept of public lending rights in the near future. Still, all writers have a stake in the outcome of this battle, and you ought to be aware that the fight is going on.

Magazine Contracts and Permissions

Eventually there will come a point at which you and the publisher must spell out what each is to gain from your relationship. Magazine publishers often handle this on an informal—sometimes sloppy—basis: a conversation over the telephone, a verbal assignment, a promise and a handshake. Where the money at stake is less than a couple of hundred dollars, the publisher can feel downright casual about it. Why not? He has everything going his way. After you submit your article he has it at his disposal, and he also has his money, to pay you or not, as he sees fit.

Not that all publishers are out to cheat you; most are as honest as any other businessman. But—as in other businesses—a publisher has a variety of creditors wanting money and a limited amount of funds at any given moment. The people who can cause the most trouble tend to get paid first: the office staff, the typographer, the printer, the paper supplier, and the distributor, because the published work won't get to the public without them; *they'll* get paid on time. Writers are another matter. There are more than enough of them, all begging for approval, and if one refuses to work for him he can easily find another. This puts writers pretty low on the priority list—especially writers without a written contract that can be waved around in court.

Before going any further, we should define a few terms. There are different types of contracts, depending on how much control the publisher will have over your work. There is an *all-rights* contract, in which you give total control of the work to the publisher forever. Such a contract probably would not be terribly long or involved, since the work belongs entirely to the publisher. (Works for hire are a subset of all-rights agreements.) There is also a *flat-fee* contract, in which the publisher agrees to pay you only a set amount for the work, with no provision for royalties or subsequent earnings.

Please note that these two terms are not synonymous. A flat-fee contract may not give the publisher all rights, but just specific ones for which you receive a specific amount. Magazine contracts are usually flat-fee contracts. An all-rights contract need not involve a flat fee since, though you sell all the rights, the publisher may still agree to pay you royalties and a percentage of the income derived from subsidiary sales. There are contracts that give only limited rights and get royalty payments based on sales; most book contracts fall into this category. And there are, of course, contracts that are both all rights *and* flat fee. Ghostwritten books are a good example; sometimes the author hands the manuscript over to the publisher, gets a check, and never sees another cent, no matter how popular the book is.

As you climb up the ladder in the publishing world, agreements become much more formalized because there's more money at stake. Magazine contracts can be as simple (sometimes deceptively so) as a rubber stamp on the back of a check, or as complex as a lawyer can devise in a page or two. When you reach the realm of book publishing, a contract can run on for many pages, covering a wealth of esoteric and obscure subjects that could be of interest only to lawyers—but as we've shown in the past two chapters, legal and copyright matters are of crucial concern to writers as well. Many writers don't want to bother learning the complicated legalese involved in contract negotiations—and as a result, there are many fine authors who spend their lives shackled to bad agreements they made early in their careers. If you are going to be a professional, you must learn to look out for your own interests.

Magazine Contracts

There are usually only six points of discussion that need to be mentioned in a magazine contract: (1) the rate of payment; (2) when payment will be made; (3) what rights are being bought, and with what limitations; (4) whether there will be a "kill fee" and, if so, how much it will be; (5) the details of the copyright notice that will appear with the article; and (6) how many free copies you'll receive. (There should be at least two: one for your files and one to register with the Copyright Office.) It should be a simple matter to work these details out satisfactorily, but a great number of problems can occur in practice.

Most magazine freelancers start out by submitting an unsolicited complete article or story. One day, a letter (or, worse yet, a telephone call) comes from the editor, saying, "I like your piece and want to buy it. Will you accept a hundred dollars?" The beginning writer is overjoyed at the thought of getting money to see his words in print and in the heat of the moment answers "Yes," without inquiring further. In due course, he receives a check from the publisher with a little rubber-stamped note on the back:

> Endorsement of this check by the payee is an agreement to sell all rights to the article "Running for Dogcatcher."

Something about that phrase "all rights" sends a chill up the writer's spine, but what is he to do? He wants the money but he can't cash the check without endorsing it—and to do so is to agree to something he might not want.

The problem really started a lot earlier, with that unthinking acceptance. Many professionals write specifically on their manuscripts, under their name and address, what rights they're offering for sale. The theory of this is that, in the absence of any other written contract, the manuscript itself can be taken into court to show that the writer did not agree to sell some disputed rights to the work. This method is of dubious legal value (although it certainly can't hurt), since in the absence of any written agreement, under the new copyright law, all the magazine buys is nonexclusive publishing rights. Most magazines have their own policy of what rights they routinely buy. The editor will ignore those little notices of yours and send you a standard agreement form.

The real mistake here was in not questioning the terms of the sale at the time. Instead of replying with an unqualified "Yes," this writer should have taken the trouble to ask what rights the editor was buying for that sum, at what point the money was to be paid, and whether the magazine would print a separate copyright notice for the article. If they are discussing the matter in a telephone conversation, the writer should ask for a letter verifying the details before giving written acceptance. Admittedly, this requires great presence of mind for the neophyte facing such euphoric prospects—but it has to be done.

Even an experienced professional, though, can sometimes make a mistake and be faced with a back-of the-check contract. At that point, there are three options. You can swallow hard and endorse the check as is, muttering curses under your breath. Or you can send the check back unsigned, saying that the offer is not acceptable. This is a particularly brave action; writers quickly learn how hard it is to get *any* check from a publisher, and sending it back means you may never see it again. In light of this, the alternative offered by the publisher may not look so bad after all. But the situation is not hopeless.

If a magazine publisher has issued a check (unless payment is on acceptance), it usually means your article has already been typeset. It may be at the printer's. It may even be on the newsstands. If you send the check back unendorsed, that suddenly puts pressure on the publisher, who is now in a position of having appropriated your work without a definite agreement. Theoretically, you have grounds for a lawsuit. Submitting your manuscript was only a display of your wares, after all, not a bill of sale. Without some evidence of an agreement, the magazine has no right to publish your work. (We've never heard of any writer who actually sued a publisher on those grounds, but we do know of one who came close.) The publisher is now under a little more pressure to make a reasonable offer.

The third alternative is the shakiest, and that is to try beating the publisher at his own game. One writer we've heard of stamps such checks FOR DEPOSIT ONLY and deposits them in his bank account without putting his signature to them. (His bank's policy is not to bother about an endorsement as long as the check is made out in the name of the account holder.) Without an endorsement, he can claim he never agreed to the publisher's demands.

Other authors have simply crossed out the objectionable phrase on the stamped agreement and written in their own terms. They might, for instance, cross out "all rights" and insert "1st N.A. serial rights" instead, then endorse it as usual. This is of dubious legality, however; a legal contract must be agreed to by all sides, and the publisher could argue in court that he never agreed to the changes the writer made. To make it official, you would have to make the necessary changes and send the check back for the editor to initial.

It has been stated that back-of-the-check contracts probably aren't enforceable anyway. The people who say this are usually writers, not lawyers. We don't know of any instance where a contract like this was challenged, and we really don't think it would be worth your while to become a test case. Better to avoid the problem altogether and settle the matter before it reaches the check stage.

Some magazines we've worked with have asked us to submit an invoice with our completed articles. Ostensibly, giving them a "bill" just like, say, the printer makes it easier for their bookkeeping department. This is really very little trouble for you, and it can actually give you more control since *you* make up the wording of your invoice. The crucial information includes the names of both parties, the date you make up the invoice, the date payment is due, a description of the work, a list of the rights being sold, rate of payment, and the fact that the publisher must print the copyright notice in your name. The pay rate, rights sold, and payment date should have already been negotiated. You might use a sample format like Figure 2.

INVOICE

```
FROM:        Arthur Penman, Author
             111 Literary Lane
             Freelance, California

TO:          Midwest Swimmers Magazine, Publisher
             666 Printer Street
             Mimeo, Iowa

DATE:        October 31, 1983

FOR:         1st World English language serial rights to the
             200-word article "Championship Swimming Style"

TERMS:       5¢ per word = $100.00 for the article.  Publisher
             must print copyright notice in the name of the
             Author.

PAYMENT DUE:  30 days from invoice date.



_____
(Author's signature)
```

Figure 2. Sample invoice for a magazine.

You would submit the original of that invoice along with the article to the editor, keeping, of course, a copy for your own files. You might also want to record a copy, signed by you, with the Copyright Office. You would mark your copy "Paid" when the check is received.

Most magazine publishers use their own form of contract, either the back-of-check kind or else a printed form. These can get complicated, depending on what rights the publisher is demanding. Some publishers may want a period of exclusivity before you publish the story or article elsewhere, or in another form. (This is because they want people to buy their magazine. If readers learn that a story will appear somewhere else next month, they might wait to buy that instead.) Some publishers may request exclusive or nonexclusive reprint rights, or an option to republish the work in a collection or anthology of pieces from the magazine. Some rights may revert to you if the publisher doesn't use them within a given time period. If you grant any exclusive or first rights, you should put a time limit on them for your own protection—otherwise the publisher could hang on to your work for years without publishing it, holding up your own chances of a resale.

If you end up doing repeat business with particular publishers, you get to know their methods of operation. You know what the rate of payment will be and you know what rights you'll be selling. You may get onto a first-name basis with the editor. But there can be some dangers in a close relationship too—the danger of taking each other for granted. Perhaps the editor gave you an extra cent a word on your last piece and you expect the new, higher rate on your next one, not realizing it was intended as a bonus rather than a raise. Editors do want to remain on good terms with their regular writers, and squabbles like these can often be worked out amicably—but a friendly relationship is no reason to take business dealings for granted.

After you reach a certain level, when the editor has confi-

dence in your abilities, he may give you assignments instead
of waiting for you to come up with ideas of your own. At this
point, you should ask for a "kill fee." This is a guarantee in
advance that, even if the editor ultimately rejects your story
for one reason or another, you are still entitled to some money for all the time and energy you put into the work *at the
editor's request.* You may have to fight for it, but get it (and
get it in writing).

The amount of the kill fee you ask for should depend on
various factors: how much expense will come out of your
pocket, how much time you spend on the project, and (perhaps most important), how much the magazine can afford.
The kill fee is only payable, of course, if your piece is rejected
(and in that case, you should retain the right to sell it elsewhere without returning the kill fee); if the work is accepted,
you get paid at the agreed-upon rate.

A note of caution on kill fees, however. Such things *must*
be agreed upon in advance. You can make yourself very tiresome demanding, after the fact, that an editor pay you for
something he doesn't want. One editor friend of ours received
a story from a young writer. He rejected it but took the time
to give the writer some suggestions, with no indication that
he would buy the story if rewritten. The writer rewrote the
story and resubmitted it; the editor rejected it again, with
more comments made out of the kindness of his heart. This
went on for a few more rounds, until finally the writer gave
up—and then demanded a kill fee for having done so much
work. The editor at this point lost all patience and told the
writer to get lost. At no time had he ever said he would buy
the story and had made suggestions only to be helpful; the
writer had done all that work purely on speculation. You're
only justified in asking for a kill fee if, somewhere along the
line, the editor has actually agreed to buy the piece.

Beware, too, of oral agreements and telephone assignments. As Samuel Goldwyn said, "A verbal agreement isn't

worth the paper it's written on." If you're talking to an editor in his office or on the phone and he proposes a deal, ask for confirmation in writing. If he's too busy, you can do it yourself. As soon as you get back to your typewriter, write a letter saying:

> As I recall from our conversation of 28 June, you proposed the following deal with the following terms. . . . If the above details are agreeable to you, please sign this letter and return a copy to me.

Then you sign it and send him two copies—one to return to you, and the other for his own records. Don't worry about hurting the editor's feelings by giving the impression that you don't think he's trustworthy; this is for his benefit as much as for yours, to avoid arguments and disagreements later. As long as you're polite about it he won't mind and will probably respect you for your professional attitude.

Permissions

After your work has been published, you may receive requests to reprint part or all of it somewhere else. These requests may come to you directly, or they may be forwarded through your publisher or agent. The nature of the request can vary. In the simplest case, another writer might want to take a quote or a small section out of your work to use as an illustration for his own writing; we then come up against the problem of fair use. Some writers believe in charging for every use of their words, no matter how slight. Others are inclined to be more generous; as long as the excerpt is small and they are given proper credit, they waive payment. This is entirely a matter of your own personal ethics and what you think you can get away with.

The situation becomes more involved when permission is requested to reprint large sections or entire articles. In this case, you should unquestionably receive payment; some writers have made more on reprints of their stories and articles than they made on the original sales. Say, for example, you wrote a magazine article on the subject of living in a condominium. An editor who is compiling a book of essays on modern living sees your article and wants to include it in his book. He will usually write to you proposing a payment scheme in return for reprint rights, and sometimes he will even be sharp enough to ask you how the copyright notice should be printed. He may have a standard contract already written up included with his request.

What's fair in these cases? A lot depends on the contract that the editor has with *his* publishing company for this book. He obviously can't give you a better deal than he has himself, and this becomes the bottom-line consideration. If you ask for some term and he says he isn't entitled, by his own contract, to grant it, then you must either give in or withhold your permission. But since you can safely assume that the publisher and/or the editor are making some money off this venture, why shouldn't you as well?

What you would ideally like is a share of the book's royalties. More and more anthology editors are sharing their earnings with the writers whose works they're using. The standard procedure in these cases is for the editor to keep 50 percent of the earnings to pay for the time and trouble of putting the book together—a not unreasonable amount. The other half is divided among the writers represented in the book—sometimes equally, more often on a pro rata basis. That is, a writer with a 10,000-word article in the book would be paid twice as much as a writer with a 5,000-word article. This division of wealth should remain standard for all the book's earnings, whether from royalties, book club, paperback, foreign editions, or other subsidiary sales; every time the editor receives a check from the publisher, he keeps half for himself and divides the rest among his writers.

Sometimes a generous editor will give contributors a larger percentage of the split—but ethics should prevent *him* from taking more than half.

There are occasions, most notably in the textbook field, where the publisher and/or editor insists on giving you only a flat fee. If you even suggest the idea of royalties, the publisher will give you an elaborate story about how competitive the textbook field is and how the extra bookkeeping required to figure out royalty payments is prohibitive. Nobody gets royalties, he will claim, not even the biggest names in writing. Whether this touching story is true or not, the fact remains that textbook publishers are adamantly opposed to paying their contributors royalties.

There may be a way around this, and that is to invoke the system used for licensing books in Europe. Many European publishers don't bother with royalties either. What they do is buy the right to print so many copies—say, fifty thousand— of a given book. If the book is a success and sells out, then the publisher has to pay you some more money for the right to print another twenty thousand, and so on. It's essentially a pay-as-you-go system and in some respects is preferable to the elaborate games American and British publishers can play with royalty statements.

If this method works for European publishers, there's no reason why it can't work for textbook publishers in the United States. If the publisher refuses your request for royalties, which is likely, see if you can arrange a limited permission. State in your release form that your permission to reprint this story is for this edition of the book only, and that further permission must be obtained from you before the story may appear in any subsequent or revised editions. That way, the publisher only has to pay you more if the book is an unqualified success (for which your work will be partly responsible.)

Some publishers will accept this and others won't. If yours

is one of the latter, your next alternative is to ask for a higher flat fee. If the publisher balks at this suggestion too, perhaps you may want to reconsider how badly you want your article to appear in this particular textbook.

Some textbook companies are notorious for not even mentioning the subject of money when asking for your permission to reprint. This has happened to us on several occasions. The editor or the permissions chief writes you a polite, flattering letter saying how good your story was and how much the company would like to use it in their upcoming anthology. If you'll just sign the enclosed permission form, everything will be taken care of.

As with prepared foods, when someone "saves you the trouble" of doing something yourself, the savings generally come out of your wallet. The company's own permission form would give them the right to use the story in that textbook free forever. *They* intend to make money on these books, but none of it will ever reach you—and it's *your* work.

How can they expect to get away with that? Well, some writers are willing to sign anything to see their names in print. And, let's face it, we all had to read textbooks when we were going to school; it's a wonderful boost to the ego to think that some kid will be assigned to read *your* story for homework. There is also the fact that, in the nonfiction field, many of the articles chosen for reprint are written by college professors with a publish-or-perish mentality. Their salary is already being paid by the university. Technical journals don't always pay their contributors, so perhaps the professors may be forgiven if they fail to wonder whether other publishers should.

If you receive such a request, don't fire back an angry letter accusing the publisher of trying to cheat you. Instead, write a polite note of thanks for the interest expressed, saying that the permission form, as written, omitted a few pertinent details and you have taken the trouble of drawing up a more acceptable one, enclosed herewith. Then you write one asking for royalties and as much money up front as you think you can get away with. This is known as a counter offer. The publisher will either accept it, give up on your story altogether, or else bargain in earnest.

We have found it wise to include in the permissions form the exact wording of the copyright notice that should accompany the story. Some publishers' legal departments have been known to botch it up if not given specific instructions. If your piece was originally copyrighted in someone else's name, make sure the copyright notice contains the phrase "reprinted by permission of the author." This is so future anthologists will know whom to contact if *they* want to reprint it. A sample permissions form similar to the one we use is shown in Figure 3.

Many textbook companies balk at paying before the book is published, and you should take this into account when stating your fee. If you asked for $200 when you signed the contract in 1983 and the book isn't published until 1986, you'll still only get $200—even though inflation will probably make those dollars worth considerably less by then. The publisher will also have had the use of your money, interest free, during the interval. Kathleen Sky once offered a publisher a choice: one amount if he paid within 60 days, or twice the amount if he paid on publication three years later. He chose the second option.

With this type of form, you need only send one copy to the publisher, keeping a separate copy for your own records. (You don't even have to record the transaction with the Copyright Office, since you're not granting exclusive rights.) You don't need a countersignature, because if the publisher uses your story at all it implies he's agreed to the terms in your permission form; your permission is contingent on that. If the publisher doesn't like your terms, further bargaining is in order.

Arthur Penman
111 Literary Lane
Freelance, California

January 6, 1982

Ms. Jane Dithers
Permissions Department
High Fallutin Textbooks, Inc.
333 Smart Avenue
Literary, Wisconsin

Dear Ms. Dithers:

In return for the considerations listed below, I hereby give you permission for you to reprint my article "Reading for Fun and Profit" in the first edition of your forthcoming textbook, TURNING A PROFIT ON SCHOOLWORK. This permission includes the nonexclusive use of my article for distribution of this first edition in the English language throughout the world, as well as for Braille and large-print copies of this edition. It is understood that separate permission must be obtained to use the article in any foreign language, revised, or subsequent editions of your textbook.

High Fallutin Textbooks, Inc., agrees to pay me the sum of two hundred dollars ($200.00) for this nonexclusive use of my article, payable within sixty (60) days from the date of this permission. Publisher also agrees to send me three (3) complimentary copies of the textbook upon publication.

Copyright notice for the article shall read:

"Reading for Fun and Profit" by Arthur Penman, copyright 1975 by Schoolhouse Magazine, Inc.; reprinted by permission of the author.

Sincerely yours,

Arthur Penman

AP/jds

_____
Jane Dithers
High Fallutin Textbooks, Inc.

Figure 3. Sample reprint permission form.

Book Contracts

Few authors enjoy dealing with book contracts. The language is legalistic, convoluted, and harsh; the subjects involved are technical and obscure; and there is the reinforced romantic notion in our culture that a true Artist is beyond such mundane considerations. Most writers try to find an agent to deal with the problem.

The trouble with this approach is that you probably won't even *get* an agent until you have one or more books under your belt. And while agents will get you the best deals they can, they aren't mind readers; how do *they* know you want something a certain way unless *you* know enough to say so? Then too, even the best agent is only human and could miss a spot where the publisher says "net gain" instead of "gross profit."

The final word, though, on why you should know about your own contracts is that your agent is not legally liable for what you agree to. Even if you have a superb agent, with all the legal acumen of F. Lee Bailey and the negotiating skills of Henry Kissinger, *he* does not end up signing that piece of paper; you do. If there are any disagreements, you are the one who will be dragged into court, not your agent. Your name is signed on the bottom line, and that makes you legally responsible for every sentence, clause, and comma. That concept should scare you; if it doesn't, we suggest you consider a less risky line of work.

There is no such thing as a "standard" contract throughout the publishing industry. Each is unique unto itself, which is perhaps as it should be, since each book and each writer are different from all the others. Contracts can vary in length from a single page up to more than twenty pages of typeset material. But they all have one thing in common which you should keep firmly in mind: Each publisher has paid a lawyer—or a staff of lawyers—to create a standard form, which is called the "boilerplate" contract. It's only logical to expect the boilerplate to be slanted in the publisher's favor. If you sign it as is, you will be giving all the advantage to the publisher and little or none to yourself.

It's not that publishers are deliberately out to cheat every writer they can. Most of them are decent, honest sorts—but they're also hard-nosed business people. Every contract, they will tell you, is negotiable to some extent; if you're too stupid to know or demand your rights, they're not in business to teach you otherwise. The burden falls entirely on you.

Writers' groups have been fighting to combat their members' ignorance by drawing up "model contracts" that are weighted in the author's favor instead of the publisher's. In the following discussion we'll use some of these models to illustrate what you should be striving for. We've studied the Authors Guild Trade Book Contract, the Science Fiction Writers of America Model Contracts (for both hardcover and paperback), and the model contract of the Society of Authors' Representatives and have tried to take the best features of each. There is no way on earth you will get a publisher to sign such an ideal composite contract; but by giving you a range of options, we hope to increase your negotiating ability to the point where only your clout as a writer, not your ignorance, determines the deal you get.

While it's true that there is no standard form or wording

throughout the industry, there are certain features that are—or *should be*—in every contract: a grant of rights, delivery date, acceptance and publication, warranties and indemnities, galley proofs, copyright, advance, royalty rates, subsidiary rights, accounting and payments, author's copies, reversion, and a bankruptcy clause. In addition there are other clauses a publisher may want to force on you, and some you may try to foist off on him in return. Conduct your negotiations in the manner we described in Chapter 4. We'll discuss each clause individually.

Most contracts begin by stating the author's name and address, the publisher's name and address, and the date of the contract. (Contracts invariably capitalize "Author" and "Publisher," and also refer to "the Work," meaning the book under discussion. We shall follow their example in our sample wordings.) Sometimes, if you're represented by an agent, the contract will list your address as c/o the agent. Otherwise, this is the simplest section of the contract. Make sure the publisher spelled your name right and listed your correct address.

Grant of Rights

If this book is a work for hire, the contract will usually say so right in the opening clause. A typical wording might be:

> Author acknowledges the Work as work for hire and hereby irrevocably assigns all rights to the Publisher.

That says it all; you've given away everything. Even if the second half of the sentence isn't there, the fact that this is a work for hire gives the publisher all rights.

If, however, this book is yours, there's no need to give anything away. The work continues to belong to you; you merely grant, or license, the publisher to publish it for you, without giving up ownership. The grant of rights, which is almost always the first clause in every contract, says, in effect:

> The Author grants to the Publisher the exclusive right to print, publish, distribute, and sell the Work in the English language for [*a stated period of time*] throughout [*a specified marketing area*].

Sounds simple, doesn't it? For the most part it is, although there may still be some hitches that can go wrong along the way.

For one thing, few publishers will let you pin them down to a limited time duration for the grant. Some contracts will say things like "for the full length of copyright" or just ignore the matter entirely by not mentioning any interval. Publishers would like to hold onto the work until it falls into the public domain at the end of the copyright, on the chance that, even if the book was a loser the first time around, it might become popular later—in which case they'd dust it off and bring it out of mothballs. This situation is not good for the writer, however; if the book is out of print instead of being on bookstore shelves where people can buy it, you can't earn any royalties.

There are two remedies for this situation. One is to insist that your contract have a reversion clause, giving the book back to you under specified conditions; the other is the automatic reversion built into the new copyright law. A good reversion clause is by far the better solution.

The other major point to watch carefully in the grant of rights is the marketing area you allow the publisher. Most publishers would like to stick "the world" into that blank in the contract—in which case you've just given up the ability to sell your British subsidiary rights yourself. This can be a good or a bad thing, depending on your circumstances. If you don't have an agent or any connections with British publishers, it may indeed be to your advantage to allow your American publisher to handle your work abroad—provided he doesn't take an overly large share of the proceeds.

If you *do* have an agent or, for some other reason, don't want your American publisher to handle your British rights, the language in this clause will have to be more restrictive. The narrowest you can expect to get is to grant *exclusive* rights to publish in English throughout "the United States of America, its possessions, Canada, and the Philippine Islands" and *nonexclusive* rights to publish in the English language throughout the "open market"—which is to say, territory other than the above-named places and the British Commonwealth. Denmark, for instance, would be part of the open market, and your American publisher could try selling English-language editions there—but he'd have to compete with your British publisher. The Danish market for books printed in English might not be large enough to warrant such competition, but there you have it.

Often within the grant of rights there will be some description of the book this contract is for. It may be a two-line synopsis or merely the tentative title. For instance, the contract might say, "The Work is to be a novel about a group of squatters who occupy an abandoned coal mine," or "The Work shall be an investigation into corruption within the recording industry"—but something, at least, to define "the Work" so that there are no claims later about misunderstanding what the contract was for.

Delivery Date

If this sale is based on your submission of a completed manuscript, you have nothing to worry about here; you've already done your end of the job and delivered the work to the publisher. But many authors sell a book on the basis of a proposal—one or more chapters plus an outline of the rest. The publisher may be willing to gamble that you'll complete the book to his satisfaction, but he wants some legal assurance that you intend to finish what you started.

This unfortunately is not an idle worry; there are some writers who take a partial advance and never complete the work—or, if they do complete it, turn it in so late that the publisher no longer cares about it. Their excuses are usually plausible, such as illness or a death in the family, but too many of them piled coincidentally atop one another can become suspicious. (We've heard of one writer whose grandmother died three times in a one-year period.) These writers eventually get a reputation as deadbeats and find that publishers will be reluctant to deal with them again, but in the meantime they make hardworking and dedicated writers look bad.

The delivery clause is intended solely to protect the publisher from these chiselers. All that would really be needed is a statement such as:

> Author agrees to deliver a completed copy of the Work to the Publisher on or before [*date*]. If the Author fails to deliver the manuscript by that date, Publisher may, upon written notice, terminate this agreement. In such case, the Author agrees to repay to the Publisher any monies advanced to him under this contract.

Publishers seldom leave it at that, though. For one thing, many of them are asking that you send them *two* copies of the manuscript instead of one—or, if you only send one, that they can make photocopies of it and charge the expense to your royalty account. This shouldn't be too objectionable, as having an extra copy on hand helps the publisher's production department and speeds the book's publication. In our case, since we live in a big city with plenty of cheap photocopy services available, we generally submit two copies anyway, even if the contract only calls for one. If you live in a small town or find photocopying prohibitive in some other way, you might prefer to let the publisher handle the matter and bill your account. (It may cost you more this way, though, since a publisher may not shop around for the cheapest photocopy prices.)

A far more serious matter is that most contracts require the delivered manuscript to be "satisfactory in style and content" as well as complete, with no definition of what "satisfactory" might mean. This gives the publisher an escape clause that can be dangerous to you, the writer—because even if you work diligently to produce the best possible book and turn it in on time, the publisher can still reject it as "unsatisfactory" for some obscure reason and demand the advance back.

The Authors Guild of America has recently taken aim at this clause, calling it unfair to the writer. The Guild points out that this clause makes the entire contract merely an option—rather than a binding commitment—on the publisher's part, since he's always free to reject a work for any reason whatsoever. The Guild would like to substitute the wording, "The Author shall deliver a manuscript which, in style and content, is professionally competent and fit for publication." The Guild also maintains that the writer shouldn't be made to refund an advance if the book is turned in on time—or, if the publisher insists, that the refund should be no more than 30 percent of the money advanced, and *that* only when and if the book sells to another publisher.

If you're writing a nonfiction book, you may need additional material along with the written text: photographs, charts, maps, drawings, bibliographies, or other graphic materials. These will usually be required at the same time your manuscript itself is due; if there are to be any complications, you may ask for separate due dates to be listed when the contract is drawn up. Usually the contract will state that it's your responsibility to supply these materials; again, if you anticipate any problems it's wise to mention the matter up front, when the contract is being negotiated. There may, for instance, be heavy expenses incurred in obtaining the necessary drawings, and you might want to insist that the publisher pay a share of them. Contract terms can be spelled out as to what percentage the publisher agrees to pay for which specific items.

We know one writer who had problems with his publisher over such additional matter. He turned in his book, a biography of a contemporary figure, and the publisher decided it needed some photos. Without asking the writer's opinion or checking to see whether he could provide his own pictures, the publisher went to a photo agency and bought the rights to some pictures for $500, then charged that amount against the book's royalty account. If your book may require illustrative material, ask for a clause requiring the publisher to check with you before purchasing any matter from outside sources.

If you need permission from others to reprint their work, your publisher will expect you to go to the trouble of tracking them down and getting their permission in a form that's satisfactory to his own legal department. (His lawyers will usually be willing to give you advice on how to word the permission form.) Again, if you anticipate a heavy outlay, try to convince the publisher to give you a permissions budget, which you may then dole out accordingly.

For nonfiction the publisher may also require an index because libraries prefer them; a book without an index faces a serious loss of potential library sales. The index would normally be due promptly after page proofs are available from which to make one. This again is your responsibility. If you don't want to do it yourself, you have the choice of finding a professional indexer and paying for an index out of your pocket or leaving that task to the publisher—who will usually charge the cost against your account. You can usually get it written into your contract that the publisher will pay at least half the cost.

Since even the most well-meaning authors are frequently late turning in their manuscripts, groups representing authors and agents suggest a slightly different wording to the delivery-date clause. Instead of allowing the publisher to cancel the contract and demand the advance back if the book fails to come in on time, they offer wording that such action can only be taken if the manuscript is more than ninety days late—and then only if the publisher gives written warning first. Publishers are used to getting manuscripts late and, while they don't like it, you may find them willing to accept this.

The Authors Guild model contract goes even further by stating that if the author is unable to complete the manuscript because of illness, disability, military service, or other reasons beyond his control, the deadline will be extended until ninety days beyond the disruption. Again, this is not an unreasonable request; publishers insist on a clause that lets them delay publication if prevented from publishing by events beyond *their* control, and there's no reason why you shouldn't be granted the same courtesy.

Acceptance and Publication

Again, if you've sold your book on the basis of a completed manuscript, you have no need to worry about an acceptance clause; the very fact that the publisher is offering you a contract is proof of acceptance. But publishers who buy books based on a proposal need some assurance that they won't ultimately be forced to publish something they don't like.

What you as a writer want to avoid is having to pay back money if a book is good, but the publisher and/or editor have changed their minds about it in the time between signing the contract and delivery of the manuscript. There are all sorts of reasons for rejection that have nothing to do with your book's quality.

Perhaps, in 1978, a publisher agreed to buy your proposed book on the history of the Olympics, anticipating a large interest in 1980. Suddenly, along came the Soviet invasion of Afghanistan and the U.S. Olympic boycott, reducing interest in the Olympics considerably. None of those events was your fault, yet most contracts would allow the publisher to back out of the deal and demand that you return your advance no matter how hard you worked to produce a good book. Or perhaps the editor who bought your novel left that publishing house, and the new editor doesn't like your style. Perhaps the firm was bought by a large conglomerate that wants to change its editorial direction. Perhaps you wrote a mystery novel and the house decided to cancel its mystery line. Perhaps you wrote a book on how to build a home computer, but between the time of your contract and the time you finish the work, eighteen other books on the same subject have come out and the publisher no longer feels he can market yours successfully.

You did your end of the job in good faith; it's not your fault the publisher decides not to use it. Writers should not be held responsible for market conditions, any more than publishers should be forced to make further payments for books they don't want to publish.

Some publishers try to deal with this by inserting the word "satisfactory" into the *delivery* clause, but this is not the best way to handle the problem from your point of view, because it forces you to return the *entire* advance even though you may have worked earnestly and hard on the book. What is more acceptable is to put the entire matter into a separate clause—which some publishers do anyway. (And there are always some who put it in both places, on the theory that even if you catch the trick in one clause, you may miss it in a second one.)

What would be ideal here is a clause allowing the publisher to decide, within a reasonable period of time, whether the manuscript is acceptable; if it isn't, you should be entitled to keep the initial part of the advance, since it was for work you did at the publisher's request and for the publisher's benefit. Upon rejection, the contract should then terminate and you would be free to sell the book elsewhere. Wording for such an ideal situation should read:

> Publisher shall notify Author within sixty (60) days after receipt of manuscript if the Work is unacceptable. The Author shall then have sixty (60) more days in which to make changes as requested by the Publisher. If Publisher still finds the work unacceptable after that time, and notifies the Author of this in writing, then this agreement shall immediately terminate and all rights granted herein shall revert to the Author, and the Author may keep all payments previously advanced to him under this agreement. Failure to so notify the Author of the Work's rejection shall constitute acceptance.

Unfortunately, you can seldom get publishers to agree to this ideal. Many boilerplate contracts contain no time-limit provision. "Acceptance" is whenever the publisher chooses to say it is; theoretically a publisher can hold on to your book for years trying to decide whether to accept it (and in the meantime, you're left waiting for the "on acceptance" share of the payment). This clause as we've worded it puts all the burden on the publisher by assuming that the work is accepted unless you are specifically told otherwise within a reasonable period of time; for that reason, you can usually expect a publisher to object if you insist on it.

Some publishers, too, will demand a return of *all* the money they advanced if the work is ultimately rejected, even though you worked hard at it and even though they knew they were taking a gamble in the first place. If you can't get your publisher to budge on this demand, at least have it written into the contract that you must return the money *only* if you ultimately sell the book to another publisher. This clause is within accepted industry standards, and most publishers should agree to it as a fair compromise.

In fact, until recently those knowledgeable in the field would have said it was so standard there was no need to put it in writing—but that has drastically changed, thanks to a 1979 ruling by a justice of the New York State Supreme Court in a case involving publisher Stein and Day and writer Al Morgan. Morgan had received an advance of $35,000 on a contract for two books. He turned in the first book, *Anchor Woman,* and it was published by Stein and Day, eventually earning $21,620 in royalties. When the second book was turned in, Stein and Day rejected it (as did several other publishers to whom Morgan later submitted it). Stein and Day then sued Morgan to recoup the remaining $13,380 of the advance.

Justice Martin B. Stecher wrote in his decision that Morgan "offered testimony that the custom of the publishing industry with respect to an unsatisfied manuscript required that all sums advanced to the time of the submission of the manuscript be retained by the author; that no further installments of the advance need be made; that if the manuscript is thereafter sold to another publisher, it is the author's obligation, from the new consideration, to reimburse the first publisher to the extent of the advance; and that in the absence of sale to a new publisher, the publisher making the advance absorbs the loss represented by the advance. The testimony as to custom was uncontradicted."

Yet despite the fact that Stein and Day did not bother to contradict this impression of the traditional way of doing business, the judge ruled in their favor—because Morgan's contract specifically said he had to pay back the money if the book wasn't accepted. Specific wording in a contract takes precedence over industry custom.

Moral: If you don't want to pay back the on-signing advance—or at least not until you've sold the book to another publisher—make sure the contract explicitly states that.

In the case of a book that the publisher feels might be a long-term seller—a textbook, for instance, or a nonfiction work that may need updating—there may be a clause requiring you to make revisions at specified intervals for no additional money; and if you can't, or won't, make these revisions, the publisher has the right to hire someone else to do it and pay that other writer—either on a flat fee or a royalty basis—out of your royalty account. In its analysis of its model contract, the Authors Guild suggests the following additions to such a clause: first, that revisions may be required only at specified fixed intervals, and not more often; second, that such requests for revision be subject to the author's approval, which may not be unreasonably withheld; third, that if a second author is called in, your share of the royalties may not be reduced to less than two thirds of what it was originally; and fourth, that you have the right to look over the revisions and to take your name off the work if you find the revisions unacceptable. (That has happened on more than one occasion.)

So far, in our discussion, the contract has given the publisher *permission* to publish the work and has laid out terms for the book's acceptance. Many contracts stop there, giving the publisher unlimited time to hold on to your book before publishing it. This isn't to your advantage. If your book contains dated material, you'll want it out as soon as possible. Even if it won't become dated, you can't earn any money on it if it's not in print where people can buy it. There has to be a clause *requiring* the publisher to publish the book within a reasonable time. Standard wording of such a clause might be:

Publisher shall publish the Work no later than [*period of time*] after acceptance, in a manner and style of its own choosing, unless prevented from doing so by events beyond its control, in which case publication will be no later than six months after the termination of such events. Upon Publisher's failure to publish the Work within the specified period, Author may, upon written notice, terminate this agreement. In such case, all rights granted herein shall revert to the Author, and the Author shall be entitled to keep all monies previously advanced to him under this agreement. Deadline for publication may be extended by mutual agreement in writing between the Publisher and the Author.

It normally takes between six and nine months for a book to travel through the publishing process; individual problems and publishing schedules at different houses can vary this time either way, sometimes more than doubling it. In no event should the time period in the blank be longer than two years. (Some companies try to ask for three, or even five.) If the publisher, through ineptitude, fails to meet the publishing deadline, it's only fair that you get the book back and the publisher be out the money. The last sentence of the clause gives enough flexibility for any reasonable situation. (Sometimes, for instance, a publisher may feel it's advantageous to both of you to wait until the next selling season, such as the fall line of books, and that sales will be better if you wait. Forcing publication at an inopportune time could be a spiteful act that would end up hurting you as well.)

Warranties and Indemnities

Publishers have a right to protect themselves from a writer who is plagiarizing someone else's work or who is deliberately defaming someone. That's what this clause is about: The publisher makes you swear that you do indeed have the right to offer the work for publication and that you're not using the publisher to settle personal grudges against someone else in print.

Unfortunately, the language of most boilerplate contracts seldom leaves the matter at that—which is why this particular section is one of the most potentially dangerous ones for the writer. Publishers try to make you indemnify them against anything that can legally go wrong with the book— and if you aren't careful, this could cost you large amounts of money.

The first part of the clause is not controversial. It is usually worded something like:

> Author warrants that he is the sole proprietor of the Work and that it does not infringe on any existing copyright.

That's simple enough to understand. If the publisher prints the book and someone sues for plagiarism, this clause says the publisher is innocent of intentional wrongdoing because you promised it wasn't plagiarized. If the plagiarism can be proved in court, then morally and legally you should be forced to pay the damaged party.

According to various model contracts, the rest of the clause *should* say:

> The Author warrants that the Work does not contain any libelous matter or violate the rights of privacy of any other person. The Author indemnifies the Publisher from any claims finally sustained for breach of these warranties.

The legal departments of most publishers, though, want the clause to be more generalized and to cover more contingencies.

For instance, most contracts also ask you to warrant that your book contains no "scandalous," "obscene," or "unlawful" material—without ever bothering to define those terms. As we saw in Chapter 6, the 1973 Supreme Court decision on obscenity left it up to local community standards to decide what was permissible—and how can you, a mere human being, know what the community standards are everywhere in the United States? As for what would be scandalous or unlawful material, your guess is as good as ours. These are words you should try to have stricken from your contract, though publishers' lawyers seldom like to part with them.

The phrase "finally sustained" is a crucial one, and you're not likely to find it in many boilerplate contracts. Without it, you're exposed to financial ruin from any number of nuisance lawsuits. Suppose some nut claims you libeled him, and files suit in court. The suit might be totally groundless, but it could still take thousands of dollars in legal fees to defend—and without those words "finally sustained," you have guaranteed to protect the publisher from *all* claims. You will have to pay the publisher's legal expenses as well as your own. Most contracts give the publisher the right to choose his own counsel in any suits filed jointly against both of you but make *you* responsible for the bills, even if the suit is won. This is grossly unfair; most publishers can afford such legal costs, while most writers can't.

(In fairness, most publishers *do* pay the bills to handle nuisance lawsuits, but this is only a matter of custom and courtesy. With more and more publishers being taken over by large, impersonal conglomerates, there is no guarantee they will continue this practice. As with everything else, your best bet is to get it in writing.)

To make matters worse, many contracts enable the publisher to settle a suit out of court without your consent and then make you pay for it. If you know you're innocent, you shouldn't be forced to concede merely because the publisher finds it inconvenient to pursue the matter. Your contract should contain some phrase like:

> No out-of-court settlement of any action involving Publisher and Author jointly may be made without the written consent of both parties.

Furthermore, many contracts give the publisher the right to withhold some or all of your royalties if a suit is filed, just in case you lose. This is again unfair to writers, who often need those royalties to survive, and is a clear violation of the principle of "innocent until proven guilty." You should try to eliminate such a clause from the contract altogether or, failing that (which, unfortunately, is likely), try to limit the percentage of royalties that can be withheld. The publisher should not be allowed to hold back more than half the royalties due, and the Authors Guild recommends a limit of 30 percent.

Writers' organizations have been fighting the inequity of the indemnity clause for many years, with no relief in sight. Publishers, they claim, can get insurance against losses suffered from legal claims, but that insurance doesn't cover their authors. In effect, writers are required to go into the insurance business themselves, insuring the publisher against lawsuit. The publishers counterargue that without those guarantees from writers, insurance companies won't insure them; publishers would then have to be more careful about which manuscripts they accepted, and some otherwise good books might never be published.

Even the wording "finally sustained" wouldn't have helped author Gwen Davis Mitchell after the Bindrim libel case (see Chapter 6). Doubleday helped her fight the battle all the way to the U.S. Supreme Court, where the decision was upheld in Bindrim's favor. Doubleday then turned around and tried to get all its legal fees back from Mitchell. Although Doubleday was probably within its rights to do so because of clauses like these, various writers' organizations interceded on Mitchell's behalf and asked Doubleday not to press the matter. Doubleday and Mitchell eventually reached an agreement acceptable to both parties.

The Bindrim libel case is bound to have a chilling impact on the publishing industry. Any book, fiction or nonfiction, dealing with contemporary topics will be reviewed very carefully, and anything that looks as though it *might* be libelous will have a harder time getting published. The publishers aren't likely to relax their demands for a strong indemnity clause after a decision like this. Nevertheless, you should try to hold tightly to the phrase "finally sustained" or "after all appeals are tried."

Galley Proofs

If you take any pride in your work at all, you'll want to see that it comes out as close to the way you intended it as possible, free of errors and unnecessary editorial changes. Most contracts have a clause requiring the author to read galley proofs, which is a way of catching typesetting mistakes before the book is printed.

A couple of definitions for the uninitiated are in order here. *Galley proofs* are sheets of paper, often about a yard in length, on which uncorrected typeset material has been printed, traditionally in long columns but now often already divided into pages, as a sample of how the typeset book will look; a typical book may require fifty to sixty of such sheets to contain it all. The printed material may run continuously down the paper in a long strip. In *page proofs,* the process has been taken a step further; the material has been corrected and then divided into page-sized units as it will appear in the book. It may still be on long strips of paper, but now instead of a continuous column of type there will be two or three "pages" of text per strip, each one numbered as it will be in the actual book.

The typical boilerplate contract says that the author will be sent galley proofs, to read and correct and return within twenty days of receipt with all corrections marked. Any expense involved in resetting the type, other than correcting the printer's errors, which is more than 10 percent of the original typesetting cost will be paid by the author. (That 10 percent figure may vary a bit.)

The reason for the last stipulation is to discourage you from rewriting your entire epic once it's been typeset—a very expensive prospect. Any final polishing of your prose is supposed to be done *before* the book goes to the typesetter; if you want to act as an eccentric writer, changing everything about at the last moment, you should expect to pay for the privilege.

What you want to make sure of, though, is that you are sent galley proofs, not just page proofs. At each step of the way, making changes in your book becomes more expensive —and making changes in page proofs requires a lot of time and money.

As a practical illustration, the following incident happened to Stephen Goldin. On one of his novels, the publisher waited until the book had gone to the page-proof stage before sending him a copy. When he read the proofs, Stephen realized that almost a full page of what he considered very important material had been chopped out by the copy editor. He demanded that it be put back, but at this stage of the game that could only be done if *other* material in the book was deleted; if the original material were just reinserted where it was supposed to be, that would throw off the page numbering, and all the subsequent pages would have to be remade. To complicate the problem still further, the newly deleted material would have to come from the same approximate part of the book where the reinstated material was to be put—again, to avoid having to redo an exorbitant number of pages. Stephen spent an entire week agonizing over how to restructure that section of the book with a minimum of disruption.

The problem could have been avoided if, earlier in the publishing process, the publisher had sent him galley proofs instead. Then it would simply have been a matter of inserting the deleted material in the proper place, before it was all parceled out into made-up pages. This is why you should stress to your editor that you want to see the galleys; it saves everyone involved a lot of time, effort, and money.

In fact, some writers try to take this a step further by insisting in their contracts that they be allowed to review the copy-edited manuscript before it's even sent to the typesetter. That way, if an editor has changed your words around in some unacceptable fashion, you can holler about the alterations before the typesetter has even begun, making any changes even cheaper. Although most book editors and publishers have no objections to this contract addition, magazine editors will fight the concept of sending copy-edited manuscripts to their authors. We're hard put to understand why they should feel this way, since it could save everyone a lot of needless typesetting expense; perhaps the publishers think writers would delay too long in returning the manuscripts, or would spend too much time arguing about changes with editors who have other things to worry about.

The *ideal* situation is to be allowed to inspect copy-edited manuscript, galley proofs, *and* page proofs, so you can check the quality of your product all the way down the line. Some companies do this as a matter of routine, but even they would be reluctant to write it into your contract.

Copyright

Just as you want to *require* the publisher to publish the book, you also want to require the publisher to copyright it. If your book is not a work for hire, then it should be copyrighted in *your* name, not the publisher's. Putting it in someone else's name, even if it's held in trust for you, can complicate matters no end if, for instance, you have to file suit against someone for infringement. No reputable publisher should argue very hard on this point.

Even if your book *is* being done as a work for hire, the publisher should be required to copyright it in *someone's* name. If you expect to earn any royalties from it, you don't want to see it lapse into the public domain because of a publisher's mistake (although the new copyright law makes that harder to do). Of course, if you just received a flat fee for it and have no further interest in the matter, you probably won't care what happens once you get paid.

Typical wording for a copyright clause should be:

Publisher agrees to copyright the Work in the name of the Author, and to take all necessary steps to copyright the Work under United States law and under all international agreements. Publisher agrees to see that proper copyright notice is printed in every copy of the Work, and to take all necessary steps to ensure copyright protection for all subsidiary interests licensed by the Publisher.

If a publisher omits the proper copyright notice, it may hurt some of your protection in case of infringement—but if you have an agreement that the publisher was *supposed* to print the correct notice, you may be able to collect damages from him. Therefore, it's in your best interest to include a clause insisting that the publisher is responsible for proper copyright notices in *all* versions of your work he sublicenses. When the publisher subsequently grants licenses for reprints, he'll insist on the copyright notice on your behalf.

Even if you're writing under a pseudonym, the new copyright law can simplify the matter of *which* name to put in the copyright notice. The book can be copyrighted under the pseudonym with an explanation on the registration form about your true identity. The copyright still belongs to you, and you've not lost a scrap of protection. If you're adamant about not even letting the Library of Congress know your true identity, the book can be registered pseudonymously—but in this case you'll get a flat 75 years of protection rather than life-plus-50-years, because the Library of Congress won't know who you are or when you die.

Advances

Most book publishers will pay their authors an advance sum, based on what they expect the book to earn. This advance is an interest-free loan, to be repaid out of the book's earnings as they come in. Once the advance has been all paid off, or "earned back," the author goes on to collect further "royalties" depending on how well the book sells.

No one in the industry has ever devised a foolproof formula for determining how well a given book will do, and so each advance represents a gamble on the part of both publisher and writer. Some books that received large advances have failed on the stands, while others with low advances have been known to make the best-seller lists. The publisher tries to offer as low an advance as possible, in case the book bombs and doesn't earn back. For that very same reason, you want to get as *high* an advance as possible, to make sure your efforts are adequately rewarded.

Most contracts specify that the advance will be paid in several installments. Generally, the arrangement is half to be paid on signing of the contract and half on acceptance of the completed manuscript. Sometimes publishers try to withhold a portion of the advance until, or even after, publication of the book. This is a practice you are justified in complaining about, since *your* share of the work has already been completed, and publishers' schedules can fluctuate enough to delay publication for years. The wait for the final portion of your advance can be very trying.

There may be some instances where other payment schedules are advisable. If your book is to be a very long one, for instance, the publisher would be justified in checking on how the work was proceeding, just as it might be better for your financial state to receive several payments before completing such a lengthy project. In that case, you might agree to a partial payment on signing, part when you turn in the first half of the manuscript, and the balance upon completion. If, on the other hand, you're making this deal based on a completed book, you should get the entire advance on signing the agreement.

As has been stated earlier, it is most desirable that the advance money *not* be considered repayable. The on-signing portion should be yours free and clear; at the very worst, if the publisher ends up rejecting your book, this portion should not be repayable unless and until you sell the book elsewhere—and then only to the extent of the advance paid by the first publisher or the amount of the new sale. (That is, if the new publisher pays you less than the first one did, you should only be liable for the amount you got from the second advance, not for the total of the higher first advance.) And it should be stated *explicitly* in your contract that the advance is *not* repayable if the book's royalties don't fully earn back the advance. That's a gamble the publisher should be willing to take.

Royalties

If your book sells 500,000 copies, you should receive more money than an author whose similarly priced book only sells 50,000 copies. This is the principle behind royalties, which are used as a gauge of how much an author should receive from the publisher. For each copy of your book that sells, you get a certain amount of money. The more sales, the more money.

This simple principle has endless numbers of refinements, depending on whether your book is a trade book or a textbook, whether it's published in hardcover or paperback, what the publisher's discounting procedures are, and how the accounts are figured.

Let's first take the example of a trade hardcover book. ("Trade" books are ones offered for sale to the general public, as opposed to textbooks or technical volumes with specialized audiences. Trade books may be either fiction or nonfiction.) A typical contract will contain a clause like this:

Publisher agrees to pay the Author the following royalties on each net copy of the regular trade edition sold in the United States: _____% of the retail list price per copy for the first _____ copies sold; _____% on the next _____ copies sold; and ____% for all copies sold thereafter.

Several points need explaining in that clause. The first is the use of the term "net copy." (Some contracts will use phrases like "copies sold, less returns.") Trade books are sent to bookstores around the country, and the stores are billed for the number they get. If they don't sell that many, they'll return the rest for full credit. Use of the phrase "net copy" only means that the publisher pays you just for the copies actually sold, not the number sent out.

The second point is that the royalty percentage should be based on the *retail* price, not on the wholesale or "net" price the publisher gets from the bookstores, which may be considerably lower. Textbooks and technical books frequently do have their royalty rates calculated on wholesale price, which means that the author's percentage should be higher to compensate.

As for filling in the blanks, this is a matter of some negotiation. The more clout you have, the better deal you can get. There are some figures that have become almost a standard minimum in the U.S. book field. For an adult hardcover trade book, royalties start at 10 percent for the first 5,000 copies sold; after the so-called breakpoint at 5,000 copies, the royalties escalate to 12½ percent for the next 5,000 copies sold; and after these 10,000 copies have been sold you're entitled to 15 percent for each additional copy. The reason for these breakpoints is that after a certain number of copies the publisher has made back the major costs of typesetting and design, and so the per-unit cost of manufacturing the book drops considerably. The publisher doesn't have to pay to reset the book in order to print and distribute some more copies, so the profits go up. Since the retail price doesn't usually drop when costs go down, these profits become even bigger. It's only right that your share of those profits increase, since your writing ability had some part in the book's success.

As we said, those numbers represent a minimum these days, and you may be able to negotiate an even better deal. Some authors start out at 12 or 12½ percent and make jumps to 15 percent or even as high as 17 or 18 percent. Some writers are able to lower the breakpoints, so that higher royalties will be paid earlier. It's not uncommon to have the second breakpoint set at 7,500 copies rather than 10,000 and some best-selling authors can even get the first breakpoint lowered as well.

Sometimes you can get a better royalty deal from a small publisher than a large one. Small publishers don't have lots of free cash to pay large advances, so they try to make it up to their authors with a better royalty package. This could mean more earnings in the long run—but if a small publisher has bad distribution, that will cut into your sales figures. All these factors must be carefully considered for each contract you sign.

The contract is generally the same for a juvenile trade book, but the numbers are different. Royalty rates are usually 10 percent for the first 10,000 copies and 12 percent thereafter, with a possible rise to 15 percent after 20,000 or 25,000 copies. Since pictures are an important part of juvenile books, you might be asked to split your profits with the illustrator. Also, since juvenile books don't sell as quickly as adult books, you have to stay with the lower royalty rate for a longer time (because the publisher has to keep them in the warehouse longer, and handling charges are higher). On the positive side, juvenile books usually stay in print far longer than adult books, so they become almost like blue-chip stocks—never amassing any spectacular profits, but being steady, solid sellers that produce their dividends quietly.

A recent category of books that has become popular is the large-sized quality paperback, or "trade paperback." These editions have started selling well because they fit into the intermediate price range between escalating hardcover prices and cheap paperbacks (which aren't so cheap anymore). Minimum royalties for these are 6 percent for the first 10,000 sold and 7½ or 8 percent thereafter. Through some hard bargaining, you might be able to lower the breakpoint to 7,500 copies, or get a flat 7½-percent rate for all copies, or get a second break at 20,000 or 25,000 copies with 10 percent royalties thereafter.

Paperback books are usually referred to in contracts as "cheap," "reprint," or "mass market" editions. We've heard of some contracts, back in the 1950s, that called for royalties of a flat 2 cents per copy. This was reasonable then, when paperback books cost 35–50 cents—but as time progressed and publishers raised their cover prices, the authors who signed those early contracts became very annoyed at receiving minuscule amounts of money for their efforts. These days, most reputable publishers pay a percentage of cover price. We think this is a great feature in these days of escalating inflation, because it gives you a built-in cost-of-living increase; as book prices rise, so does your share of the money.

There was a time when the standard paperback royalty was 4 percent, escalating to 6 percent after 150,000 copies were sold. This should be considered the absolute minimum today; anything less (except for special deals like movie and TV novelizations) is highway robbery and should not be accepted. Actually, the standards have been raised so that royalties of 6 to 8 percent are almost the norm, and royalties of 8 to 10 percent are possible for established writers. Even higher percentages, such as a flat 10 percent or better, are not unheard of. The 150,000-copy breakpoint is pretty rigid, but best-selling authors can sometimes get it lowered to 100,000.

In negotiating your royalty rates, be wary of editors who say, "It's only a 2-percent difference, why put up so much of a fuss?" It is *not* a 2-percent difference. When you're talking about raising the rate from 4 to 6 percent, you're talking about a 50-percent increase; from 6 to 8 percent is a 33⅓-percent increase. If those numbers are so trivial, let *the publisher* be the one to give in. Some numbers will illustrate the point.

Suppose your paperback novel retails for $2.00 and sells 100,000 copies. At 4-percent royalties, you'd earn 8 cents per copy, or $8,000 on that number of sales. At 6-percent royalties, you'd earn 12 cents per copy, or $12,000 total—which is 50 percent more than you'd have earned at 4 percent. At 8-percent royalties, you'd earn 16 cents per copy, $16,000 total—one-third more than you'd earn at 6 percent, twice as much as you'd earn at 4 percent. A difference of 2 or 4 percent on your contract can make an enormous difference in your bankbook. Editors and publishers are well aware of those differences; it's time that writers were too.

Textbooks and technical books, as we said, frequently earn royalty rates based on *wholesale* price instead of retail price. The practice is so standard through the industry that it's hard to change. In this case, you have to ask for a higher royalty percentage just to earn the same amount of money.

These books are sold to bookstores at discounts from 20 to 45 percent, depending on various factors. This means a book retailing for $10.00 will only pay you royalties based on a figure of $8.00 down to $5.50. Nevertheless, many textbook companies try to get you to sign contracts that start at 10-percent royalties and escalate in two jumps to 15 percent. Because of the lower wholesale price, you really want your percentage to *start* at 15 percent and escalate to 18 or so. At worst, you shouldn't have to start at less than 12½ percent.

These initial percentages for U.S. sales are the simplest part of the royalty clause. Unfortunately, because of complications in real life, the clause becomes more complex as you go further into it. Most of the additions describe ways in which the publisher may reduce your royalty percentage for special categories of sales.

Sometimes it's to both your advantage and the publisher's to keep a book in print even if its sales are relatively small. Many contracts have a clause that permits a publisher to reduce your royalties in these circumstances—but you should make sure the circumstances under which this can happen are spelled out explicitly. First of all, this shouldn't occur before the first eighteen months or two years after first publication, nor should it occur on books from the first printing. But suppose your book is still selling regularly after a couple of years; nothing spectacular, but maybe 200 copies every six months. Neither you nor the publisher wants it to go out of print, but at the same time that level of sales isn't enough to justify a large print run of more copies. Small print runs are more expensive per unit, so the publisher asks you to reduce your royalty. Such a clause might equitably be worded:

> If, after two years from the date of first publication, sales of the Work do not exceed 250 copies in any six-month royalty period, the Author will accept ¾ the stipulated royalties on such semi-annual sales of 250 copies or less, provided such copies are sold from a second or subsequent printing of 2,000 copies or less.

This clause limits the cases in which lower royalties can be paid: less than 250 copies sold in six months, from a small reprinting of less than 2,001 copies. If any of the numbers are greater than that, the publisher has to pay you at the full rate. The publisher may try to talk you into reducing the royalties to *half* rather than three-quarters; this is another variable you have to bargain over.

There are other times when the publisher will ask you to take a cut in royalties, and all of them will be spelled out in painstaking detail in your contract. You'll be asked to reduce your royalties by 50 percent on sales to Canada, on sales made directly by the publisher (rather than through booksellers or distributors) through the direct mail or special sales departments, sales of unbound sheets, copies of the publisher's trade edition exported to foreign countries, and so forth. The theory behind this is that the publisher goes to extra expense to make these sales and should be reimbursed appropriately. If the publisher sells off *remaindered* copies at a discount greater than 51 percent of the retail price, the contract may state that your royalty share is 10 percent of the actual amount received. It will also state that no royalties be paid on copies given to you free or given away for promotional purposes, or on copies sold at a price less than or equal to manufacturing cost.

In general, such clauses are tolerable. No one likes having his royalties decreased—but on the other hand, these various categories normally amount to only a small percentage of total sales. One case where this is *not* true is in children's books. Many publishers ask for a reduction in royalties on library-bound editions—but about half the sales of children's books are to libraries, and this reduction should be fought.

Sometimes publishers will get a large order from a distributor or some other source for a lot of different books. The larger the order, the bigger the discount usually is. For an order of 1,000 books or more, the discount may exceed one of the limits on your contract, thereby bringing about a reduction in your royalty rate. But there may be only a handful of *your* titles in that group; the rest are other books. You should try to limit the discount clauses by insisting that they be for single-title orders, but the publisher is bound to fight you on that issue.

While your publisher can make something of a case for reducing your royalties in special situations, you may try to salvage something from the situation by asking that copies sold in Canada, through mail order, direct or special sales, copies exported, and copies sold in library-bound editions be counted as part of the total sales. This way, if you get lower royalties for them, at least they'll count toward helping you reach your breakpoint sooner and thus raise your royalties on regular sales. You'll have to ask for this clause specifically, however; most publishers' contracts either ignore the subject altogether or else state flatly that those sales are counted separately.

For works of nonfiction that promise to be long-term sellers, the publisher may include a provision similar to the following:

> If a new edition of the Work is published which requires resetting of more than half of the Work, royalties will revert to the original scale.

This is reasonable, since typesetting is a major expense in book production. If more than half of it must be redone for updates or other revisions, it'll cost almost as much as a new book to produce and should start its earnings from the zero point again.

Subsidiary Rights

There are as many different kinds of rights to a work as there are ways to communicate it. You've already given the publisher the right to print, distribute, and sell the work in the Grant of Rights. In the ideal world, that's all the publisher would need or ask for. Since we don't live in the ideal world, the contract will ask for a wide variety of other rights as well, sometimes presented in such a bewildering array that the author doesn't know which to give and which to retain. The deal you make will depend a lot on whether you're selling to a hardcover or paperback house, so we'll discuss each in turn.

Hardcover Books. Most people assume that hardcover publishers make their money by selling books. That may have been true once, but it certainly isn't today. The sad fact is that about 75 percent of all books printed either lose money or, at best, break even. Publishers have to keep afloat on the 25 percent that *are* successful. As any economist can tell you, that's a precarious position to be in.

Hardcover publishers these days survive not by selling books but by selling the *rights* to the books. In many cases the earnings from subsidiary rights sales can make the difference between a book that's a total flop and one that manages to succeed. We've even heard of some companies which publish books merely as an excuse to sell the rights to them. In such instances, the company prints up a small run of books and is satisfied if it can make a few thousand library sales, without even trying very hard to sell the book in the general market; the firm is gambling on making its money selling book-club or paperback rights.

Because they're so dependent on these sales, hardcover publishers are adamant about holding on to the rights for them. Unless you are a very important writer, you will have to give a hardcover publisher the exclusive authority to license book-club and paperback rights. There's virtually no room for compromise on *that* issue.

You may, with hard bargaining, win some concessions over *how* the proceeds from those licenses are divided between you and the publisher. For book-club rights, the publisher will usually offer to pay you 50 percent of "the net amount received by the publisher." The first thing you want to do is delete the word "net"; otherwise, the publisher has the right to deduct various expenses involved in running the subsidiary rights department before splitting the proceeds with you. The publisher should be willing to absorb these costs, just like an agent would. The next thing you want to do is aim for a graduated escalation similar to the royalties clause. The Authors Guild recommends a 50-50 split on the first $10,000 of book-club income; a 60-40 split in favor of the author on the next $10,000 of book-club income; and a 70-30 split of all income over $20,000. These numbers, of course, are all subject to negotiation, and don't expect to win anything on your first few contracts. The 50-50 split on *all* book-club money is far and away the most common deal.

The same is true of paperback rights: Most publishers will demand a 50-50 split. The best you can usually hope for is a graduated scale, jumping up to a 60-40 split after the first $50,000 or $100,000 of paperback income.

These days, most major paperback houses are owned by or affiliated with hardcover publishers, and sometimes a hardcover publisher will offer you a deal for both hardcover and paperback publication by the same firm. This has the advantage to you of giving you normal paperback royalties, without having to split them with the hardcover company. On the other hand, you miss out on the chance for the really big money: the paperback rights auction.

When a hardcover company thinks it has a blockbuster book on its hands, its subsidiary rights department sets up an auction. Copies of the book are given to a number of interested paperback companies, and an auction date is set. On that date, the companies make bids for the paperback rights. The hardcover publisher announces the top bidder, and if anyone wants to continue bidding higher there are more rounds until the best offer is reached. It's no longer uncommon for potential best-sellers to bring in bids over a million dollars. Half that money goes to the hardcover house that conducted the auction, the rest to the author.

(There is also a phenomenon known as a "floor bid" in an auction. Before the actual auction starts, one company pledges a floor bid. This sets a minimum level for the bidding. The company that offered the floor bid also gets the right to top anyone else's best offer by 10 percent if it chooses. The advantage to you of a floor bid is that it guarantees a minimum offer. At the same time, however, a high floor can discourage some bidders from even entering the contest; other bidders may be put off by the fact that, no matter how good their offer is, the floor bidder always has the right to top it, so why should they bother?)

Some writers, seeing that all the real money is in paperback these days, wonder why they should bother with hardcover publication at all. More and more paperback companies are issuing their own originals (whereas they used to deal exclusively in reprints sold to them by hardcover houses); why not sell directly to the paperback company and not have to split half the money with a hardcover publisher?

The figures can look attractive. Suppose, for example, you sell a book to a hardcover publisher for $10,000, and he sells the paperback rights for $50,000; you get half the paperback money along with the initial advance, earning you a total of $35,000. That's not bad, but you look at the $50,000 for the paperback sale and realize you've lost $15,000 you *would* have had if you'd sold directly to the paperback company yourself. Was the deal really worth it?

Most of the time it is. Paperback publishers have a curious inferiority complex about their medium. Although many paperback originals these days are every bit as good as hardcover originals, hardcovers still have a certain prestige associated with them. Because of this prejudice, paperback publishers are likely to offer more money for a book that's been pretested in hardcover than they'll offer for an original, on the theory that prior hardcover publication will create public interest and spur sales of the book. This prejudice is dying slowly, but it's still an important factor to consider. Thus, while the hardcover book got a $50,000 offer for reprint, it might only have gotten a $20,000 offer if you'd sent it originally to a paperback publisher. Like everything else about the writing business, this hardcover vs. paperback question is a gamble you'll have to weigh carefully each way.

(There are intangible factors to consider as well. One prolific writer we know has said he could make more money selling directly to paperback, but he continues to sell hardcover first. The reason is that most libraries stock hardcover books, and our friend contends that there are few better forms of advertisement than a long row of books on a library shelf with your name on them.)

Most hardcover contracts will contain a clause saying that no reprint edition may be published earlier than one year from the date of original hardcover publication. This is to give the hardcover edition a chance to sell on its own, without competition from a cheaper form. If your contract doesn't have such a clause, try to add it; most publishers will go along.

It's educational to see a reprint contract a paperback company will offer a hardcover company, as opposed to an original contract it will offer a writer; the terms are far less demanding. A reprint contract asks only for the rights the reprinter needs, and it also usually contains a very strong reversion clause. The reprinter only gets the rights for a fixed period of time, and the book may revert directly after that.

Sometimes, after a book is published, there will be interest in publishing it in newspapers or magazines. This is particularly true for a work of nonfiction, although some novels are done this way too. Since these publications could also hurt the sale of hardcover copies, the publisher will usually ask for second serial rights too, demanding the exclusive right to deal with magazines, newspapers, syndicates, and book digests. Some publishers want a 50-50 split on these sales also; others are willing to accept a 75-25 split in favor of the author. You naturally want to negotiate to get the better deal, but in no case should you give the publisher more than 50 percent of the take.

There are several other minor rights that customarily go to the hardcover house: filmstrips, microfilm, computer programs, sound recordings, photocopies, and the right to license excerpts or abridged versions. The 50-50 split is pretty typical for these rights; since they don't usually involve large sums of money, most authors don't put up much of a fight about them. Sometimes you can get the publisher to give in on these rights, though, so you might as well try to get them all for yourself.

Sometimes, too, a contract will authorize the publisher to allow Braille editions or phonorecordings of the work for the handicapped at no charge. This is a personal decision for you; your publisher probably wouldn't object if you chose to delete it. If you leave it in, it's wise to add a clause saying that if the publisher *does* receive some money for such usage, it has to be split with you at least 50-50.

Those are the rights you can usually expect to give up when you sign a trade hardcover contract. They're *not* the only ones the publisher will ask for. Most hardcover contracts also request publisher control over World English-language rights, first serial rights, foreign translation rights, film, radio, TV, and dramatic rights, commercial and merchandising rights, and almost every other right the publisher can think of.

If you have an agent, most of these clauses will be eliminated as a matter of course, because the publisher knows the agent will want to handle those rights for a percentage of the sale. If you don't have an agent, the publisher may be more insistent on keeping them—and, depending on your situation, it could be advantageous to agree.

If you don't have contacts of your own with foreign publishers or film producers, it might be worthwhile to let the publisher sell these rights for you—acting in effect as your agent. As long as the publisher doesn't take a larger cut than an agent would, you're no worse off than you'd be if you kept the rights yourself (and sometimes better, since many publishers have good connections in other areas). Unfortunately, most contracts call for the publisher's share in the sale of these rights to be anywhere from 25 to 50 percent, far more than an agent would charge you. If you want to let the publisher act as your agent, you should make sure he doesn't get more than 10 percent of the gross proceeds from any of those sales.

(The only exception to this is for sales of foreign rights. If you had a regular agent handling them for you, he would probably be working through a foreign representative. In that case, you would be charged a double commission: 10 percent for your agent and 10 percent for the foreign representative, and perhaps a charge for expenses as well. Thus, if a publisher asks for 20 percent—or at most 25 percent—for selling foreign rights, there is a reasonable basis for the request. Any higher percentage is to be strongly resisted.)

Some writers have a cavalier attitude toward subsidiary rights. "These rights will never be sold anyway," they reason, "so what does it matter who has them?" This is particularly true of some nonfiction and most textbooks and technical books. While that's usually true, it's not the point. Why should you give away anything of yours for no good reason? If the publisher has no intention of selling those rights either, why ask for them?

Take the case of this book. It's oriented very strongly toward the publishing business in the United States. There will probably not be much demand for it overseas, and even less likelihood of its being made into a movie, play, or TV show. Nevertheless, we kept all those rights for ourselves because—you never know. If you don't care about those rights, perhaps you can use them as bargaining chips when negotiating your contract; you can offer to give the publisher some of these rights in exchange for some other point you do want to win. The publisher, though, might not value those rights very highly, either, and might not make major concessions on that basis.

(Besides, strange things can happen. *Sex and the Single Girl* and *Everything You Always Wanted to Know About*

Sex were both nonfiction books with few prospects for film sales; yet their titles became so recognizable that movie rights were bought so films could be made to cash in on their popularity.)

Paperback Books. The major difference between hardcover and paperback book contracts in terms of subsidiary rights is that paperback books don't have a separate "mass market" clause, since they already *are* mass market. There's been a strange transition lately, though, with respect to subsequent hardcover sales after paperback.

At one time, the traffic flow was all one way: Books would originate in hardcover and then become paperbacks. But as more and more paperback lines began developing originals of their own, some of these originals started finding their way into hardcover. Sometimes this occurs after the fact; a book sells so well in paperback that a hardcover edition is printed to sell to libraries and collectors. Increasingly, however, a paperback company may originate a project with good potential and sell hardcover rights before the paperback edition is published.

Naturally, the publisher will want a cut of this sale. However, a paperback company typically asks for only 25 percent of the proceeds from a hardcover sale, leaving the rest for you—plus you get 100 percent of the paperback royalties as specified in the contract. This is another way in which dealing with paperback companies is becoming more and more attractive.

Like a hardcover publisher, a paperback publisher will demand a large share of book-club rights—usually 50 percent, although a paperback publisher may be a little more likely than a hardcover publisher to give you a larger share of this revenue after certain breakpoints.

Some publishers' contracts, hardcover and paperback, contain the clause, "All rights not specified herein are granted to the Publisher." This is a ripoff of the highest dimensions, and you should never leave it unchallenged. What you want to do is change those last four words to "retained by the Author." If there's no clause like this at all, try to get it included. Even though the new copyright law protects you by not allowing any exclusive transfers except in writing, it's still good policy to include in the contract a notice that everything you haven't specifically granted the publisher is still yours.

In the Authors Guild model contract there are three clauses that you won't see in a standard publisher's contract with regard to subsidiary rights. These call for author approval of any licensing, the termination of subsidiary-rights grants after a specified period of time, and a reduction of the publisher's share of a subsidiary-rights sale more than ten years after the initial publication.

The standard boilerplate contract gives the publisher complete control over who gets the license for subsidiary rights. You can generally rely on the publisher's greed to get you a good deal, since he wants as much money as he can get for his own share. But there may be occasions when you disagree with his judgment. If you'd had very bad dealings before with one reprint company, you might be unhappy to have your publisher sell subsidiary rights there. Then too there are times when, to avoid reverting a book through the out-of-print clause, a publisher may offer your book to a sleazy reprint house just to keep it in print. You want a clause to protect you from having bad deals being made against your will, something like this:

Publisher shall not grant licenses for any subsidiary rights without approval by the Author, which approval shall not be unreasonably withheld. Publisher shall submit terms of any proposed license to the Author; if the Author does not respond within thirty (30) days, he shall be deemed to have consented to the terms of the license. The Publisher shall provide the Author with a complete copy of every license promptly after its execution.

You also want some guarantee that the publisher won't hold on to rights he isn't using or selling. You may grant the publisher some subsidiary rights because you don't have an agent to handle them for you, but five years later you may have an agent eager to sell them and the publisher still holds them and refuses to do anything with them. To protect yourself this way, you want a clause that says something to this effect:

> At any time after _____ years from first publication, the Author may terminate the Publisher's authorization to license any subsidiary rights granted above by sending written notification to the Publisher. Such termination will not affect any licenses made by the Publisher before receipt of the termination notice.

Most publishers want to hold on to those rights as long as the contract is in force; the Authors Guild suggests a term of seven years. This is obviously a matter subject to negotiation.

The rationale most publishers have for handling subsidiary rights at all is that your book gained a certain prestige by their publishing it, and they should benefit from that added value. This assertion is unprovable, but it makes a certain amount of sense. That prestige doesn't last forever, though; after a while, other factors may influence subsidiary sales more than the publisher's name. You may have become better known as a writer, for instance, and it's your name, rather than the publisher's, that spurs the renewed interest. Also, after that long a time, the publisher's own edition is not as likely to be competing financially with the subsidiary works. This is why you'd like to have a clause such as:

> If the Publisher licenses any of the above subsidiary rights more than ten (10) years after initial publication, the Publisher's share of the proceeds from those licenses will be reduced to one-half the amount stated above.

These three protectionary clauses are by no means standard in the industry, and you're bound to have a fight on your hands to get even one, let alone all three.

Accounting and Payments

Most contracts that aren't flat-fee agreements provide for regular royalty payments. The basic wording is:

> The Publisher shall compile semi-annual royalty statements of the Work's earnings as of June 30 and December 31 of each year, and will send the Author a statement, along with any payments due, within _____ days after the end of the accounting period.

Some publishers may agree to pay royalties more often, such as quarterly, but the semi-annual period is standard in most of the industry. A few publishers may try to get away with only annual statements, but you should fight against this; the longer the publisher holds onto your money, the more interest you lose.

The dates mentioned in that clause may vary too, depending on the accounting practices of the publisher. The January-to-June and July-to-December intervals are basic, but every so often you run across a publisher who has a different fiscal year. Such a publisher might use the periods April-to-September and October-to-March, or any other six-month periods. As long as the accounting periods are stated specifically in the contract and adhered to consistently, this should present no problem.

You should pay more attention to the number of days between the end of the accounting period and the date the publisher must send your royalty statement. The longer the publisher is allowed to hold onto *your* money, the more he can use it for his own benefit rather than yours. We know one writer who is convinced his royalties are invested in a three-month Treasury bill to earn interest for the publisher before they're paid to him. Other writers are sure the publishers are loaning *their* money out at short-term loan rates (sometimes 30 percent or higher) during the interval between the end of the accounting period and the time the publisher has to send out the statement. This may sound petty in terms of an individual writer's royalties, which may only be a few hundred or a few thousand dollars; but if you multiply it by *all* the money owed to all the publisher's writers, it can easily be an amount in the five- or six-figure range.

The publishers would like us to think their accounts are all done by bookkeepers with quill pens and green eyeshades. They usually ask for a 90-day interval in which to report; some companies ask for 120 days, and some even have the gall to ask for six months. In the old days *before* accounting departments were computerized, royalty statements were promised within 30 days. Now the standard is 90 days, and it's almost impossible to get anything less. You should strongly resist anything more.

The reason publishers can't predict exact sales is that most hardcover books are shipped to booksellers and wholesalers on a fully returnable basis. Therefore, the number of copies sent out during any given six-month period is not an accurate reflection of the book's sales, because some of them may be returned during the *next* six months. If the publisher paid you royalties based on the number of copies shipped, he might end up overpaying you—and *no* publisher wants that to happen!

Most hardcover contracts therefore have a clause allowing the publisher to set aside a "reserve against returns." This is permissible, but you should try to get the details spelled out in writing. The publisher should only be allowed to do this for the first two or three six-month royalty periods; after that, sales should have stabilized enough that returns won't be significant. You should also specify how much of a reserve can be held back. Some contracts allow a "reasonable amount" to be withheld against returns, leaving it entirely up to the publisher to decide what's reasonable. Some publishers have withheld 50 percent or more of the money owed when they thought it was justified. It's better if you can pin yours down to a firm number in advance; the Authors Guild Model Contract suggests 15 percent, and one publisher we've dealt with has that number in its contract. Many publishers today, though, insist on higher percentages—when they'll specify a figure at all.

Let's illustrate the principle with some actual numbers. Suppose you got a $2,000 advance for a book that retails for $10.00, and your royalties are 10 percent. During the first royalty period, the publisher's records show sales of 3,000 copies. You total royalty earnings are $1.00 per copy, or $3,000 for that royalty period. If your contract allows the publisher to withhold a 15-percent reserve against returns, that's $450, leaving the payable earnings at $2,550. Subtracting your $2,000 advance, the publisher would then send you a check for $550.

Suppose your next royalty statement shows additional sales of 1,000 copies. That's a profit of $1,000 for you, plus the $450 withheld last time, meaning the publisher owes you $1,450. Fifteen percent of that, or $217.50, may be withheld, so you'll get a check for $1,232.50. And so on.

Like anything else, this reserve clause can be abused. Unless it's properly worded, the publisher may withhold 15 percent of *all* monies coming in. If, for instance, the publisher sells movie rights or foreign translations, nothing should be withheld from that money, because it has nothing to do with returns. To ensure this, you should try to insert a clause to the effect that only 15 percent of the revenue from sales of the publisher's edition of the work may be withheld.

(Some paperback companies don't have a reserve clause; they just figure the reserve into the total sales before giving you your money. Paperbacks are marketed in a different way from hardcover books; instead of returning the physical book, the bookseller or wholesaler strips the cover off and sends *that* back for full credit. He is then supposed to destroy the coverless copies. Instead, some distributors and stores sell these coverless copies to used bookstores or donate them to charities. This is, quite literally, a ripoff of authors and publishers. If you have any respect for your fellow writers, never buy a paperback book with its cover torn off. You can help end this practice by telling everyone you know not to buy these books either. Anyone who buys or sells a coverless paperback book is dealing in stolen property.)

Most contracts don't say anything about how much information has to be contained in a royalty statement. At a minimum, it should tell you how many copies of the book were sold and how much your earnings were, but this information is often presented in a confusing form. Ideally, a royalty report should be a complete financial record of the book's publishing history. It should list the number of copies sold during this royalty period, the total sales to date, the list price, the royalty rate, the amount of royalties, the number of copies printed, the number of copies distributed free for publicity, and the number of copies returned—and it should list those figures for each category of the publisher's sales (trade edition, library edition, direct mail, export, etc.). It should also list, for each subsidiary right licensed by the publisher, the gross amount received, a list of itemized deductions, and the percentage that goes to the writer. In the case of reprint or book-club sales, there should be a copy of the paperback or book-club royalty statement as well.

Publishers seldom do this elaborate a statement. For one thing, it involves a lot of bookkeeping, and for another, it's too easy for a writer to catch them if they try to pull a fast one. For instance, a publisher might claim a book is still in print to prevent it from reverting to the author—but if the royalty statement says that the total number of copies sold plus the number given away for promotion plus the number returned and destroyed is equal to the total number of copies printed, even a child can see that there aren't any copies left to sell. By trying to keep the facts out of your hands, the publisher may hamper your efforts to obtain your rights. Anyone who fails to read his royalty statement could end up losing money without realizing it.

You can try to add to your contract a description of what the royalty statement should contain, but the publisher will fight it. Even if he doesn't intend to be dishonest, the information you ask for will probably be different from what he gives on the royalty statements to his other authors. The royalty department won't want to do a special form just for you. The Authors Guild and other writers' organizations are pressuring publishers en masse to adopt a standard royalty statement format.

You *should* insist on a clause allowing you—or an accountant paid by you—to examine the publisher's books. That way, in case of a discrepancy, you can take action against the publisher. Such a clause might say:

> The Author or his duly authorized representative may, upon written request, examine all the Publisher's accounts and records with regard to the Work. If an error of more than 5% of the total monies paid is found to exist in favor of the Publisher, the Publisher shall pay the cost of the examination; if not, the cost shall be borne by the Author.

This is fair, since the cost of a detailed accounting will be high and should scare off authors who have only trivial complaints, but at the same time, if there is massive inaccuracy the publisher is penalized. Most publishers should go along with a clause like this.

There's another trick for delaying your payment, and that is for the publisher to hold on to money from the sale of subsidiary rights until the next royalty statement. Suppose, for example, that your accounting period is from January to June, and the publisher gets the money from a reprint sale in February. Under many contracts, you don't have to be paid until the *next* royalty statement at the end of September— meaning that the publisher has had seven months to use your money, interest free. The publisher also may apply that money against your unearned advance, reducing the amount paid you still further. At best, only the sales of the publisher's edition should make up the advance—or, at worst, only a certain percentage of the subsidiary money should count toward the advance, the rest going to you.

A clause to take care of these payment problems might read as follows;

> The Publisher shall pay to the Author any monies due from sale of subsidiary rights within thirty (30) days of receipt by the Publisher. The Publisher may withhold no more than _____% of these sums as a charge against unearned advance, and may not withhold any of it as part of a reserve against returns.

A figure of 30 percent in that blank might be acceptable. It's particularly important that you try to get a clause like this when you realize that some book clubs pay royalties to the publisher quarterly, but the publisher only pays royalties to the author semi-annually.

Just to guard against the frightening possibility of making an overpayment to an author, many publishers put a clause into their contracts stating that any accidental overpayment may be deducted from payment to the author under subsequent royalty statements. This is fair—but make sure there's a clause stating expressly that the term "overpayment" doesn't refer to any unearned advance against royalties. The advance is the only *sure* money you get for writing this book; you did the work, and you shouldn't have to give any of that money back.

Some publishers go even further, trying to withhold money

you may owe them "under this or any other contract." This is a blatant grab, and you should try to delete the words "or any other." Each book should be treated as a separate venture, independent of any others. If you let a clause like this get by, you're asking for trouble. If your first book was a flop, for instance, and your second book is a big success, your publisher could try withholding some of your profits on the second book to make up for the loss on the first.

In order to avoid cluttering their bookkeeping departments with trivia, publishers sometimes put in a clause saying that if, any time more than two years after publication, the royalties in any given six-month period are less than $10, they don't have to issue a royalty statement until the amount owed you is more than $10. This isn't unfair, although you should try to add that you have the right to demand a statement anyway if you want it. Also, be careful about the amount quoted; sometimes the publisher will stick in $50 or $100 instead of $10. We don't know many writers who consider those amounts trivial.

Sometimes a contract will contain a limitation clause, saying that the publisher is not to pay you more than a certain sum of money per year, no matter how successful the book is. This is supposed to help you with tax problems; if you have an enormous best-seller you could be pushed into a very high tax bracket unless it says specifically in your contract that the publisher may only pay you so much in any given year. There may be writers who need a clause like this, and we envy them. We can't help thinking, though, that this gives the publisher more time to hold on to your money and earn interest on it; the *publisher* certainly isn't worried about being pushed into a higher tax bracket.

Shere Hite had such a clause in her contract with Macmillan, stating that she could not receive more than $25,000 per year for her book *The Hite Report.* In 1979 she filed suit against the publisher, claiming that, although the book had earned her more than $875,000 in royalties and reprint advance, she had only received $95,000 as of that date—the initial $20,000 advance and $25,000 for three years. Macmillan, she claimed, had not put the money into a trust fund for her, nor was it paying her interest. By doling out just $25,000 a year, the publisher could be making use of the balance for more than thirty years, even if the book never earned another cent. There would also be the danger that, if the company should go bankrupt within that time, the money that by rights belonged to her might end up as part of the company's assets and be distributed to its creditors. As of this writing, we don't know what has become of her lawsuit; the wheels of justice can grind very slowly at times.

If you're in the same position as most writers, we think it's poor policy to let the publisher hold your money longer than necessary. Our advice is that unless your financial adviser *specifically* asks you to put a limitation clause in your contract, you should have the publisher delete it. If you do have a limitation clause, you should try to insist on some arrangement to safeguard the money in case the publisher goes bankrupt.

Bankruptcy

Publishing is a very risky business, and occasionally a publisher—particularly a smaller one—may go bankrupt. Every writer mourns when a potential market is lost, but if the publisher owns any rights to your books you could have additional reasons for dismay. Those rights, along with the physical copies of the book, are part of the publisher's assets; as such, they could be put into a receivership or assigned to his creditors to help liquidate his debts. If the publisher owes you money for royalties you simply become another creditor, and your royalties may be lumped into the general pool and paid out to everyone.

To protect yourself, you should try to have a bankruptcy clause in your contract covering all contingencies. If anything dire happened to the publisher, this clause would give you back all your rights immediately so those rights couldn't be bartered away as part of a settlement. A bankruptcy clause looks terribly legal and complicated—but, like the indemnity clause, it's meant to cover a complicated subject. An ideal bankruptcy clause might be worded as follows:

> If a petition in bankruptcy shall be filed by or against the Publisher, or if it shall be judged insolvent by a court, or if a Trustee or Receiver of any property of the Publisher shall be appointed in any suit or proceeding by or against the Publisher, or if the Publisher shall make an assignment for the benefit of creditors or shall take the benefit of any bankruptcy or insolvency Act, or if the Publisher shall liquidate its business for any cause whatsoever, this agreement shall terminate automatically without notice, and such termination shall be effective as of the date of the filing of such petition, adjudication, appointment, assignment, or declaration, or commencement of reorganization or liquidation proceedings, and all rights granted hereunder shall thereupon revert to the Author. All payments made to the Author prior to such date shall belong to the Author without prejudice to any other remedies the Author may have.

There are many different ways in which bankruptcy or liquidation can occur; this clause says that if any of them happen, all rights *immediately* revert to you, that you can keep any money the publisher gave you before the bankruptcy occurred, and you can stand in line with other creditors to collect money owed you as royalties.

Getting a good bankruptcy clause is not always an easy matter. Just as people afraid of death refuse to make a will or discuss their funeral arrangements, some publishers refuse to even consider including a clause like this in their contracts. One publishing company we've dealt with is owned by a large conglomerate; the publisher asked, "Does the author really think our conglomerate will go bankrupt?" Actually we don't, but that doesn't mean we shouldn't have a bankruptcy clause anyway. What if, sometime in the future, the conglomerate sells the publishing company to some other owner whose financial situation is much worse? Without a bankruptcy clause, there's no protection if the new owner goes under.

Many publishers do have a form of bankruptcy clause in their boilerplate contracts—but even so, you have to be careful about how those clauses are worded. One variation you'll frequently find is that the contract doesn't automatically terminate as soon as any of those nasty conditions befalls the publisher; instead, you have to send a written notice of termination. This puts the burden on you to know about these goings-on and take action. If you don't learn about the bankruptcy proceedings until after they've gone through the courts, you may have missed out on some of your rights. Sometimes you can convince the publisher to switch to the automatic termination; other times you may have to settle for this method of requiring a notice. It's still better than having no bankruptcy clause at all.

A sneakier approach in some publishers' bankruptcy clauses is that the "right of publication" will revert to you in case of bankruptcy—but if you sold the publisher any other rights, they will presumably remain as assets to be distributed to the creditors. You should make sure that *all* rights revert to you; most publishers will give in on this point.

Some of the model contracts we studied demand you be given the first option to buy up all remaining copies, sheets, and metal plates for your book if the publisher goes bankrupt. If you choose not to do so, those items may be sold at fair market value, and the proceeds should be split between you and the publisher. This is worth asking for, at least, although there's no guarantee you'll be able to get it.

Reversion

Just as you don't want to grant too many rights the publisher can't use, you want the ability to recover any rights that the publisher *refuses* to use. If your book is out of print, no one can buy it and you can't be earning royalties. If the publisher doesn't want to keep it in print, you should have the right to take the book back and look around for another publisher.

(This doesn't always mean you'll find one; frequently books are out of print because there's no market for them at all. But as you continue your career, your name acquires more value, and years later publishers may want to reprint your earlier works. If the original publisher didn't want to help promote you by keeping your book in print, why should that publisher be able to reap the benefits by reprinting the book after you're a success?)

A typical reversion clause might read as follows:

> If the Work shall go out of print any time after two years from the original publication date, the Author may send a written request to the Publisher to put the Work back in print within six months, and Publisher must state its intentions within thirty (30) days after receipt of such request. If the Publisher fails to respond within that time or if, having responded, fails to put the Work back in print within six months, this agreement shall automatically terminate without further notice and all rights granted herein shall revert to the Author. Such termination notwithstanding, the Publisher shall continue to share in the proceeds from any subsidiary licenses it granted before the termination of this agreement.

This is fair. The clause outlines a simple procedure you can follow to force the publisher either to reprint your book or to give it back to you. The publisher is entitled to profit from subsidiary rights he sold while he had the right to sell them. Even so, you might want to put a limit on this. Some model contracts say that, after termination, the buyer of the subsidiary rights will pay *your* share of those proceeds directly to you, rather than paying the whole amount to the publisher, who might delay in making the payment to you. Some model contracts also state that the publisher's right to share in subsidiary sales ends when his grant to the subsidiary buyer ends, and that he can't renew the subsidiary agreement after his own edition has gone out of print. You're bound to get a fight if you ask for these provisions.

The tricky part of this clause is the definition of "out of print." Many publishers' contracts have no definition of the term at all, and if you try to enforce the reversion clause they can fight you for months or years on those grounds. For your own protection, you should insist on some clear definition of "out of print" written into the contract.

There have been a number of definitions used in the field. One definition might be that if less than a certain number of copies are sold in a year—say, 100 for a hardcover book, 500 or 1,000 for a paperback—then the book is out of print. This is the easiest for you to check, because the information will be on your royalty statement. Another definition is that if the publisher has less than a given number of copies in stock— say 50 for hardcover, 150 for paperback—then the book is out of print. This is hard to determine, because publishers these days seldom give you much information about numbers of copies printed, sold, destroyed, etc. Another definition is that if the book is not listed in the publisher's current catalog (or the catalog of the reprint publisher, if a reprint license has been issued), then the book is out of print. (Publishers *have* been known to play games with their catalogs, however; your book may be listed in a catalog, and yet when people try to order it they're told it's not available.)

The most common definition a publisher will try to give

you is that a book is out of print only when it isn't available for sale in the United States in either the publisher's edition or in any subsidiary edition licensed by the publisher. This way, a hardcover company can publish one printing of your book and then keep it in print in paperback forever, taking its share of the royalties off that. This definition is the hardest to prove because it's the one with the most loopholes.

You can have more than one definition in your contract. The more the better, in fact, because it gives you more chances to invoke the clause. (The publisher knows that too, which is why you'll probably get a fight if you try for too specific a definition.) The ideal situation is to say the book is out of print if *any* of those conditions applies.

There are several ways to check whether your book is being offered for sale. Sometimes you can glean the information from the publisher's own royalty statements. Or you could ask your publisher to send you a copy of the latest catalog, to see if your book is listed. If the publisher won't do that, talk to the clerks at a local bookstore and ask to see *their* copy of the catalog. You can try to find a copy of *Publishers' Trade List Annual* (PTLA), in which major publishers collect and bind their yearly catalogs. You can check the latest edition of *Books in Print* to see if your work is listed there. If these sources list the book as being in print and you suspect it isn't, you'll have to resort to sneakier methods. Ask a friend to order five copies of the book directly from the publisher. If the books arrive, well and good; if the publisher can't supply them, you've got grounds for a good case.

(Sometimes a purchaser will be told that a work is TOS—temporarily out of stock. In that case, write to your publisher and ask for details on when your work will be back in stock.)

Some contracts say the book reverts to you only if the publisher fails to "undertake" to arrange a reprint contract within the specified time limit. This is an attempt to weasel out.

In this case, all the publisher has to do is say, "Well, I tried but I couldn't find anyone interested," and he still keeps the rights. Trying isn't good enough; the publisher ought to succeed or give the book back to you. Make sure that there either *is* a reprint edition in print or else a definite contract for one in the near future; if not, the book should revert to you.

If you're going to invoke a reversion clause, read it over *very* carefully and follow its terms exactly. Most hardcover book contracts say you can't invoke the clause earlier than two years from first publication; most contracts for original paperbacks give the publisher between two and seven years, with the average around five. (It shouldn't be longer than five in any case.) We've known writers who got in trouble by not following the procedure properly. In their cases, they sent the notices by ordinary mail (not *certified,* as they should have) when the book was out of print and then didn't wait the required period; instead, they sold reprint rights themselves and then were angry when the original publisher demanded a cut. Stephen Goldin got a book reverted and then resold it elsewhere. The original publisher tried to object, but Stephen had followed the clause exactly and the publisher backed down.

Most hardcover contracts, and some paperback ones, have a clause whereby if the publisher decides to get rid of any overstock of your book, it may be "remaindered" by selling the copies at a cheap price—sometimes at or below manufacturing cost. (This means you get no royalties on the sale.) You can't expect the publisher to keep copies of your book in stock forever, but you do need some protection against a publisher who'll print a small number of copies and then remainder them quickly, preferring to live off the reprint share of the book's earnings. Most publishers will accept a clause stating that they can't remainder copies of your book sooner than eighteen months or two years after the first publication date.

You might also try for a clause giving you 10 percent of the *gross* (not net) amount received by the publisher for such remainder sales, although you could have a fight on your hands.

You might also ask for a clause granting you the first option to buy any overstock or remainder copies at the remainder price. This is entirely up to you, but we've found it can be very handy to have a large number of our books available. If you do a lot of lecturing or public appearances, you'll find people more than willing to buy copies of your work from you right there on the spot—and buying books at the publisher's remainder price is an incredible bargain. (You can also turn these remainders into a signed and numbered limited edition and charge for them whatever the market will bear.)

A reversion clause may even help you if a publisher refuses to give you a bankruptcy clause. If the publisher goes bankrupt and your contract is assigned to a creditor, the creditor may still have to honor the agreement because most contracts state that they are binding on all heirs, successors, and assignees of both parties. If your book was unpublished at the time of the bankruptcy, the new owner may be forced to publish it within the period specified in the "Acceptance and Publication" section, or the work could revert to you. If the book was published, the new owner should arrange to keep it in print according to the terms of your reversion clause, or else he might lose it. A reversion clause is not a substitute for a bankruptcy clause, but it could aid you in a pinch. A good reversion clause is one of the most important things you can have in your favor in a contract. (You can always use the reversion provisions in the new copyright law, of course—but who wants to wait 35 years?)

Neither a reversion clause nor a bankruptcy clause will do you any good if your book is a work for hire. Since you never owned the rights in that case, you can't expect to get them back.

Infringement

If someone infringes on your copyright it damages both you and the publisher, and so either or both of you should have the right to sue an infringer. Many contracts have a clause to this effect. The wording varies slightly, but such a clause should contain the following points: (1) Either the publisher or the author has the right to sue an infringer separately, or both can sue jointly; (2) the party bringing the suit pays the legal costs; if the suit is brought jointly, both sides share the cost equally; (3) if damages are awarded, they must first be used to pay the legal fees; any balance should be divided between author and publisher at an agreed-on ratio; (4) each side shall promptly notify the other when it learns of any infringements.

The only point of any controversy here is the division of the damages awarded after legal fees have been paid. One model contract says that it *all* should go to the author, since it was the author's rights that were infringed, unless it can be proved that the infringement damaged the publisher's ability to sell or distribute the work, in which case both parties share equally. The more customary wording is that the author and the publisher will share the balance equally. You may be able to get a provision that, if the rights infringed were subsidiary rights, the split of the award should be in the ratio spelled out in the subsidiary rights part of the contract.

Option

The option clause is generally one of the most innocuous looking—and potentially pernicious—clauses in the entire contract. It gives the publisher the first look at your next work but doesn't require him to buy it. To the beginning writer who's worked hard to find a market for his books, this might seem like a good foot in the door—but a badly worded option clause (and most of them are) can have a chilling effect on a writer's career.

It's our opinion—and the opinion of most writers' organizations—that option clauses are unnecessary and should be deleted entirely from your contract. If your first book for a publisher is a success and you were treated well, you'll naturally want to do business with that company again. Loyalty between author and publisher can be a beautiful thing. But if your first book flopped—or if it was a success but you didn't like the way the publisher treated you—you may want to look elsewhere for a better deal, and you should have the right to do so. No option clause ever written forces the publisher to buy a book he doesn't want, yet it could force *you* to deal with a publisher you don't like.

Many publishers realize that they can't enforce loyalty any more than they could buy love and will delete the option clause if you ask them to. But there are still a good number who feel that if they've invested the effort to promote your first book they should have a piece of your subsequent career, and they'll insist on some sort of a option clause. If you *must* accept an option clause, be very particular about the way it's worded.

A reasonable option clause might be expressed as follows:

> The Author grants the Publisher the right of first refusal for his next similar book-length work. The Author shall submit a detailed proposal to the Publisher, who shall not be forced to consider it before thirty (30) days after acceptance of the present Work. After that time, the publisher shall have sixty (60) days in which to accept or refuse the proposal. Failure to respond within that time shall constitute refusal, and the Author shall thenceforth be free to submit the proposal elsewhere.

A number of points need explaining. First, the option clause unfairly penalizes prolific authors in favor of ones who work more slowly. Some publishers are reluctant to publish too many of one writer's books too quickly for fear of devaluing all of them. If your publisher will publish your mystery books but doesn't want to print your nonfiction, the option clause could force you to write only mysteries. The word "similar" is a way of getting around that; you can submit your next mystery novel as the option work, and other books elsewhere. Or, instead of "similar," you might put in a description of the particular type of work, such as "nonfiction book," "Western," a book under a specified pseudonym, or even "mystery novel about the detective character Mr. Smithers" if you have a series going. Most contracts simply say "next book-length work"; try to pin the publisher down as precisely as you can.

Many option clauses demand that you submit a completed manuscript for the publisher to decide on. If you can afford to write an entire book on speculation, fine. Many writers live from advance to advance, though, and can't afford to finish the entire book before knowing whether it will sell. The option clause we've written calls for you to submit a "detailed proposal"; considering that the publisher has already bought one book and presumably knows the quality of your work, that's all you should have to provide.

Sometimes a publisher doesn't want to buy a second book from a writer without knowing how well the first book is selling. Many option clauses therefore say that the publisher doesn't have to consider your new proposal until several months after the first book is published. This can be several years after you turned in the manuscript, and you'll be left hanging in limbo while the publisher holds your proposal without having to make a commitment or pay you a cent. Our suggested clause says he has to start considering it when you turn it in, but no sooner than thirty days after accepting the previous work. Making you wait until after the first book is published, unless you're a slow writer or have no intention of writing another book, is totally unacceptable.

Many option clauses also put no time limit on how long the publisher may hold your new proposal before deciding whether to accept it. If you don't put a limitation on the time he can consider your work, the publisher could agree to look at your proposal right after accepting your first manuscript and *still* hold on to it until well after publication; until he says yes or no, you can't send it to anyone else. Our sample clause gives the publisher two months in which to decide; the length of time is a subject for negotiation, as long as the publisher keeps it within reason. If he hasn't made an offer by deadline time, you may assume he's turned it down and submit it elsewhere. (Although it would certainly be polite to send him a note and ask for a formal rejection.)

This is *all* a legitimate option clause should have. Some publishers load their clauses down with more conditions, every single one of which is detrimental to the writer.

The worst is the clause specifying that the contract for the new book will be at the same terms as this one. This is slavery, pure and simple, because if the next contract is identical to this one it will have the same option clause, which means your next book, and the one after that, *ad infinitum,* will all have to be under the same conditions and your career will be locked into the terms of this one contract.

An only slightly better variation is that the terms of the next contract will be similar to this one except for the advance and royalty rates. This gives you some room to improve your situation, but not nearly enough because it leaves the publisher with the same subsidiary rights, reversion clause, etc., as in your first contract. As your career advances, you should be able to win more and more concessions on all aspects of your contracts. If the option clause mentions future contracts at all, it should simply say that the terms will be subject to mutual agreement and bargaining in good faith. If you can't agree on terms, you should be free to submit the work elsewhere.

Sometimes writers who are trapped by restrictive option clauses like the ones described above will write "contract breakers." These are books that are deliberately so bad that no sane publisher would print them. Once the publisher rejects the contract breaker, the option clause is no longer in force; you submitted your next work to the publisher and it was turned down, so now you're free to do whatever you want with your future work.

Unfortunately, publishers have caught on to this trick and are prepared with a new clause. Some of them now insist that if the work they rejected is not sold to another publisher within a given period of time, the option clause goes back into effect. This is just as reprehensible as insisting that all contracts be identical to the original and should be fought just as strongly.

Some publishers try to keep a hold on your optioned manuscript even after they've turned it down. The option clause will say that if the publisher rejects the work—or if you both fail to reach an agreement on the contract terms—you can't sell the book to anyone else on terms *less* favorable than he offered . . . and if anyone offers you *better* terms, the original publisher has the right to match that offer and get the book back.

Imagine our ubiquitous Arthur Penman. He wants to get away from his original publisher, Wretched Press, because he doesn't like the way he was treated there. Wretched offers Penman $10,000 as an advance against 10 percent royalties and refuses to allow a bankruptcy clause. Penman turns down the offer and goes to Top-Flite Publishing Company, which has a more prestigious line. Top-Flite offers Penman an $8,000 advance against 10 percent royalties and agrees to a bankruptcy clause. Wretched immediately raises a fuss because Top-Flite's terms are "less favorable." (This is a matter that could be argued in court, but Penman doesn't want the aggravation.) Frustrated, Penman goes to Press Gang Books, which offers him a better deal all around: $15,000,

12½-percent royalties, and a bankruptcy clause. Penman accepts—and then Wretched steps in and agrees to buy Penman's book on those same terms. According to this option clause, Penman has to go back to Wretched even though he doesn't like it.

In reality, this kind of a clause puts a damper on your future negotiations. After all, why should another publisher go to the trouble of reading a work, discussing it in editorial conferences, and negotiating terms if some other publisher can calmly waltz in when the entire process is finished and take the book away? Unless your book is a potential blockbuster, the new publisher might feel it's not worth the time to make such an effort—which leaves you right back with your original publisher again.

Some publishers ask for an option clause on your next *two* books, wording their demand in such a way that even if they reject your next one, they still have an option for the one after that. This ranks about even with the publisher who wants to keep your contract terms the same for the rest of your publishing life and is totally unacceptable.

Recapping briefly: There is no such thing as a good option clause, and you should try to have it deleted in its entirety. If you can't remove it, remember that some clauses are worse than others, and a bad one can tie you in knots for years to come. If a publisher refuses to deal unless you sign a contract with a bad option clause, you might be well advised to seek a different publisher.

Other Possible Clauses

Depending on how busy the publisher's lawyers have been, there may be a lot of other miscellaneous clauses you'll encounter in a contract. We'll list some of the most common ones briefly.

Author's Copies. The publisher normally gives you a number of free copies of your book. The number printed in the contract may be anywhere from 6 to 25. If you need more than the contract initially calls for, the publisher is usually amenable to changing the number—but anything over 25 starts getting greedy. There should also be a provision to allow you to buy more copies at trade discount (usually between 40 and 50 percent). Try to add a provision that the publisher supply you with 5 copies of every reprint or foreign edition he licenses.

Competitive Work. Many standard contracts say that, for the duration of the contract, you will not allow any other publisher to publish a work of yours that directly competes with this one. The reason behind this is that if you're doing, say, a cookbook for one company, it's unfair to do one for another company that might detract from this one's sales. The situation becomes murkier, however, if two works aren't in direct competition. If you do an adult biography of Winston Churchill and then do a juvenile book on the same subject, are they competing? The definition breaks down completely when it comes to fiction. If you write two different science fiction novels, could they be considered competing against one another? If your book is nonfiction, try to get a specific definition in the contract of what is meant by "competing"; if your book is fiction, this clause probably has no place in the contract and should be deleted.

Interpretation. Most contracts say that, regardless of where the contract is executed, it will be interpreted according to the laws of the publisher's home state, usually New York. House lawyers are usually most familiar with their own state law—but you can always get yourself a lawyer there if you have to.

Assignment. There's usually a clause forbidding either party to assign the contract to someone else without written approval of the other party. This is to prevent you from hiring some other writer to write the book for you; it also prevents the publisher from selling your contract to some other company. (There's usually an exception if another company takes over the publisher's business.) There should also be a clause stating that this contract is binding on all heirs, successors, or assignees of either party.

Agent. If you're represented by an agent, there'll be a clause in the contract saying that all payments are to be made to the agent and that doing so discharges the publisher's responsibility. What the publisher is saying is that if your agent's a crook and skips town with your money, don't blame the publisher. You'll have to try to get the money back on your own.

Arbitration. There may be a clause saying that any dispute between you and the publisher shall be settled in arbitration through the mediation of some impartial entity like the American Arbitration Association. Such arbitration may be binding. You should insist that you have the right to refuse arbitration in cases of failure to pay royalties, and to pursue other legal remedies in such cases. Compromise on most issues is fair, but you don't want the publisher able to withhold your royalties hoping to split the difference in an arbitration compromise.

Notices. Some contracts specify that any notices called for in the contract (such as a demand that an out-of-print book be put back in print, for instance) should be sent by certified mail. This is a good idea in *any* case, whether your contract calls for it or not. Certified mail, with a return receipt, is proof that the document was sent and received.

Monies Owing. As mentioned under statements and payments, some publishers have a clause stating that any money you owe under this agreement may be collected under any other agreement, and money owed under any other agreement may be collected out of this one. Our opinion of this is not fit for publication in a book that may be read by minors. Each book should be a separate venture, to succeed or fail on its own. This sort of clause should be deleted.

One thing to watch out for is a practice publishers call "basket" or "joint" accounting. This means that if you have more than one book with a given publisher, the books' records are lumped together in an attempt to make the better-selling books pay for the advances on the others. This way you won't get any money until *all* the advances have been earned back. The publisher takes less risk than you do, and may be able to hold on to money that would otherwise be yours. This sort of accounting should be avoided; don't let the publisher get away with it!

Freight Pass-Through. These are tough times for bookstores, and particularly for the small, independent booksellers. One of the many problems they face is rising freight costs. Bookstore owners must pay shipping costs once to receive books and a second time to return unsold copies (in the case of hardcovers). In any other retail business this added expense would simply be passed along to the customer—but book prices are already printed on the dust jackets. If booksellers try to charge more than is listed for the books, customers will think they're being swindled. Raising the printed cover price is no solution either, because the bookseller's discount from the publisher is based on the cover price; the bookstores would simply have to pay more as well, and the savings would be eaten up again.

To deal with this problem, a growing number of publishers are instituting a "freight pass-through" policy. This is still in the experimental stage and different publishers use different methods. Harper & Row's policy may be taken as an example of how this works. Basically, each book will have two prices: the "suggested retail price" printed on the dust jacket and the "invoice price" on which the bookseller's discount is based. The suggested retail price will typically be higher than the invoice price by about four or five percent, to cover the cost of shipping.

Here's how it works. Suppose your book has an invoice price of $10.00 and a suggested retail price of $10.40 (4 percent higher). If the bookstore's discount is 40 percent of the invoice price, the publisher gets $6.00 for each copy sold. The publisher will get that amount regardless of whether the bookseller charges $10.00 or $10.40 for the book (or even if the bookseller offers a discount and sells the book for $9.00). The store that sells your book at the suggested retail price earns the $4.00 difference plus the extra 40 cents to defray the freight costs.

How does this affect you? Well, your contract states that your royalties are based on a percentage of the retail price. This has traditionally meant the price printed on the cover or dust jacket. Publishers are quick to point out that *they* aren't making any additional money on this new system, so they're asking you to base your royalties on the lower *invoice* price. If you don't agree, no price at all will be printed on the dust jacket; your royalties will still be based on the invoice price, and the bookseller can charge whatever the market will bear.

Is this fair? It's certainly to the advantage of all writers that bookstores stay in business, so this system is at least an indirect benefit. It's also true that the system, as described, doesn't bring in any more money for publishers than they would have gotten under the old single-price system, so you're not being cheated that way. The Authors Guild has given the idea a tentative okay and is monitoring the process carefully to make sure nothing shady takes place. The thing to avoid is having your royalties be a percentage of the *wholesale* price, or a percentage of the net amount received by the publisher. If your contract has a freight pass-through clause, make sure it specifies that the suggested retail price can be no more than 5 percent higher than the invoice price on which your royalty percentage is based.

Promotion. There's usually a clause allowing the publisher to give away copies of the book for advertising or promotion without paying royalties on those copies. This is reasonable. Most authors complain that publishers don't do *enough* to promote their books.

Counter Demands

The publisher isn't the only person entitled to ask for beneficial clauses. There's nothing to stop you from asking for a few things that aren't in a standard contract, but which will help you. We've indicated some of these as we went along. There are a few others that should be mentioned as well. Some of these are far out of the ordinary, and publishers aren't likely to grant them—but these clauses can always be used as bargaining chips during negotiation. Maybe the publisher will give you some of these things to make you accept a clause you dislike.

Revisions. You may ask for a clause forbidding the publisher to make any editorial revisions in your work without your approval, and that you be shown the copy-edited manuscript before it's sent to the typesetter. Most companies do this as a matter of policy, but it's nice to have it in writing.

Subsidiary Sales. Many contracts give the publisher total control over subsidiary sales; some say you're entitled to see a copy of the subsidiary contract agreement *if* you ask for it. You may try to get a clause requiring your approval before any subsidiary sale is made, and demanding that you receive a full copy of all subsidiary agreements.

Advertising Budget. An oft-heard complaint among authors is that the publisher isn't promoting the book enough; the author is sure more people would buy it if only the publisher launched a major campaign to tell them about it. Publishers counter that such campaigns are rarely cost-effective and that word-of-mouth advertising is usually the best. Some authors have been able to get a clause forcing publishers to spend a certain minimum on various forms of advertising.

Publishers hate this. They prefer to treat each book as an individual case, and to have the freedom to advertise it according to market conditions existing at the time it's published, not when the contract is signed. Still, they have been known to grant advertising clauses when they want a book badly enough. (The best way to ensure lots of advertising, though, is to get a large advance; then the publisher will *want* to promote the book, if only to recoup his investment in it.)

Cover Control. Many authors have complained about the horrible covers foisted off on their books by publishers' art departments, or about misleading or salacious blurbs on the covers. You might ask for a clause allowing you to write the cover or dust-jacket copy yourself (a right seldom granted), or at least giving you the veto power over any wording you find offensive. Similarly, you may ask for veto power over any artwork selected for the cover (again, seldom granted), or at least the right to consult with the publisher over the choice of the artist.

Advertising Inserts. In the early 1970s, some paperback publishers tried an experiment of printing full-color ads (usually for cigarettes) in the middle of their books. This experiment was largely a failure and it isn't done much anymore—but that doesn't mean it won't be tried again sometime. You could try asking for a clause that no advertising or other extraneous matter be inserted into copies of your book without your permission, and that you be granted a share of any revenues generated that way if you do give permission.

Manuscript Return. Ask that your manuscript be returned to you within 30 days after publication. Additionally, you may ask that the publisher also send you a set of the galleys after publication. The reason for this (aside from cluttering up your files with old paper) is that, in case you become famous, you might want to donate your papers to a library or museum, and it's best to have as complete a set as possible. There used to be a tax deduction for such things, based on the appraised value of the papers. As of this writing that law has been changed, and now all you can claim is the cash value of the paper. Authors' groups are continually lobbying Congress to change the law back again, and someday they may succeed. This clause is a reasonable thing to ask, and most publishers shouldn't object.

A Horror Story

To illustrate how important it is to read a contract carefully and insist on changes in clauses that could be detrimental, we offer the following horror story. The contract terms quoted are taken verbatim from the contract offered by a major publishing house, which we'll call Zyx Publishing Company for fear of lawsuit. (This company, by the way, has since changed its basic contract after many complaints and threats by writers' organizations.) We won't quote the entire contract, which went on for several pages of very small type. There were many objectionable clauses in it we won't even mention. We'll only talk about the ones that illustrate our point; they were bad enough. We've filled in the amounts of the advance ourselves as an illustration.

Suppose young Arthur Penman has hopes of being a novelist. After years of rejections, a proposal of his reaches the desk of Editor Smith at Zyx Publishing. Smith loves the concept and sends Penman a glowing letter of praise, along with a contract all filled out and ready for Penman's signature. Among other things, the contract contains the following numbered clauses:

4. If the complete manuscript (or related materials) delivered by the Author is not, in Publisher's sole judgment, acceptable to it in content and form, Publisher may terminate this agreement by written notice and upon such notice (or upon Publisher's failure to accept the manuscript within the acceptable period pro-

vided in Paragraph 5(b)), this agreement shall terminate without further obligation or liability between the parties except that all sums paid to the Author by the Publisher hereunder shall be repayable by the Author, and except as provided in Paragraph 22 hereof.

5. (a) Within ninety (90) days after delivery of the complete manuscript and related materials the Publisher shall determine whether the same are acceptable to it in content and form. In lieu thereof Publisher may request the Author to make revisions, changes or supplements (herein "revisions") thereto. If Publisher requests one or more revisions in the manuscript of the Work or the related materials as submitted or as thereafter revised, the Publisher's time to determine the acceptability thereof shall be extended for an additional ninety (90) days after resubmission by the Author, or written notice by the Author that no further revisions will be made. Author will make revisions as promptly as possible after Publisher's request therefor. No request for revisions shall be deemed to obligate the Publisher to accept the final revision or to constitute a conditional acceptance thereof.

(b) If Publisher fails to accept the complete manuscript (including related materials) or a revision thereof within the time above provided, the Author shall thereafter have the right to notify the Publisher in writing that unless the manuscript is accepted within forty-five (45) days after the delivery of such notice, the manuscript will then be deemed unacceptable and this agreement will terminate in accordance with the provisions of Paragraph 4 above. . . .

13. Subject to the provisions hereof, Publisher agrees to pay the Author as an advance against all amounts accruing to the Author under this agreement, the sum of ten thousand dollars ($10,000) payable as follows:

(i) $2,500 on signing of this agreement;

(ii) $2,500 on approval by Publisher of the first half of the manuscript of the Work;

(iii) $2,500 on acceptance by Publisher of the complete manuscript of the Work as satisfactory to it in content and form;

(iv) $2,500 on the date the Work is first published by Publisher. . . .

18. Publisher shall have the exclusive option to acquire upon mutually agreeable terms the publishing rights to the next (i.e., written after the Work hereunder) full-length work written by the Author until sixty (60) days after submission of the manuscript for such next work or sixty (60) days after publication of the Work hereunder, whichever is later. During the period of this option the Author agrees not to submit the said next work to other publishers, nor to seek offers from nor negotiate with others, directly or indirectly, with respect thereto. If Publisher wishes to publish the said next work, the parties shall negotiate in good faith the terms of a publishing agreement. If the parties are unable to reach agreement before the expiration of the option herein granted, then the Author shall be free to offer the next work to others, but only on terms more favorable than those offered by the Publisher, and Publisher shall retain the option to publish the next work on terms no less favorable than those offered by any other publisher.

19. (a) During the term of this agreement the Author agrees not to write or participate in writing nor publish or authorize publication of any other book-length work upon the same subject matter as the Work which would be competitive with the Work without the prior written consent of Publisher.

(b) The Author warrants that the Work will be his next book (whether under the Author's own name or otherwise), that he will not undertake to write any other work for publication in book form before delivery to the Publisher of the complete satisfactory manuscript of the Work, and agrees that in no event will he publish or authorize publication of any other book-length work of which he is an author or co-author until six months after publication of the Work. The Author further agrees not to submit any full-length work or proposal therefor in any form to the Publisher or to any third party until he has delivered to the Publisher the complete satisfactory manuscript of the Work. . . .

22. (a) The Author hereby warrants and represents (i) that the Author is the sole author of the Work, the sole owner of the rights herein granted and that the Author has not and will not assign, pledge or encumber such rights or enter into any agreement which would derogate from or conflict with the rights granted to Publisher herein and that the Author has no prior agreement, commitment, or other arrangement, oral or written, to write or participate in writing any other book-length work and will enter into no such agreement, commitment, or other arrangement until after delivery of the complete satisfactory manuscript of the Work hereunder. . . .

Penman is overjoyed. Ten thousand dollars advance! He's figured it out, and he's sure he can write the book in six months. The encouraging letter from Editor Smith suggests she'll be wanting to buy other books from Penman as well. The prospects of earning $20,000 a year strictly from writing are fascinating indeed.

Penman looks the contract over, but all that legalese makes his head ache. He's sure it's all right, though—after all, Smith likes his work and wouldn't give him a bad deal. Penman signs the contracts without changing a word. On January 2, Penman receives the on-signing check of $2,500. He immediately quits the job he's had and sets to writing full-time.

Working hard, he finishes the first half of the novel and sends it in for approval on March 1. It takes a month before he hears anything, but then he gets a letter from Ms. Smith on April 1. Smith is delighted with the work and encourages Penman to finish. Along with the letter is a check for the second installment of the advance, another $2,500. Penman gets busy on the second half of the book, confident his successful literary career is assured.

Just as he finishes the manuscript in June he gets a letter from Smith, who has just taken a more prestigious job with

Abdef Publishing Company. Smith wishes Penman well and says that editor Jones will handle the manuscript from now on. Penman is sorry to see his editor leave, but he submits the completed manuscript to Jones on June 30, right on schedule.

Unfortunately, Jones hates the book. He hates the plot, the characters, the style—everything. He lets it sit on his desk while he works on other projects he prefers. Three months, the period specified in Paragraph 5(a), go by. It's now September 30, and Penman is wondering what happened to his on-acceptance money. After all, the year is three-quarters over, and all he's earned is $5,000; he's had to take money out of his savings account to pay his bills. He's spent the intervening time writing up a proposal for his next book, but Paragraph 19(b) says he can't submit it until Zyx tells him this first book is satisfactory. He decides to take advantage of Paragraph 5(b), so he writes a letter to Jones, asking for a decision within forty-five days.

Because Jones hates the project, he puts it off until the last minute. Finally, on November 14, he writes a long letter to Penman saying that the manuscript is not satisfactory. He suggests a lot of changes that make Penman's head swim. This will mean rewriting the entire book from beginning to end. He knows, though, that he won't get paid the third installment until the book is accepted, so he goes back to his typewriter. Working like a demon, he finishes a complete rewrite of the book in just a month and a half. It's now December 31. Penman's entire income for the year is $5,000, well within the federal poverty level. His savings are getting low, but he sends the new manuscript in, hoping Jones will like it.

Another ninety days go by, and still no word. It's March 31, with no additional money. Penman's bank account has reached bottom, and he's started asking his creditors to wait until next month when his acceptance check comes in. He writes a letter to Jones, demanding that Jones either accept the manuscript within forty-five days (as per Paragraph 5(b)) or reject it. Then he waits some more. To keep busy, he completes the novel he'd done the proposal for last year.

April passes without word. Desperately, Penman tries calling the Zyx offices, but Jones is always in conference and never returns his calls. Finally, on May 15, Penman gets a letter from Jones asking for more rewrites. Penman is furious at this treatment and writes back an angry letter saying he's already done enough work on the book; either Jones must accept it as it is now or reject it, again citing Paragraph 5(b).

Another month and a half passes. Penman's had no income from writing this year, and has had to take a temporary (he hopes) job at a hamburger stand to pay his bills. Finally, on July 1, Jones's answer comes in: Zyx finds the manuscript unacceptable. As per Paragraph 4 of the contract, Penman must now pay back the $5,000 he received earlier. It doesn't matter that Penman spent all that money last year just to survive; Zyx wants it back now.

Penman is stunned, but in the back of his mind is the spark of hope that Smith really liked the book, and Smith is still editing for Abdef. Smith, he's sure, will buy it and make up for all the anguish he's suffered. Using every scrap of collateral he has, Penman borrows $5,000 to pay back Zyx. In his triumphant letter to Jones that accompanies the check, he mentions that he intends to sell the book to Abdef where they appreciate him.

Jones writes back quickly this time, reminding Penman of Paragraph 22(a)(i), which states that Penman can't enter into any agreements for book-length work with anyone else until after he's delivered a complete satisfactory manuscript of the book. Since he did *not* deliver a satisfactory copy, this means he can never make an agreement with any other party.

In desperation, Penman sends Jones the novel he did while awaiting acceptance of the first book. Jones, deciding to be spiteful after the nasty things Penman said in his letter when he paid back the $5,000, holds onto it. After another two months (it's now September 1) Penman asks Jones to make a decision. Jones says that, according to Paragraph 18, he doesn't have to decide on the novel until sixty days after the *first* book is published, which will be never. Nor, according to that same clause, can Penman submit his novel anywhere else, or even *talk* to Smith about it, until Jones sends it back.

Penman is a bitter man. Twenty months of his life have been completely wasted. His career as a novelist is over without a word seeing print; because of the terms of that first contract, he can never sell another book again. Of course, he can still write short stories, articles, plays, movies, radio or TV shows—but the prestigious world of book publishing is forever closed to him.

In creating this little tale, we've used the worst possible case to show what can go wrong. Most publishers are reasonable people, and the odds are they wouldn't have been so petty and spiteful as to hold to the letter of the contract in *all* cases. Even if this publisher did, the contract is so blatantly unfair that Penman could probably fight it in court (which would take more time and money, by the way). The point is, the contract gives the publisher the *right* to do all these nasty things—and other clauses we didn't quote gave him the power to make life hell for an author in other ways as well. A smart author doesn't give a publisher the chance to do this.

What is the moral of the story? An obvious one is never to sign a contract without checking it thoroughly. More than that, however, is to look at the overall package. In this case, the individual clauses weren't completely out of hand, but the way they *interacted* with one another—particularly Paragraphs 18, 19, and 22—were deadly. Look at each clause from the standpoint of worst possible case when you evaluate a contract, to give yourself a better picture of what might lie ahead.

When you get a contract, read each clause carefully, even if it takes time away from your writing. Spending a day or two now to determine the trouble spots may save you months of grief later.

9

Agents

One of the two questions asked most often by beginning writers (along with "How do I keep editors from stealing my ideas?") is "How do I get an agent?" Beginners think that having an agent will solve every problem. All their work will instantly sell, and they won't have to bother with the messy details of contracts and marketing. Besides, it's a well-known fact (they think) that all big-name authors have agents, and so getting one will put them in the upper strata.

Our answer to the question is that you get an agent the same way you get a bank loan: by proving you don't need one. A number of major authors don't have regular agents; some rely only on lawyers to handle contracts and other legal matters, while others handle all the business themselves.

It's possible to build yourself a very respectable career without an agent. An agent markets your work—but you can learn to do that for yourself. An agent negotiates with editors—but you can learn to do that too. In movies and TV you *must* have an agent; producers refuse to even look at un-agented material. But in the publishing world there are only a few things agents can do that are difficult or impossible for you to do on your own, like maintain overseas connections to sell foreign rights or conduct an auction of your work.

If this is true, why bother with an agent at all? There are

several reasons. First, an agent is a specialist. While you have to learn to market your writing and negotiate with editors as an important *adjunct* to your work, these aspects are the agent's total business. You have to put some of your energy into actually writing the piece before you can market it and negotiate for it; the agent devotes full attention to marketing and negotiation, thus freeing you to do what you really want to do, which is write.

Second, being a specialist, the agent is more up to date on the affairs of the publishing world, constantly keeping an eye on the field, getting to know the editors and their tastes, learning which publishers make better deals than others, finding out which publishers are buying certain kinds of material and which are filled up, knowing what terms he can demand and which he'll have to compromise on. While it's true you can do these things for yourself, a good agent can do them better and faster.

Third, an agent brings an air of detachment to the work. Because he knows the market, an agent can give you criticism if your manuscript isn't salable. While representing you, he can make claims on your behalf sound more acceptable than if you said them yourself. For instance, to walk into an editor's office and say, "I'm a great writer and this manuscript is fantastic," sounds terribly boorish. If your agent goes to that same editor and says, "My client is a very promising writer, and this book has great potential," it sounds much better. The editor knows an agent screens his clients, so the manuscript has at least a minimum level of quality; depending on their previous dealings, the editor also knows to what degree the agent exaggerates such claims and therefore how to approach the project.

In short, writers have agents because it makes life simpler for them. It lets someone else worry about those particular aspects of the business and gives them more time to devote to their writing. It doesn't free them from all responsibility, however. After all, if they don't know about marketing and contracts, how can they know whether their agent is doing a good job on their behalf?

There are no schools on how to be an agent, no certification tests that must be passed, no licenses that have to be periodically renewed. An agent becomes an agent by saying so—and, as with everything else, there are good agents and bad ones. The only way to tell which category yours falls into is to judge the agent's performance against your own. An agent who is getting better deals for you than you could yourself is worth 10 percent of your writing income; if you think you could do as well or better, why pay an agent part of your earnings?

What Agents Do

The basic and ongoing activity of an agent is to know what's happening in the publishing world. Agents are continually meeting and talking with publishers, editors, and other agents to learn the status of this everchanging field. This knowledge is their stock-in-trade; an agent who is poorly informed about market conditions can't sell his clients' work effectively and will soon be out of business.

For this reason, an agent must be located where the action is. In the publishing field, this means your agent should be located in the northeastern metropolitan area—either in New York City itself or within commuting distance (Massachusetts, Connecticut, New Jersey, or Pennsylvania). A film and TV agent should be either in New York or, preferably, in Los Angeles. An agent located anywhere else could have difficulty keeping up with the rapid changes in the field.

We've talked to some literary agents in California who claim they can keep up with the business through long-distance calls and occasional trips back east. We also know of one very successful agent who started out in Minnesota (though he moved to New York when his business picked up). It's possible for an agent to do well away from the center of activity, but the odds are against it. One of the reasons we pay our agent 10 percent of our income is so that *he'll* live in New York for us.

When a client's new work comes in, the agent reads it and evaluates it in terms of market potential. If he doesn't think the piece will sell under current market conditions, the agent may suggest changes. As the author, of course, you are the ultimate judge of the way a book should be. You should listen to your agent's advice and temper it with your own visions of the work. In the final analysis, an agent should either try to sell the work the way you, the writer, say it should be, regardless of his personal feelings—and agents have sold books that they didn't particularly like or have confidence in—or else he should return it to you to sell on your own.

The agent develops a marketing strategy for each work, much as you would do yourself, except that agents know the market better and should make fewer mistakes before getting an acceptance. An agent sends the work out to different markets until either it sells or he is positive he can't sell it—in which case it may go on the shelf until market conditions change or else it will be sent back to you.

After selling your work, the agent must then negotiate terms of the deal with the editor. This can be a faster process than if you do it yourself. For one thing, the editor and agent may have done business before, so they know approximately what each will demand and what each will settle for. For another, many publishers will send a different contract to an agent than they would to an unagented writer; they know an agent wouldn't sit still for some of their grabby clauses and they'll routinely tone down their demands. Generally all the agent needs is a phone call or two to settle the basic terms. Then the agent contacts you, explains the deal, and advises you whether or not to accept it. If you have any further suggestions for contract changes, the agent will either offer them to the publisher for you or tell you why they're impossible. In the end, the ultimate responsibility for agreeing to the deal is yours, and *your* signature is on the contract.

You may be in direct contact with an editor about the writing aspects of your work, but all financial and contract decisions should go through the agent. Most editors realize this and won't even mention terms to an agented writer. If your editor does, politely say that your agent handles such matters and change the subject. Once you agree to a deal, nothing can be done to change it, so the best strategy is not to do anything that will undermine your agent's bargaining position on your behalf.

In addition to this correspondence between the agent, the editor, and you, the agent is also in contact with foreign agents, film producers, and other people who might be in the market for subsidiary rights. When payments and royalty statements come, the agent deposits the money in a special account and pays your percentage out of that. The agent forwards fan mail to you after receiving it from the publisher. The agent may also suggest projects for you to work on and, in general, tries to guide your career along lines that will be most rewarding for both of you.

These are the more or less official duties. Agents have also been known to serve as friends, sympathetic ears, money-lenders, financial advisers, and mail drops, as well as fulfilling a thousand other unofficial functions. Your agent is the person you turn to when things aren't going right or when an emergency arises. Naturally, the best agents are people you can depend on.

This work takes time and energy—particularly when you realize that the agent is performing these services for *all* his clients simultaneously. Sending out your manuscripts time after time also takes money. In compensation, the agent takes a commission on everything he sells for you. The standard commission is 10 percent, although if the agent works through another representative on a subsidiary rights deal—a foreign translation, for instance—you may have to pay an additional 10-percent commission to the other agent as well.

We know one writer whose agent upped his commission to 15 percent; the rationale was that, since he had to live and work in New York with its attendant higher cost of living, he needed the additional 5 percent to meet his overhead. Our friend considered how much his agent had done for him and decided to go along with the raise. Nevertheless, 10 percent is still the norm, and you can probably find a perfectly good agent to handle you at that rate.

Because agents live on a small percentage of your earnings, they have to make sure you will earn enough money to be worth their time and energy. This is why most agents don't want to handle beginners. If you're selling articles or short stories and earning $500 a year, the agent's share would only be $50—not enough to justify all the effort to keep you as a client. That's why most agents won't even consider you unless you're already earning at least $5,000 or $10,000 a year from your writing.

This is also why many agents refuse to handle poetry, articles, or short stories; their share would not be worth the trouble it takes to make the sale. If an article sells for $200, the agent's share would be $20—scarcely enough to pay for the postage of several submissions these days, let alone the effort of sending it out several times. Our agent expects us to handle our own short-story sales (unless there's a chance of selling to the high-paying slicks), which we're quite willing to do. He handles the book deals which make up the bulk of our income, as well as first serial rights for those books.

Fee Agents

From time to time you may see ads from agents who charge a fee for their services and will look at manuscripts from anybody, established or not. These ads claim the agent will read your manuscript and offer it for sale if it's salable; if not, the agent will give you criticism to help make it salable. Many beginners, eager to say they have an agent—any agent, it doesn't matter who—answer these ads.

How legitimate is this deal? Well, it's legal in most cases, and there are even some large, well-established agencies that engage in this practice. The rationale they give is that it takes a great deal of time to read and properly criticize a manuscript (this is certainly true) and that, with a beginner, there is no guarantee that the agent will earn enough money on a sale to justify his time and energy. By charging a reading fee, these agents say, they can open their doors to beginning writers who otherwise could not get an agent. These agents usually promise to drop the fee after several sales and thenceforth handle the client's work on a regular commission basis.

Most established writers and commission agents look down their noses at these procedures—and most editors distrust submissions from these fee agents because they're not as selective about the material they represent as a commission agent is. Even the large, respected agencies that charge fees for beginners segregate their fee-charging department as an operation entirely separate from their normal business.

We know writers and editors who worked for a time in the fee-charging department of a large agency. Knowing the caliber of their own work, we're sure the advice they gave their "clients" was probably very good. Nevertheless, they were under strict orders *never* to discourage anyone; the last paragraph of their criticism was supposed to be an encouragement to try again with something else. No matter how hopeless the writer was, no matter how obvious it was that he was wasting his time and money on this endeavor, hope was always held out to keep him sending in more manuscripts—and more money. This critical promiscuity throws doubt on the entire operation. How can you be sure whether the agent is being honest or just leading you along to collect more money?

Even if a fee agent agrees to send your work out, you still have no assurance of being well represented. He's already gotten paid for the job, so he doesn't have as much incentive to hustle on your behalf as does a commission agent, who doesn't get paid until the work sells. To be a good salesman, an agent must be at least as enthusiastic about your work as you are.

Many beginners send their works to these fee agents because they don't know any other way of getting professional criticism. Relatives and friends are notoriously unreliable; for one thing, they generally don't know much about the business, and for another, they tend to be complimentary and tactful even if a work is wretched. Most editors would *like* to give helpful suggestions, but they're so overworked that all they usually have time for is perhaps a word or two on a printed rejection slip.

If you want criticism, there are other ways of getting it. All across the country there are writers' clubs where aspiring beginners gather to read and criticize each other's work and to discuss matters of writing in general. (Check the writers' magazines and the annual volumes for addresses.) Many high schools offer adult education programs in writing; colleges, too, offer extension courses. These teachers aren't necessarily looking for your repeat business, so they may be more honest with you. There are scores of writer's conferences and workshops held around the country every year, many run by established professionals who can give practical advice. These conferences are again listed in the writers' magazines and annuals, as well as *Literary Market Place* and *Coda,* a magazine published by Poets & Writers, Inc.

If you want to pay for professional criticism, you might also consider freelance editors or editorial consultants. There are a number of these listed in *Literary Market Place.* While some of them may also resort to flattery to get your repeat business, they're at least a little more honest in that they don't hold out false hopes of selling your work for you.

It's our opinion that, unless you can get an agent to handle you on a regular commission basis, you're probably better off marketing your work yourself. If you've read our chapters on marketing, negotiating, and contracts you'll know enough of the basics to get by—and you'll bring to the effort more enthusiasm and understanding of your work than a fee agent is likely to feel.

Getting an Agent

Once you've reached the point where an agent might be interested in you, the search may begin in earnest. A good agent may be hard to find, because the ethics of the profession discourage advertising for clients. (Good agents don't have to advertise, anyhow; clients gravitate to them, and unless they're careful they'll wind up with more than they can handle.) How do you go about finding one?

If you've been selling steadily in one particular field, you may have come in contact with other writers in your same genre. Ask them who their agents are, whether those agents are interested in new clients, and whether they would recommend you to their agents (and vice versa). This will help you find an agent who specializes in the same field you do. Word of mouth is a strong force within the writing community. You'll have to proceed cautiously with any recommendations, though, since the agent-client relationship is a personal one and the perfect agent for one writer may be a horrible one for you.

If your writing contacts fail you, try asking the editors you've been selling to. This advice sounds strange to beginners, who think editors and agents must be deadly enemies. There is—or should be—no adversary relation between the two. In fact, many editors prefer to deal with agents. An agent's behavior is normally calm, predictable, and business-like; a writer may be none of those. A shorthand develops between editor and agent; editors don't have to explain the same set of facts to an agent over and over again as they do to individual writers.

An editor usually knows from personal experience who is a good agent and who isn't, and when an agent may be looking for more clients. There have been times when an editor and an agent conspired for their mutual benefit, to the detriment of a writer, but these instances are rare. Most editors can give you good advice about agents, particularly if you're one of their regular writers.

If you can't get a personal recommendation, you can check other sources. The most comprehensive listing is probably in *Literary Market Place;* to qualify for a listing, an agency must have sold at least three books to major publishers in the preceding year. LMP lists commission agents and some who do "mixed" business (i.e., some fee charging on occasion). The Society of Authors' Representatives (address listed in Appendix C) will provide a list of its members free if you enclose a SASE with your request. SAR members must have sold to reputable publishers and must not charge fees, so you can be sure of their quality. A point to remember, however: Membership in SAR is voluntary, and there are many good agents who *aren't* members.

Another place to check is the Independent Literary Agents Association (address in Appendix C), another voluntary association that will send you a list of its members if you enclose a SASE with your request. *Writer's Market* and *The Writer's Handbook* list agents (including some who charge fees), but you're probably better off exhausting the other references first.

Sometimes you'll see a brief notice in *Publishers Weekly* or a writer's magazine that a new agency has opened and is willing to take on new clients. This is an ideal opportunity. The fact that an agency is new doesn't necessarily mean the agent is inexperienced. What frequently happens is that an agent who's been working at a large agency decides to form his own; or sometimes an editor decides to jump the fence and open an agency (because a successful agent can earn a lot more than a successful editor). A brand new agency *may* be run by someone with many years of experience and expertise in the publishing field.

Now that you've acquired a list of possibilities, you have to find an agent who's willing to take you on. This process is remarkably similar to marketing a piece of writing, only now you're selling yourself instead of your work. You want to convince an agent you'll be a worthy client.

As with story marketing, the multiple query letter is an effective tool to cover a lot of ground quickly. Each letter should be individually typed rather than photocopied, to give the impression you care about each particular agent. You should explain that you're querying others as well, and you should enclose a SASE out of courtesy.

Your letter should include a *brief* biographical summary, just enough to let the agent know a little about the kind of person you are. If you have any special background or educational qualifications that affect your writing, mention that too. Go on to discuss your writing career to date: your chosen genre, how long you've been writing, how long you've been selling, what markets you've been selling to and how regularly, whether you write full or part time, and what your current projects are. Then go on to discuss your ambitions and how you think the agent can help you achieve them. Offer to show him some of your current work, and include your address and phone number so the agent can contact you. Close with thanks for considering your request.

Some of your queries will get no response, others just a polite "no." If some agents do express an interest, you may be asked to send in a manuscript for evaluation (at no charge, since the agent isn't promising you detailed criticism but just deciding whether your project is worthwhile). If the manuscript interests him, he'll take you on; if not, he'll return it with regrets. (Be sure you include a SASE with the manuscript, just as you would to an editor.)

As with marketing manuscripts, you run into the problem of simultaneous submissions. An agent doesn't want to waste valuable time reading a manuscript that may already be in someone else's care. On the other hand, you don't want to waste time sending a manuscript to one agent at a time, only to have it sent back repeatedly. Poets & Writers, Inc., in its worthwhile booklet on literary agents, suggests a compromise: Send your manuscript exclusively to one agent on the express condition that, if he doesn't respond within a reasonable period of time, you'll send a copy to another agent who's expressed an interest, although the first agent may still consider it after that date. Naturally, when you send the manuscript to the second agent, mention that the first is still looking at it and that, if you don't hear from the second by a certain date you'll send it on elsewhere, exactly as before. This is admittedly awkward, but it's a compromise many agents may accept.

If, after going through all these procedures, you still don't get an agent, don't despair. Continue marketing your own work as before. Then, the next time an editor offers you a book contract, don't agree to any terms right away. Instead, say you're thinking about getting an agent. Maybe the editor can suggest one, or maybe you'll go back and try one who'd been on your list before.

Write to the agent you've chosen and explain that you've got a book offer. Ask if he'd like to represent you on this book as a one-time deal, with no obligation to handle the rest of your work. The chances are good that he'll say yes. After all, the hard work of selling the book has already been done; the negotiation of contract terms is a far less risky proposition. The agent is sure of some reward for representing you;

how much reward will depend on his or her own negotiating skills.

This book will then be a test case for you and the agent. If the deal works out well for both of you, he may consider taking you on as a regular client. If he doesn't do as good a job as you'd hoped, then you've learned at relatively small cost that this wasn't the right agent for you. And if you're happy with the deal but the agent still doesn't want to represent you further, you will at least have gotten a good contract out of it.

Author-Agent Relations

The agent is, to some extent, your partner. If you are successful he shares that success, and you both are working toward that same goal. But in part the agent is also your employee. He performs services on your behalf, but he can't make any deals without your consent. You're paying for the agent's expertise and advice, but *you* must be the ultimate judge of whether that advice is good for you. If you don't like it, you're free to "fire" your agent and find another. If you ignore his advice too often, your agent may quit in frustration.

The author-agent relationship has been likened to a marriage—an apt analogy. Two people are voluntarily linking their futures for mutual benefit. The writer develops a strong dependence on his agent and, if the relationship must later be dissolved, the details are apt to be as messy as any divorce.

Each writer is looking for different qualities in an agent— so, just as with a spouse, the perfect agent for one person may be horrible for another. Some writers want minimal contact with their agents. They just want to send off their material and get back to work on other projects; they know the agent will contact them when the work is sold, and they don't want to worry about all the rejections in the meantime.

Other writers may want the agent to hold their hand constantly, keep them informed of everything that happens, and give them long explanations of why works were rejected or why a book is being marketed a certain way. (We tend toward this side ourselves. It's a little frightening when our work is out of our hands and we have no direct control over its fate.) An informed writer may be able to help the agent decide on the best strategy for a given work—after all, no one knows the work better than its author—but not all agents appreciate such interference. An agent may be dealing with dozens of clients at once and can't afford to devote this amount of time to each of them. If you make too many demands on him, he may ask you to take your business elsewhere.

It's best if you can spell out exactly what you expect of your agent at the beginning of your association. You should know something about the way your agent works, and he should know what you want of him.

Find out whether your agent is interested in your suggestions or prefers to work on his own. Find out whether he likes to give detailed criticism of your work or prefers to leave that to the editors. Find out whether he stays in frequent contact with his clients or just notifies them of sales. Find out whether he'll keep a work on the market doggedly until it sells or whether he'll try it at a few places he thinks are best and, if it doesn't sell there, put it on the shelf until another ideal market opens up. Find out whether the agent wants to handle all rights to all your works or whether there are limitations on what he will sell. (An agent may not be interested in foreign translations, or poetry, or short articles or fiction, and may allow you to handle these things on your own or through another agent.) Find out whether the agent will charge you for unusual expenses like photocopying and long-distance phone calls on your behalf or absorb these costs as a part of operating expenses.

It's a good idea, too, to discuss what happens if the association between you and the agent breaks up. This is akin to discussing property settlement, alimony, and child custody on the night before your wedding; you hope it won't be necessary, and you don't want to look like a cold-blooded pessimist by bringing the subject up. But so many relationships have ended with ill feelings that this should be a practical matter for both of you.

The agent will expect to keep earning his percentage from all rights that he sold, whether he's still representing you or not; in the case of a popular book, this could go on for years after you terminate your relationship. But more than this, an agent may also want a share of sales he *didn't* make, if his work cleared the way for them. For instance, your agent may have negotiated a sale with a publisher and fought hard to retain the film rights for you; if you later switch to another agent who makes a big movie deal, the first agent might demand a chunk because the original contract made that sale possible. Or, in another example, an agent may have worked hard to sell a book of yours, only to have you switch to another agent who takes advantage of the first agent's groundwork and completes the deal.

What's fair? That answer varies from writer to writer and agent to agent. We feel the following compromise is reasonable: that the agent should benefit from all contracts he negotiated as long as they're still in force, whether he's currently representing you or not; that either side may terminate the relationship by giving thirty days' notice to the other; that within a certain period of time after the termination (the period could vary between sixty days and two years) if you or another agent sell rights to a work that the first agent handled and get a deal no better than the first agent could have gotten, then the first agent is entitled to a commission on the sale; and that the agent is entitled to *no* commission on sales of any works he didn't handle while he was representing you.

Many agents have only a verbal agreement with their clients. Others, including many of the larger agencies, insist on a full written contract spelling out the relationship in detail. These contracts are for a fixed term—usually one year—and are automatically renewed each year unless one party gives the other thirty days' notice of cancellation. Some of these contracts can be very prohibitive, demanding full control forever over all rights to any book the agency has ever sold. Some agency contracts also have option clauses saying that work you wrote while under contract to the agency will be represented by the agency even after you leave it, regardless of whether it was sold before you left or not. This is to prevent a writer from holding back an upcoming work until he gets a new agent, but it's still unfair; if relations between agent and author have deteriorated that badly by then, there's no good trying to enforce a relationship. Our advice is to read an agent's contract every bit as carefully as you'd read a publisher's, and question everything that doesn't look right.

Regardless of whether your agreement with your agent is verbal or written, there are certain ethics that bind both parties. On your side, you shouldn't keep secrets from your agent; report any contacts you've had with other writers, editors, or publishers that might affect your work. When you send material to your agent, include a list of where it's been submitted before to avoid wasting time covering the same ground. Pay close attention to your agent's advice; after all, you're paying for his expertise. If a deal falls into your lap without your agent's help, let him in on it anyway, even if you've done all the selling; there'll be other deals on which your agent will have to work very hard for his commission, and he's entitled to his share on the easy sales too. Above all, don't discuss contract terms with an editor when you're making your own sales pitch. You're employing your agent to be a professional bargainer; it's sheer stupidity to undermine his position and authority.

On the other side, your agent should notify you promptly of any legitimate offers on your work, even if he personally disapproves of them. Your agent should offer advice if he feels you're on a wrong course but he should follow your instructions or resign if you go against his counsel. Your agent should pay you promptly when money comes in from a publisher and should keep his clients' money separate from personal funds. If the relationship ends, your agent should return all unsold manuscripts to you with a detailed list of where they've been submitted so *you* won't waste time going over old ground.

Large vs. Small Agencies

A small agency may be as simple an operation as one person working at home. A large agency may occupy a suite of offices and employ dozens of agents working in different departments to handle various aspects of a sale. There are advantages and disadvantages to dealing with each.

A small agency—one agent (perhaps with a few assistants) or several agents working in partnership—is a more personal operation. You and your agent get to know one another well, and he handles all aspects of the sale. He gets personally involved in all your projects and gives them closer attention. On the other hand, he must be a jack-of-all-trades; he must know the subsidiary markets as well as the regular ones or else farm that work out to someone else. He must be a combination of salesman and laywer. He must know how to market all kinds of books, from romances to suspense to nonfiction.

A large agency may be more specialized. There may be one person who handles nothing but foreign rights, another who handles film and other subsidiary rights, as well as a legal department to check on contracts, in addition to the agents who handle book sales—and these agents may also specialize. One, for instance, might handle all the science fiction while another handles all the mysteries. Each agent thus has the specialized knowledge of each department as backup—but on a complicated deal you might find yourself frustrated by the hassle of dealing with several different departments at once. There may also be a lack of continuity at a large agency. Perhaps you've been working with one agent there for a number of years, when suddenly that person quits to form an independent agency and you find yourself working with someone new who doesn't know you and isn't familiar with your work. We know one writer connected with a large agency who experienced a constant changeover of agents handling her books; the agency kept handing her account to whoever was the most junior agent on staff at the time.

A large agency may have more muscle behind it by virtue of the fact that it represents more writers, and you may benefit from that clout. On the other hand, if you're not one of the agency's major writers, you may get overlooked a little more easily than you would at a small agency. It all comes down to the question of whether you'd prefer to be a big fish in a small pond or a small fish in a big pond—and that's a decision you'll have to make for yourself.

10

Vanity Publishing vs. Self-Publishing

If we were writing this book ten years ago, we wouldn't have included a chapter like this. We'd have given you a warning about the dangers of the so-called vanity press, probably somewhere in Chapter 1, but the subject of self-publishing wouldn't have been mentioned. After all, this is a book for current and would-be professionals, and a professional is someone who gets *paid* to write, not someone who pays to have his work published. We'd have looked on someone who wanted to produce his own book or magazine as a hopeless dreamer fighting a monolithic system he couldn't hope to beat.

Cracks have begun to appear in that monolithic system of late, and enterprising writers have had considerable success filling in the gaps. A list of best-sellers that started out as self-published endeavors is rather impressive: *The Whole Earth Catalog, Winning Through Intimidation, Zen and the Art of Motorcycle Maintenance, The Star Trek Concordance,* and other recognizable titles all began their existence as self-published works and found their own niches in the marketplace. In theory, there's no reason why any self-published book can't hit the big time.

Self-publishing comes from a long and honorable tradition. Many writers of the eighteenth, nineteenth, and early twentieth centuries produced their works this way, and their names would make a proud addition to anyone's library: Thomas Paine, William Blake, Washington Irving, John Bartlett, Walt Whitman, Stephen Crane, Mark Twain, Upton Sinclair, Zane Grey, James Joyce, Virginia Woolf, D. H. Lawrence, Anais Nin, and Edgar Rice Burroughs, just to name a few. In the mid-twentieth century, when publishing turned to mass-marketing techniques, there seemed to be something of a lull in the self-publishing successes, but they've picked up again and seem to be doing as well as ever.

Whole books have been written on the subject of self-publishing, and it's beyond the scope of this one to cover the same ground in detail. We do feel compelled to give some of the broad outlines, however, so you'll know the choices that are open to you.

Vanity Publishing

As far as we know there is no publishing company with the actual name Vanity Press, nor do the outfits who deal this way refer to themselves by that term. They prefer to call themselves "subsidy publishers." Martin J. Baron, in his article "On Vanity Publishing" in Bill Henderson's *Publish-It-Yourself Handbook,* categorically states, "Vanity publishing is to legitimate publishing as loansharking is to banking." There's little doubt that the established literary community shares that viewpoint.

Most publishers are in business to make money; the practice that makes people regard vanity publishers as reprehensible is that they prefer to make money from gullible authors rather than from selling copies of their books. Vanity publishers have been in trouble on several occasions for misleading their authors with come-on ads and, despite all the rosy testimonials in their brochures, even they admit that only about 10 percent of their authors recoup their investment . . . and many vanity-press books are lucky to sell twenty-five copies.

Vanity publishers can be recognized by their ads, which usually sport large headlines such as "Publisher Seeks Authors" and invite prospective clients to submit completed manuscripts to them for appraisal. The appraisal is entirely financial, not editorial. Vanity publishers don't care how atrocious a book is; their only objective is to make money off those writers desperate to see their work in print at any cost. The only reason an editor reads the manuscript at all is to make sure it isn't blatantly offensive, obscene, libelous, or likely to get the publisher in any legal trouble. Literary quality is of no concern whatever.

The publisher analyzes the work purely in terms of how much money it will take to publish it. This amount varies depending on such factors as the book's length, whether it needs illustrations or other special material, and whether the customer wants it published in hardcover or paperback. The minimum for a 60-page hardcover book of poetry will probably be $1,500 for a 3,000-copy printing, and the cost can run to $10,000 or more for a novel-length work. These prices already include a hefty profit for the publisher. He'll also be quite willing to let you have any illustrations, cover, and blurbs you like; after all, you're paying for them.

The publisher sends back an estimate of the cost along with an impressive-looking contract. The contract calls for you to pay the publisher, generally in three installments: one third when you send the signed contract back, one third when galleys are sent to you, and one third on publication. The contract is for a fixed term, usually two or three years. The price quoted is for a first printing of up to, say, 3,000 copies; if there is any subsequent printing, it will be at the publisher's expense. All printed copies belong to the publisher, even though you paid for them. In return, the publisher promises you a royalty rate on the order of 40 percent, far better than any commercial publisher will ever offer you (although if there is a subsequent printing which the publisher pays for, this royalty decreases to 20 percent). There are clauses dividing up the money for subsidiary-rights sales that never materialize, and clauses guaranteeing that the publisher will spend some definite sum on advertising and promotion. On the surface, this all sounds perfectly legitimate.

If you sign the contract and pay the money, the publication process goes into action. The book receives only the most superficial editing, just enough to correct grammar, spelling, and punctuation; since most vanity-press books are totally beyond redemption, anything else would be a waste of time. Then the book is printed, and this is where one of the first real cheats comes in.

Your payment was based on an estimate of a certain number of copies printed—say, 3,000. But the publisher doesn't print that many; since he knows the vast majority of his books won't sell many copies anyway, why should he pay to print them when he could pocket that money himself? If the book *does* sell well he can always print the rest—but he knows he can get away with a minimum print run of maybe 1200 copies instead. He saves himself even *more* money by not binding all the copies he prints. He'll have perhaps 400 copies bound and ready for distribution; the rest sit around his warehouse in unbound sheets against the slim chance that they may be needed later.

The contract calls for you to get a certain number of author's copies, say 50 or 75; if you want any more, you have to buy them at trade discount, even though you've already paid for them. The publisher will send out review copies and may even consult with you on where they're to be sent. It doesn't matter; legitimate reviewers toss vanity-press books in the wastebasket the instant they see the house imprint, because they know from long experience that they're utterly worthless. The most you can hope for is a kindly notice in some neighborhood paper saying that a local writer has made good.

As for selling copies, you could probably do better by standing on a street corner and hawking them to passing pedestrians than the publisher will be able to do for you in bookstores. To fulfill the advertising clause in the contract, the publisher takes out so-called tombstone ads in some papers—long columns of type in which he gives a short description of your work along with that of his other current authors. Librarians and bookstore operators recognize those ads instantly and ignore them. Similarly, they refuse to have anything to do with books from vanity publishers, because they know the general level of quality those publishers provide. Even if your book is an exception, it suffers from the stigma of the many that aren't.

Besides, the publisher isn't going to try very hard to get anyone to buy your book. Why should he? He's already made a tidy profit on the printing. To promote the books beyond the contractual obligation to do so would mean *spending* some of that money and reducing the profit margin. The publisher even has a good incentive *not* to sell books. Consider: The average bookstore gets between 40 and 50 percent of the cover price; your promised royalties eat up another 40 percent. The publisher would receive at most 20 percent of the book's cover price. Considering overhead, bookkeeping, and taxes, he'd practically be losing money on each copy sold. How hard to you think anyone would work to sell books under those circumstances?

(If, by some miracle, your book *does* sell out its first printing, the publisher has promised to pay for the next. A second printing is always cheaper than the first because the plates are already made. And, in this case, the publisher's share of the royalties increases at your expense. In other words, if there should chance to be some gravy in this deal, the publisher gets a share of it even though he took absolutely no risk from the very start.)

Most vanity-press books spend the term of the contract ly-

ing in the publisher's warehouse. The publisher fills any orders that happen to come in—usually whatever business the
author manages to drum up—and makes no effort to sell the
rest. At the end of the term, the publisher must make room in
the warehouse for more suckers. He sends you a note offering
to let you buy up the remaining stock. If you refuse, he simply destroys it and you have nothing left to show for your
investment. If you do buy it—thereby paying for the printing
a *second* time—you'll find yourself with 400 bound copies
and another 800 copies in unbound sheets. If you want them
bound too, you'll have to make another payment to a bind-
er—and even then you'll end up with only 1,200 books instead of the 3,000 you *thought* you'd ordered.

Some vanity publishers have a variation called a "guaranteed sales" contract. This means that you guarantee the publisher enough sales of the book within a certain period of time
to earn back the printing costs, or else you have to buy the
copies yourself. You can end up getting stuck with a lot of
unwanted books this way.

In fairness, there may be some cases in which vanity print-
ings are justified. Some people may not mind paying large
amounts of money to have copies of their work to give to
their friends or to hand to strangers; if they have no ambitions beyond that, a vanity press will work fine for them.
Similarly, some large corporations turn to vanity publishers
to produce in-house instruction manuals or the memoirs of
the Chairman of the Board to distribute at stockholder meetings. People who have no commercial aspirations and go into
the venture with their eyes open may find that they indeed
get their money's worth. Our book, however, is aimed at people who hope to make some kind of income from writing, and
so the advice we give is hopelessly biased.

One final word on the subject. If, by some circumstance,
you should find yourself forced to deal with a "subsidy publisher," ask that your book be published under some new im-

print you've made up yourself, rather than under the publisher's own house name. Most publishers should be willing to go along with that—and, if nothing else, it will help you avoid *some* of the stigma associated with a vanity publisher.

Self-Publishing

There's nothing particularly mysterious about the art of publishing. Many people have managed to learn the skills involved in all phases of the operation and have produced works that can rival the big publishers. (In fact, considering how shoddy some books are these days, homemade books can be even better than mass-produced ones.) If you have time, money, and energy to devote to your project, and if you're reasonably skilled with your hands, you can produce your own book or magazine without help from anyone else. Some people derive great satisfaction from these labors.

Everything depends on how you want your work presented and what you're willing to settle for. If your message is more important than its medium, you can edit and copy-edit the manuscript yourself and type it up on a good typewriter (one with a film ribbon gives the best results). A justified (that is, perfectly even) right-hand margin isn't absolutely necessary to get your point across. You can buy a mimeograph machine or a used printing press to turn out multiple copies. Your binding can be as simple as a staple in one corner—although we know one couple whose hobby is binding books, and theirs come out looking as fine as any old editions of the nineteenth century.

If some or all of these skills elude you, or if you simply can't spare the time to do them, you can hire someone else to do them for you. There are freelance editors and copy editors who will get your manuscript into shape. There are typesetting services that can make the copy look as neat as you like. There are printers and binders ready to turn your material into finished books at your command. There are even book manufacturers and author's co-ops that house all these services under one roof and will produce a book to your specifications—for a fee.

It's fair to ask what the difference is between these people and a vanity press outfit. After all, both are charging you to print your work and both are making a profit off that end of the business; neither has any incentive to sell the book for you once it's produced. Why do we condemn vanity publishers and say it's okay to go to typesetters, printers, and book producers?

The difference is one of intent. The vanity publisher is out to milk you for all he can get; to this end, he makes exaggerated promises he has no intention of fulfilling. He demands legal control of the books *you* paid him to print, makes only the most rudimentary attempts to sell copies, and then makes you pay him again to get the books back. If, by some miracle, the books are a success, he'll be the first in line to take a cut.

When you arrange for a typesetter or printer to work on your project, you're dealing with an independent contractor, paid to perform a service for you. Once the service is done, that person's interest in the project is over. A printer doesn't promise to sell any books for you, he doesn't retain ownership of the copies *you* paid for, and he doesn't ask for a share of the profits. If you pay for 3,000 copies to be printed, you'll *get* 3,000 copies printed. Sales of the book are entirely up to you. You've paid for it *once* (and you can usually have it done for far less than a vanity house will charge), and you get all the proceeds. *You* are the publisher, and you don't have to worry about splitting the profits with some pushy writer.

There are reasons why even perfectly good books are rejected by publishers. A work of fiction may be thought too daring for its time, or perhaps the publisher doesn't want to risk a novel by a first-time author. A work of nonfiction may be considered too specialized to appeal to a large audience.

Publishing companies have an overhead that must be taken into account when they consider whether to publish a work. They have to provide salaries and benefits to editors, art directors, lawyers, bookkeepers, sales managers, subsidiary rights directors, shipping clerks, warehousemen, and scores of others—not to mention rent for offices and warehouse space. Any book they publish must have at least the potential to pay its share of the overhead. When boiled down to its basics, all *any* rejection slip ever says is, "We don't feel we could sell enough copies of this to earn our investment back."

An individual doesn't have to maintain this overhead, and so he can make back his investment with far fewer sales. This is the theory behind self-publishing. A large publisher might not be able to break even on a given book without selling at least 5,000 copies, while a self-publisher may break even with sales of only 1,000. A self-publisher can *afford* to publish a book with a limited market, while a larger publisher can't.

Publishing your own book or magazine can be a relatively simple procedure: You decide what you want it to look like, do as much as you can yourself, shop around for bids, and farm the rest of the work out to specialists. If there's any chance you might do more than this one project, decide on a name for your "publishing house." (Check with *Literary Market Place* and the *International Directory of Little Magazines and Small Presses* to see which names have already been taken.) The only hard part comes when you try to *market* the finished product. If it's any consolation, even the big publishing companies have trouble with this end of the business.

There are various marketing strategies, depending on the nature of your book and the audience you hope to reach. If your book is of interest mostly within a local community, you can cover it yourself, talking to neighborhood bookstores and other retailers, handing out fliers at supermarkets, or even selling copies door to door. (It has been done.) If your audience is more geographically scattered but still capable of being pinpointed—all owners of Volkswagens, or people with an interest in gardening, for example—you might want to try a direct-mail campaign. *Literary Market Place* mentions companies that will sell you mailing lists in any number of specialized categories; you could send brochures to these addresses and hope for sales through the mail—but be warned that a 2-percent return is considered successful in this sort of thing. (We've heard of one woman who published a guide to Haviland china and sold it through antiques shops across the United States.) You could also try taking ads, either classified or display, in publications your intended audience is likely to see. Ads that include a coupon to be sent in generally do better than ads that just list your address. If you do any business through the mail, you'd be wise to consider getting a post office box.

If you want your work sold in bookstores, you can travel to the local ones personally and talk to the managers. For stores outside your area you can send press releases, clippings of favorable reviews, and any other positive publicity you can think of to the store's manager. If you want to sell to the big chains like Walden Books and B. Dalton, try writing to their national headquarters. (You can get the addresses from the store clerks.)

Libraries form an important part of any trade publisher's sales, and they can be crucial for a small independent publisher. Sending review copies of your book to *Library Journal, Choice,* and *Booklist* (see LMP for addresses) may garner you some publicity in magazines that librarians pay attention to. Librarians used to be wary of small-press books, but they've come to distinguish between them and vanity-press books, and you won't meet with quite as much resistance as you would have in the past.

If you don't care to do all this work yourself, you can try to find a distributor to handle sales for you. There are several distributors these days who are willing to handle small-press books. *Literary Market Place* lists some of them, as does the *International Directory of Little Magazines and Small Presses.* You should also join the Committee of Small Magazine Editors and Publishers (COSMEP), whose newsletter will keep you informed on all aspects of the small-publishing field.

A distributor will buy copies from you at a discount of around 50 percent and sell them to the stores at 40 percent off, making a profit in between. Some distributors are nationwide, others operate only within a specific region. The distributor you sign with will probably want exclusive distribution rights within his area. As with any contracts, get all the details spelled out in writing before you agree.

If self-publishing sounds like something you'd like to try, there are several references that can give you more detailed instruction: *How to Get Happily Published, The Publish-It-Yourself Handbook, How to Publish, Promote, & Sell Your Book,* and *How to Publish your Own Book.* The real key to success in the self-publishing field seems to be drive and dedication; if you're the shy, mousey sort you're probably safer sticking with commercial publishers.

We still believe that your *best* choice as a professional writer is to work through the established publishers who pay you for your writing. We did want you to be aware, though, that for special projects requiring your personal attention, commercial publishers aren't your *only* choice.

11

Record Keeping

Efficient businessmen keep records of their enterprises, both for their own use and for the government's. They need to keep track of inventory, so they'll know what's on hand to sell, what sells best, and who their customers are. They have to know whether they're making a profit or whether their expenses are too great to support their business. They also have to pay taxes on their earnings or be able to claim deductions on their losses.

As we've often emphasized, writers must run their operations as a business if they hope to succeed—and that means keeping records and files. Bookkeeping is a tiresome chore, and nobody enjoys it. Many writers look on it as a distraction from their *real* job of putting words on paper. Actually it's as much a part of the job as typing. A good filing system *saves* you time and energy in the long run because it keeps you from making mistakes or tearing up your office looking for the contract you know was there *somewhere.*

You really need several separate and distinct filing systems. You need to store your work away when you aren't using it and yet have it at your disposal instantly when it's needed. You need to keep track of how each individual piece has been marketed, and what rights have been sold to whom and when. You need to keep track of special dates in the future when legal matters must be handled. If you write books, you need to know how much has been paid in royalties and whether you're due more money. And you need to keep a set of financial records, both for your own sake and to prove to the government that your tax statements are accurate.

There are as many different systems for handling these things as there are writers. Some writers, playing the part of bohemians, keep no records at all and conduct their work on a haphazard basis. Other writers use home computers to keep everything rigidly in place. Most writers fall somewhere in between those two extremes.

In the following discussions, we make no claim that our way is best, and we'll suggest how other people have handled the problem. Since all writers are different, the best system for you is the one you feel most comfortable with. The important point is to have *some* system, and to use it consistently.

Storage

Writers are collectors of paper. It's amazing how much of it can accumulate in even a short time. Rough drafts, final drafts, tear sheets, research notes, outlines, editorial correspondence, copies of contracts, fan mail—all these pieces of paper must be stored somewhere. They should be out of your way so they don't clutter up your desk and your life, but you should be able to find them quickly if you need to check back with them for any reason.

When you're just starting out, a cardboard file box is probably sufficient to hold all you need. Each story, article, or novel should have a file folder of its own, clearly labeled across the top. We use this folder not only for the notes, rough draft, and final draft of the work but also for editorial correspondence dealing with it as well (except for rejection slips, which Stephen Goldin keeps in a separate folder in his desk). You may also want to store a set of "tear sheets" in this folder. Tear sheets are actual pages from the magazine or book in which your piece appeared. The pages are torn out and pasted onto plain pieces of paper. (Don't use rubber cement; it dries out and stains the tear sheets, making them difficult to read.) You may need to destroy two copies of the publication, since your story is usually printed on both sides of a page. If an editor later wants to reprint the piece, you can send the tear sheets instead of a manuscript copy. Since tear sheets usually have more copy per page than a typed manuscript, they're more economical to mail.

Sometimes, if you've got more than one project going with a given editor, a letter may mention two or more works on the same page, and then there is the agonizing choice of *which* folder to file it in. If you really want to be thorough, you could make a copy of the letter for each folder involved—but that way lies madness. (Not to mention very heavy file drawers.) You should keep copies of all letters you *send* (except routine cover letters) as well as receive; you never know when you'll need to refer back to something you said.

We keep copies of all our contracts, agreements, and release forms in a separate folder in a desk drawer beside the typewriter. Book contracts are in a pocket on one side of the folder, short story and article agreements are in a pocket on the other side. They are arranged in the chronological order of their signing. Being all in one location, they're available for quick reference and comparison. Other writers prefer to file each agreement in the same file folder with the work it refers to; that way, all documentation on a given work is located in one place. Other writers prefer to keep their contracts together locked in a fireproof safe. The important point is not *where* you keep them, but that you have a system so that you can find a given contract in a matter of seconds if you ever need to check the details.

A word of warning: One writer we know kept all her contracts in a locked metal file box. One night a burglar broke into her apartment and found the box. He didn't have time to open it then, but he figured it must contain something valuable if it was locked so he took it with him to open later at his convenience. He probably just threw the contracts away when they turned out to be nothing of value to *him*—but the writer had to contact all her editors to ask for copies of the contracts.

After you've filled several cardboard file boxes, you'll probably want to graduate to something better. At this point, we recommend that you move up to a really good wood or metal filing cabinet with *full-suspension* drawers. These are more expensive than cabinets with drawers that just roll in and out without suspension—but file drawers filled with paper become heavy very quickly, and non-suspension drawers have a nasty habit of falling on your feet if they're pulled out too far. We guarantee that after this has happened to you the first half dozen times or so, you'll wish you'd spent the extra money for drawers that work properly. The expense in this case is well worth it.

Kathleen Sky has an office arrangement you might consider. She got a pair of two-drawer filing cabinets, spaced them apart, and spread an unfinished wood slab door over them to serve as a desk. As her files expand, more filing cabinets can be added underneath or beside the desk. This does come out to an awkward height for a typewriter, though. Kathleen dictates her books so this doesn't bother her; if it's awkward for you, a separate typing stand can be added to the assembly.

If you have a long, successful career the amount of paper will stack up incredibly, threatening to engulf you or push you out of your workplace. You might look into the possibility of donating your papers to a university library or other nonprofit institution. This can unclutter your own files and leave the problem of where to store things up to the library that accepts them. Because there is currently no tax advantage for living writers to donate their papers, you simply come to an arrangement with the institution to store the mess for you. If the law is changed at some later date, *then* you can officially donate the papers and get a tax break. If the law is never changed, you can leave the papers there until after your death, and maybe your estate can get a tax break on them.

File Cards

Every piece of work you do has a story of its own. It was conceived and written within a certain time period, it's so many words long, it was submitted to certain editors at certain times, specific rights to it were sold and some of those reverted, it was published in certain places, and you received various sums of money for it. You need a record of all these things to keep track of the work's progress. You don't want to waste time submitting the piece to an editor who rejected it before, and you certainly don't want to make the mistake of selling rights you no longer own (or the equally embarrassing situation of turning down a sale because you thought you'd sold those rights, only to learn later that you hadn't).

The system we use is basically that described in *Science Fiction Handbook, Revised* by L. Sprague de Camp and Catherine C. de Camp. Each work has a file card associated with it similar to Figure 4. The cards are filed alphabetically by title, and contain whatever information you deem pertinent. We like to list the type of work (novel, story, poem, article, etc.), its length, when it was written, where and when it was submitted, what rights were sold, how much money it received, and where and when it was published.

When you're just starting out it's tempting to ignore this work. You've only written a few pieces, and it's easy enough to remember where you sent them all. But if you intend to write a lot, over a period of time, you'll find your memory

"AMATEUR SAFECRACKING"
Article, 5,000 words
Written 8/15/82 - 9/2/82
Submissions:
Felony Pub. (S. Todd, ed.) 9/3/82; rej. 10/18/82
Crime Mag. (ed. unknown) 10/19/82; rej. 12/5/82
Larceny Ltd. (Ben Barker, ed.) 12/8/82
received $100--1/30/83 for 1st N.A. serial rts. &
option on nonexclusive anth. rts.
published in Burglar's Quarterly, Fall, 1983
Reprint House (Wm. Sikes, ed.) 2/4/84
received $50--3/10/84 for 1-time anth. rts.
published in HOW TO ROB RIGHT, 1985

Figure 4. Sample file card.

starting to grow confused. It only takes a few minutes to do
up such a card, and it can be an invaluable time-saver later in
your career. The one simple card will give you a complete
history of the work it represents.

In listing the submission history, be sure to give the *name*
of the editor as well as the magazine or publisher you submitted the piece to. As we've pointed out, editors jump from
publisher to publisher; if your only notation is the cryptic entry that the work was submitted to Really Good Publications
in 1981, you may have to rack your brain to remember
whether Smith or Jones was editor there at that time. If both
of them are now at different publishing houses, which one
rejected it before? Maybe the editor who's at Really Good
Publications *now* might like to see it.

The de Camps also use a system of numbering each manuscript. Every work is assigned an "opus number" in order of its creation. This number is listed prominently on the file card, and the manuscripts are filed in the drawer in numerical rather than alphabetical order. This has the advantage of cataloging your work chronologically rather than by the random chance of alphabetical arrangement. A quick glance at a work's file card gives you its opus number; then it's a simple matter to go to the proper drawer and find it.

Royalty Statements

File cards are an adequate system for recording the income from stories and articles, which usually get flat-fee payments. On books, which earn money continuously as more royalties come in, you might want some more detailed records.

We again defer to the de Camps' method. Each book is listed separately on a piece of looseleaf notebook paper with pertinent descriptive material at the top. There are then columns to list the royalty reporting period, the date the royalty report was received, the number of copies sold during the period, the total sold to date, the total money the publisher paid, the agent's commission (if any), and the net amount you received. You might want to use a separate page to list amounts received because of subsidiary rights, and then summarize the data on the main sheet. Depending on how ambitious you are and how complete the publisher's royalty statement is, you might even break down the sales figures by category and include them as well. A sample form is shown in Figure 5.

When a royalty statement arrives from the publisher, analyze it carefully to decipher its meaning. This isn't always as easy as it sounds. Some royalty reports don't state how many books were sold in the previous six-month period; they just list the total sold to date. By checking your looseleaf summary sheet you can tell how many total copies were sold last

Title: HOME DEMOLITION MADE EASY

Publisher: Catastrophic Press, 999 4th St., Wrecker, NY

Agent: Smith & Jones Agency, 222 S. West St., NYC 10001   Contact: Smith

Nonfiction, 65,000 words

Contract date: 6/30/81

Publication date: January, 1983

Price: $10.00

Major terms: 10% to 5000 copies; 12½% on next 25○○ copies; 15% thereafter;
publisher controls reprint, book club, 2nd serial rts, gets 50%; all
other rts retained; good reversion clause; fair bankruptcy clause;
option on next nonfiction book.

PERIOD COVERED	DATE PAID	COPIES SOLD THIS PERIOD	TO DATE	GROSS REC'D	AGENT'S FEE	NET REC'D
1st ½ of advance	7/15/81	0	0	$1000.00	$100.00	$900.00
2nd ½ of advance	2/03/82	0	0	$1000.00	$100.00	$900.00
Total Advance		-	-	$2000.00	$200.00	1800.00
1/1/83 - 6/30/83	10/04/83	3000	3000	1000.00	100.00	900.00
7/1/83 - 12/31/83	4/10/84	800	3800	1200.00	120.00	1080.00

(includes money for book club sale; see royalty statement)

1/1/84 - 6/30/84	10/07/84	300	4100	300.00	30.00	270.00
7/1/84 - 12/31/84	4/16/84	16	4116	16.00	1.60	14.40
1/1/85 - 6/30/85	10/06/85	4RT	4112	0	0	0

sent letter to Catastrophic on 10/10/85, asking to reprint book or let it
revert

on 1/6/86, paperback rts sold by Catastrophic to Quantity Books for publicatic
in late 1986. Terms: 8% for 1st 150,000 copies, 10% thereafter; $2,000 advanc
½ on signing, ½ on publication; 50% to author.

1st ½ of advance	4/03/86	0	0	500.00	50.00	450.00
2nd ½ of advance	4/08/87			500.0⊕	50.00	450.00
10/1/86 - 12/31/86	4/08/87	10187	10187	0	0	0

Figure 5. Sample sheet of royalty information.

time; the difference between the figures is the number of copies sold (or returned) in the interval.

The publisher's actual royalty report should be filed in the looseleaf notebook behind the summary sheet in reverse chronological order—that is, with the most recent one on top. The reports can then be referred to if the summary sheet doesn't give you the information you need at a glance.

There is no standard form for a royalty statement. Some can be a couple of pages of detailed information; we've heard of others that were nothing more than adding machine tapes with a few scribbled notations. Most fall somewhere in between. Using a three-hole punch you can store them neatly in your royalty looseleaf notebook. (In the case of small slips of paper, you might first paste them down on a regular-sized sheet of notebook paper.)

Tickler File

You must learn to plan ahead. Because a writer usually has several projects going at once, in various stages of completion, it's hard to keep straight all the information you need to organize yourself effectively. Some writers have found that the best way to keep track of important dates when things must get done is to maintain a "tickler" file.

In its simplest form, this is a list of dates when various actions must be taken, kept in chronological order. Some people might keep the notes on a small note pad, although we think a set of index cards is more versatile because their order can be shuffled around if needed. On these cards you list whatever needs to get done, and put the most urgent on top. When that's been done, you remove it, and the next card tickles your memory that *it* requires doing. If you keep the cards up to date, it becomes an effective reminder system.

You might find you need two different files, one for short-term items and another for long-term ones. Short-term items would be things like follow-up letters after a submission. As soon as you mail a submission to an editor, make up a file card for two or three months in the future, reminding you to send a follow-up letter asking what has become of your manuscript. Stick that card in the appropriate place in your file. You can then put that project completely out of your mind and devote yourself to your next work. When that card comes up, if you haven't yet received a reply from the editor you can send a polite note inquiring about the manuscript's fate. At the same time, you make up another card dated one month in the future for sending a second follow-up letter if needed, and so on. (If the editor does reply before the card comes up, simply remove it from the file as being no longer necessary.) This saves you the trouble of constantly checking your files, wondering how long it's been since you sent a given piece to the editor and whether you should write to him. When the proper card comes up, you'll know automatically!

A long-term tickler file is for dates that are several years away, like rights reversions and copyright renewals. Suppose you had a book published on May 1, 1980, and the contract says that if the book is out of print after two years from the initial publication date, you may write a letter to the publisher demanding it be put back into print or else reverted to you. You would make up a card for late April 1982, reminding you to begin a check on whether the book is still in print. If it isn't, you write the letter on May 1 and make up another file card for six months later, when the book should be back in print or else reverted to you. If the book *is* still in print when you first check, make a card for your short-term file reminding you to check again in six months. Keeping a regular watch on it will help you goad the publisher into action promptly.

A similar device will remind you when your copyrights need renewing. If you published three stories in 1970, they'll come up for renewal in 1998. By that time you may have forgotten all about them, and you could lose out on the additional 47 years of copyright protection. Make up a file card dated January 1 of every year in which you'll have work requiring renewal, and list all the works that have to be renewed that year. All the articles and stories can be renewed as a group; each book will have to be renewed separately. By taking care of the matter at the beginning of the year, you allow yourself plenty of time to straighten out any problems that might occur.

This can also be used to remind you of the dates for the automatic reversion, under the copyright law, of any exclusive rights you granted. Make a card up for twenty-five years in the future, reminding yourself that this is the earliest you can send a warning letter to the publisher. If you're still happy with your treatment by that publisher when the card comes up, make a card for twelve years later, reminding yourself that that is the *last* year during which you can send a warning letter.

A tickler file is a good idea even if you have a perfect memory and can keep all these dates straight in your head. If you should die prematurely, your heirs might not know when reversions come due and when copyright renewals are required. Having a tickler file to remind *them* could save your estate a lot of grief and hassle.

Tax Records

In some ways, the most important records you'll need to keep relate to your profits and expenses. Not only do they have to satisfy you, they have to meet the tough standards of the Internal Revenue Service. Just dumping all your receipts into a shoebox and hoping they'll sort themselves out by the end of the year won't work. You have to have some sort of a system.

We keep a ledger book for all income and expenses. Whenever money comes in, we record the date, the amount, what it was for, and keep a running total of the amount received to date. At the end of the year, all we have to do is look at the last figure in the column to find our gross income for the year; we've already done the complicated addition one step at a time as the year went along.

(If your system is working properly, this also gives you a detailed cross-reference check. Your file cards for each individual piece also list income and when it was paid. For books, your royalty summary sheet also lists payments that came in.)

In that same ledger book, we have a separate page for each category of deduction. Whenever we have a deductible expense we list it on the appropriate page, giving the date, an explanation of the expense, the amount, and, again, a running total for this category that makes a year-end summary very simple. If we paid for something by check, we list the check number as reference; if we paid cash, we assign a reference number to the receipt and list that. This way we can document nearly every expense we claim on our tax records.

For example, suppose you buy a package of typing paper, clearly a deductible expense. You paid cash for it and got a receipt. When you get home, open your ledger book to the page of deductions for office supplies. List the date, the nature of the supplies, and the amount you paid for them. Add this amount to the total from your last purchase as the new running total. Give the receipt a reference number. Our system is to list receipts for supplies as S-1, S-2, S-3, etc. Receipts for postage are P-1, P-2, etc. You can probably think of some equally clever method. If you bought some nondeductible items at the same time and they're also listed on the receipt, point to the costs of the deductible items with little arrows.

We keep all the receipt slips sorted in numerical order by

category in a large envelope that becomes thicker as the year progresses. Canceled checks are stored separately. If you enter each expense as you incur it, it'll only take you a couple of minutes to make each entry, simplifying your bookkeeping enormously. At the end of the year, when we send in our tax forms, we make photocopies of them before mailing them off and keep the copies in the same envelope with the receipts.

Some people prefer to keep a tax diary—a bound book in which daily business expenses are entered. Expenses by category may be totaled in the back of the book. If you're having cash-flow problems, a daily breakdown of expenses may help you pinpoint trouble areas.

You'll need every scrap of documentation if you ever have to face an IRS audit. The normal statute of limitations for an audit is three years from the date the return was filed or two years from the date the tax was paid, whichever is later. You should hang on to all records and receipts for at least that long. If you've underreported the amount of your income by 25 percent or more, however, the tax people can ask to see your records for the last six years—so if you anticipate any problems along these lines it might pay to keep the receipts a little longer. There is *no* statute of limitations if the IRS has proof that a return is fraudulent or wasn't filed at all, so watch out.

You can get rid of all the receipts and canceled checks once the time limit has expired, if only to clear your drawers of excess paper. You should, however, keep copies of *all* your tax returns, W-2 Statements, and so on. If you end up doing income averaging one day, you'll need to know what your reported income was for the past four years—and if Social Security makes any mistakes in crediting your account, it's nice to have the W-2 forms on hand to correct them.

12

Taxes

This chapter begins with a warning. Neither of us is an accountant, lawyer, or tax expert. Although we're basing our advice on information from all these sources, it's only intended as a series of general guidelines, to give you some idea of what you'll need to know when you face the maze of government forms and regulations at tax time. Your best course of action is to consult a professional in the tax field. You might not need help every year; but at the very beginning of your career, a tax expert can set up a program for you that will be tailored to your individual situation.

Similarly, we warn you that we're only going to discuss *federal* income tax problems. Each individual state and many local governments have their own systems of taxation that can vary considerably; a general book like this can't begin to cover all the variations. Many states model their forms after those of the federal government, and the same guidelines apply. But even the federal government changes the rules and regulations every year; something that's true when we write it might not be true when you read it. Again, you'd be well advised to check with an expert in your area for detailed assistance.

We're also not going to tell you how to fill out your tax returns in general. We give no instructions for completing

Schedule A if you itemize your personal deductions, nor do we talk about possible advantages to buying municipal bonds. There are plenty of good books published every year to advise you on these matters. Our concern is to show you some of the specialized problems and situations a writer faces when the ides of April roll around.

Hobby vs. Profession

Your first problem may be to prove that you are, in fact, a writer. This isn't always as easy as it sounds. The vast majority of writers only work at it part time and have a regular job that brings in a steady paycheck. Because writing is a field in which it's easy to have large expenses and small income, there's a temptation for people to *claim* they're writers just to register a loss that can be deducted from their other earnings. How can legitimate writers prove they're serious about their work?

The most common criterion is that you've got a legitimate business if it makes a profit at least two years out of every five—that is, if your records for any five consecutive years are examined and you show a profit in at least two of them, the IRS should agree that you've got a legitimate business. If the IRS questions you early in your career, before you've been working at it for five years, you can ask them to postpone their evaluation until you can show them records for five years. By careful management of your expenses—such as by delaying payment on some items until the next year—you may be able to arrange profits in two years out of the five. If you don't, and if the IRS rules that your writing is just a hobby, you may have to pay penalties and interest on the disallowed deductions over that five-year period.

The importance of establishing that you're writing as a profession, not as a hobby, is so you can claim deductions for your expenses. Expenses incurred pursuing a hobby are not deductible, while any income you'd get as a sideline is fully taxable, and you would list it simply as "other income" on Form 1040.

A self-employed person, on the other hand, lists business income on Schedule C and then is allowed to deduct from that all the expenses that are "ordinary and necessary" for the operation of the business. This can often represent a considerable savings.

The taxable income that you must report includes payments, advances, and royalties from publishers; any fees that you get from lectures and readings; and sometimes money that you get as grants or prizes. The rules can be complicated in this last category. If a prize is given to you in recognition of your past accomplishments, and you didn't have to apply or do anything special to get it, the prize money may not be subject to tax. If you get an educational grant, you may be able to exempt part of it per month, but there is a limit of thirty-six months during your entire life when you may do this. If you have any questions as to whether some of your income is taxable or not, consult either the IRS or a tax specialist.

There are a couple of basic decisions you must make about your accounting methods. First is the period you will use as the basis of your tax year. You may choose the regular calendar year, or the fiscal year of July 1 through June 30, or any other year you care to define, as long as you stick with it consistently. Most writers find the calendar year is the simplest, and our discussion will assume you're using it.

There are two different systems of accounting. "Cash basis" is when you list income as of the date you received it and expenses as of the date you paid them. "Accrual basis" is when you list income as of the date it becomes due, and expenses as of the date you incurred them. Cash basis is by far the simpler, and most writers use it. We'll assume that you will too.

Home-Office Deductions

The most complicated deduction for many writers is whether, and to what extent, they can deduct for operating an office in their homes. The government has tightened up the rules considerably, following major abuse by some businessmen who took work home with them, used a desk in one room, and then claimed a deduction based on that. In an attempt to crack down on cheaters, the government has made it harder for legitimate expenses to be deducted.

In order to claim a deduction, an office or other business area must be partitioned off by itself; it can either be a separate room or an area behind a wall divider with its own door. Just putting a screen around your desk won't do. In our case, we have a three-bedroom house and, since we have no children, each of us has one of the bedrooms as a permanent office.

Your work area has to be used for business on a "regular and exclusive" basis. The definition of "regular" is open to interpretation; several hours a week *might* be enough to qualify, depending on how you arrange them. "Exclusive" means what it says; that room may not be used to double as a guest room, living room, kitchen, bedroom, or anything else. It must be used only for business matters: writing, bookkeeping, storing files, etc. The writer who types on the kitchen table or has a desk in a corner of the bedroom is out of luck; but if you can arrange your home to accommodate these provisions, you should be able to declare a deduction.

The Internal Revenue Service has tried to get even tougher on this regulation by saying that a taxpayer can have only *one* principal place of business, and that you're not allowed to deduct any expenses for an office that *isn't* your principal place of business. It further asserts that your principal place of business is the one where you earn the greatest amount of money. In other words, if you earn $10,000 a year at your regular job and $9,999 from writing, your principal place of business is your normal job and deductions for any other place are disallowed. Tax courts have ruled that a taxpayer *can* have more than one principal place of business, but the IRS doesn't always follow the court's decisions. If your office falls within the "regular and exclusive" guidelines and the IRS challenges your deductions, stand up for your rights. The odds are the IRS will be reversed in court, and most examiners know it.

Once you've established that you're entitled to a deduction, the next step is calculating how much it will be. First, figure out what percentage of your home is devoted to business purposes. For example, if your home has a total of 1,600 square feet and your office comprises 400 square feet, then 25 percent of your relevant home expenses are deductible as maintaining your office.

If you rent, the calculations are simple. This percentage of your rent is tax deductible, as is this percentage of your heating and cooling bill and your electricity bill for lighting, electric typewriter, computer, etc. (These expenses are generally listed together as "Utilities" on Schedule C.) You may also deduct this percentage of your homeowner's insurance. The amount of these deductions, though, may not be more than the gross amount of money you earned by writing, because the IRS has ruled that the expenses from an office in the home can't be more than you earn using it. If, for instance, you grossed $1,000 from writing in the year under consideration, your deductions for rent, utilities, and insurance may not be more than that. Your deductions for other categories, however, aren't subject to that limitation.

If you own a home, the calculations become more complex. In this case, the limitation says that your deductions for your work space can't be more than your gross writing income *minus* the deductions you could have taken anyway if the area *wasn't* used for business (like real-estate taxes and mortgage interest, which you could itemize on Schedule A). Let's again quote the figures from our example, where the work area is 25 percent of the total and you earned $1,000 gross from writing. Suppose, also, that you paid $1,600 as a combined total for mortgage interest and real-estate taxes during the year. One fourth of that, or $400, is deducted from the gross income to find the limitation—in this case, $600. Your other expenses for keeping an office in your house may not exceed that amount.

Those other expenses include insurance and utilities, as before, plus some new categories. You don't pay rent, but your house as a whole may be subject to depreciation, and your working area may claim 25 percent of that yearly depreciation in our example. You could also claim 25 percent of the cost of repairs made to the house as a whole, and 100 percent of any repairs made to the specific working area. Suppose your total for these deductions came to $750. In our example, you'd only be allowed to claim $600 worth, and the other $150 would be wasted. (You would also claim the $400 in real estate taxes and mortgage interest, of course.)

Other Deductions

Schedule C lists categories of deductions alphabetically. We'll cover individually those that normally pertain to writers.

Advertising. Although most writers don't pay for their own advertising in papers and magazines, leaving that to the publisher, you might list your publicity expenses—such as special photos—in this category. If you're publishing your own work, be sure to list all the advertising expenses for it here.

Bad Debts. It's generally thought that if you write a piece on commission and the publisher doesn't pay you, that is listed as a bad debt. This is *not* the case, because the money was never listed as income. It should only count as a bad debt if you actually had the money and loaned it to someone who never paid you back. (Or, if you're on an accrual system of accounting, if you listed the money as income and later realized you weren't going to receive it, it might count as a bad debt.)

Bank Charges. If you keep a special checking account strictly for your business activity—which many advisers recommend—the checking fees would be deductible here. So would any other fees paid—for instance, if you pay for a safety deposit box to hold your contracts and writing-related papers *only,* or if you bought traveler's checks for a business trip and paid a fee for them.

Car and Truck Expenses. If you use your own vehicle in the course of business, you're allowed to deduct certain expenses in connection with it. You can figure out what percentage of your car's use is for business purposes and deduct that percentage of depreciation and insurance, as well as gasoline used to drive where you're going. A much simpler way, however, is to use the government's figure for a standard mileage deduction. Simply keep track of the number of miles you drive each year for business purposes—keeping a log of all business-related driving is a good idea—and at the end of the year multiply that total by the per-mile allowance. (Our car has a trip gauge, a resettable odometer that is very handy for figuring how many miles a given trip takes.) The government allowance changes from year to year as costs of operating a car go up; for 1981 it was 20 cents per mile. You may also include such expenses as parking lot charges, toll bridge fares, etc., in this category.

Note, however, that the IRS doesn't allow a deduction for "commutation." If you rent an office outside your home, the drive to and from the office isn't deductible—and if you drive to a business appointment directly from your home instead of going first to the office and *then* to the appointment, that drive may be disallowed.

Commissions. If you have an agent, the usual practice is for him to receive the money from the publisher, deduct his commission, and then send the rest to you. If you report the amount you receive from your agent as income, rather than the *gross* amount, you're not entitled to also list his commission as a deduction. (If you did, you'd be deducting it twice, which the IRS frowns upon.)

Depreciation. This is a complex subject. Basically, if you buy an object for use in your business which has a useful lifetime of more than one year, you can't write off the entire cost during the year you bought it. Instead, you have to deduct part of it for each year of its estimated useful life until it is fully depreciated.

In order to calculate an item's depreciation, you have to know its purchase price, how long you think it will last, and its "salvage value"—that is, how much you might be able to sell it for at the end of that useful life. Estimating an object's useful life and salvage value are guesswork at best, although the IRS does have some general guidelines; ask your tax expert or call the IRS for assistance. Most writers compute depreciation on a "straight line" basis—that is, an equal amount each year until the item is fully depreciated—although other methods are available.

Because an item depreciates most rapidly when you first buy it, the government has a deduction for what it calls "additional first-year depreciation" which may be 20 percent of the cost. Check with the IRS for the rules governing this deduction. Since the government wants to encourage business to invest in new machinery and equipment, you may be able to qualify for an investment credit as well.

Depreciable items for writers are things like typewriters, computers, office furniture, filing cabinets, and books that

---

are to be a permanent part of your reference library relevant to the subjects you write about. (For tax purposes, such books are considered to have a useful life of five years.) If your office is in a house that you own, you may be able to claim depreciation on that too.

Dues and Publications. If you belong to any professional writers' organizations, the dues paid to them are tax deductible. Dues to other organizations are deductible also *if* you need them for your work. For instance, if you write popularized science articles you may belong to several scientific and engineering societies even though you aren't a scientist or engineer yourself. Belonging to such an organization allows you to get their publications and keep in touch with developments in the field—certainly a deductible expense.

Employee Benefit Programs. If you have a regularly paid employee, such as a secretary, your contributions to his benefits are tax deductible. Most writers, though, hire outside help on an individual contract basis and don't pay employee benefits.

Insurance. A portion of your homeowner's insurance is deductible if you have an office in your home. If you pay for any other insurance with regard to your business—for instance, liability insurance against libel suits—this would also be deductible.

Interest on Business Indebtedness. If you borrow money for business purposes or buy some office equipment, like a typewriter, on a time-payment plan, the interest you pay is deductible. If your office is in a house you own, part of your mortgage interest may also be deductible.

Legal and Professional Services. This category would include any fees you pay to the Copyright Office for registration and recordation. If you have to consult with a lawyer on a matter *concerning your writing*—including a will that details your literary estate—the cost is tax deductible. The cost of preparing your business tax forms is also deductible. So is the consultation with a tax expert to set up your record and tax program, as we've urged you to do.

Office Supplies. Paper, pencils, pens, paper clips, staplers, staples, file folders, light bulbs used in your office, erasers, desk calendars, envelopes, carbon paper, typewriter ribbons, correcting fluid, postage scales, note pads—virtually every sort of stationery item is deductible if you use it for your writing. These smaller items are assumed to have a useful life of less than a year, and so can be written off completely when they're purchased rather than being depreciated. Don't forget to include the sales tax in the price of an item.

Pension and Profit-Sharing Plans. This only applies if you have any regular employees. It *doesn't* refer to any pension plan you yourself may have.

Postage. All your postage for business correspondence, answering fan letters, mailing books, and submitting manuscripts is deductible.

Rent on Business Property. If you rent an office away from your home, or perhaps just a small storage space to keep your old files and manuscripts, it's fully deductible. A portion of your home rent may be deductible if you have an office at home. If you lease a car, typewriter, or computer *for business purposes,* it may be deducted here.

Repairs. If you pay to have any of your office equipment fixed—or if the office itself is repaired—in a way that doesn't increase its useful life (in other words, just plain maintenance), the full cost may be entered here. If the repair *does* increase the object's useful life, you may have to depreciate the cost of repairs. If you have a maintenance agreement on any of your office equipment, that's fully deductible. (However, if you have a multi-year agreement payable all at once, the cost is spread out over the number of years of the agreement.)

Taxes. If your state or local community levies any special operating taxes on your business, declare them here as a deduction. A portion of your real-estate taxes may be deducted for an office in your home. If you had any major purchases for business purposes, like a word-processing system, the sales tax you paid could be entered here.

Telephone. If you maintain a special line *exclusively* for your writing business, that phone's bill is fully deductible. If you just use your normal residential line for business calls, keep a diary of what percentage of the phone's use is for business and deduct that percentage of the normal charge. Any toll calls for business reasons are fully deductible, as are credit-card calls and pay-phone calls for business purposes.

Travel and Entertainment. This is another complex category. The government has had to put a lot of restrictions on these deductions because of widespread abuse, but if you know and follow the rules you shouldn't have too much trouble.

If you travel away from home for business purposes, such as to a writers' conference or a meeting with your editor, all the expenses you incur while traveling are fully deductible. This includes transportation, meals, tips, laundry services, shoeshines, hotel accommodations, and so on. The catch is that you *must* be away from your home overnight. If you go to a conference in the morning and come home in the evening, only your transportation is deductible. (The IRS assumes you would have had to eat your meals somewhere, even if you hadn't gone, so they're not deductible.)

There is a tax break if your spouse accompanies you on the trip: You can deduct the amount you would have spent if you'd been alone, rather than half the total for the two of you. Thus, if you and your spouse stayed in a hotel that charged $80 a night for a double and $60 for a single, you could deduct $60 out of the $80 you actually paid. If you can *prove* that your spouse was along for business reasons—say, to take notes for you—you may deduct the expenses in full for both of you. (Be prepared for a hard fight on that one, though.)

If your trip was only partially for business and partially for pleasure, you may only be able to deduct that percentage of the expenses that were for business purposes. The rules on this aren't hard and fast, however. If you were talking with editors and other writers, or doing research for some of your writing, you may be able to prove to the IRS that these business activities constituted "the major part of your activities during your travel," and as such they'd be fully deductible. Check with a tax expert on the details of your individual case.

Travel outside the United States comes under even closer scrutiny; too many doctors and lawyers were holding conferences in exotic countries and then writing off vacations as business expenses. If you travel to a convention or conference outside the country, you may be required to prove that you did indeed attend events in both morning and afternoon sessions, and that the trip was necessary for the pursuit of your business. You're also allowed only two out-of-country conventions each year.

If you travel for research purposes, take plenty of notes. If and when the IRS questions you, it always helps to produce those notes to show you were actually working. (If you can point to a published work you've done based on that research, that's even better.)

On the entertainment side, you may deduct a meal if you treat an editor in hopes of possibly selling something to him, or if you're talking with another writer about working together on a project. You might be able to deduct a party for fellow writers, agents, and editors if it's *primarily* for the purpose of establishing business contacts. You're also entitled to deduct gifts to business associates, with a limitation of $25 per person per year.

Utilities. You may deduct heating, cooling, and electricity bills necessary to maintain your working areas.

Wages. Again, this is only if you pay a regular salary to an employee.

Finally, we come to the category entitled "Other expenses

(specify)." Some of the ones most often used by writers are:

Research Materials. Books that become a permanent part of your research library should be listed as depreciable items—but nonpermanent research materials, like pamphlets, catalogs, newspapers, magazine subscriptions, and so on may be listed in a separate category and fully deducted in the year they're purchased. They must be appropriate to your field of writing, of course; if your specialty is articles on stamp collecting, don't try to write off a subscription to *Science Digest.*

Photocopying. If you pay to have copies of your work made, these expenses are fully deductible.

Educational Expenses. You are not allowed to deduct any expenses you incurred while training to enter a new occupation—but once you're practicing an occupation, any education or training you take to improve your skills is tax deductible. Any courses you take in writing are therefore only deductible if you've previously filed a declaration as a writer.

Typing or Transcription. If you pay someone to do typing or transcriptions for you on a case-by-case basis (rather than as a regular employee), you could deduct the total amount under this separate category.

Casualty Loss. If your business property suffers a loss from fire, earthquake, theft, flood, etc., you may be able to deduct some of the loss that wasn't reimbursed by insurance. Check with the IRS or a tax expert to see whether any deductible applies.

Conference Memberships. If you have to pay a membership fee to attend a professional writers' conference or convention, that fee is deductible. So is buying a ticket to a writing awards banquet. (A guest's ticket might not be, unless you can prove a business relationship.)

Miscellaneous. There'll always be some expenses that don't fall neatly into designated categories; such overall expenses can be lumped together in one place. Clothing usually *doesn't* count. Even if you buy an outfit specifically to wear to a professional conference or banquet, the IRS feels that if you could wear it out on the street as normal clothing, it's not deductible. If your miscellaneous deductions are too large, the IRS might ask you to break them down into individual categories.

Once you've got all your business deductions itemized, total them up and then subtract them from your gross writing income (keeping in mind the limitation on deductions for an office in your home). This gives you your net gain (or loss) from writing during the year. Enter this amount on Form 1040 where it asks for business gain or loss. You'll also have to report this on Schedule SE.

Self-Employment Tax

If you work at a regular job for someone else, your employer pays a portion of your Social Security tax. As a self-employed writer, you have to pay the employer's share as well as your own. This is one of the hidden disadvantages of being self-employed, and many beginners are shocked to learn just how high this extra tax can be.

Use Schedule SE to compute your self-employment tax. Enter the net profit or loss from Schedule C on the appropriate line. If your total net income from self-employment for the year was less than $400, you don't have to pay any self-employment tax and can skip the rest of the form. If your earnings were more, you must continue.

The government has set a maximum amount of Social Security tax that anyone has to pay in a given year. (This amount is subject to variation at the whim of Congress, so we can't quote you a current figure; in 1981 it was $2,762.10, which is the amount you would have paid on an income of $29,700.) If you work at a regular job and had any FICA wages withheld, these may be deducted from the maximum; this gives you an upper limit on the amount of self-employment tax you must pay. The form quotes a percentage by which you must multiply your income to determine the amount of self-employment tax. (Again, this is subject to increase at congressional order; it was 9.3 percent in 1981.) Multiplying that number against your total self-employment income, subject to the maximum limitation, gives you the tax you must pay. Depending on various factors, we've found that this amount can actually be more than the regular income tax. You list the self-employment tax on the back side of Form 1040, along with any other additional taxes you may be liable for.

An important point to note: The amount of self-employment tax is affected only by your net self-employment income, which in turn is affected by your *business* deductions, not your personal itemized deductions listed on Schedule A. There are some deductions that could be listed on either Schedule A or Schedule C—for instance, dues in professional organizations, and real-estate taxes and mortgage interest on your home office. If you want to pay less taxes, it's to your advantage to report these deductions on Schedule C rather than Schedule A, because that will reduce the amount of self-employment tax you must pay.

These figures will enhance your Social Security account so that when you're disabled (which is *very* difficult for a writer to prove) or retired you can collect the proper benefits. There's a provision of Social Security that anyone collecting benefits under age seventy-two may lose some of the benefits if there is any additional earned income. This used to be detrimental to writers because, after a long career, a writer's reputation will be greatest and he'll earn larger royalties on his early works. In 1965, at the insistence of the Authors League of America, this was altered so that royalties from works copyrighted before the writer turned sixty-five don't count as "earned income."

Suppose Arthur Penman turns sixty-five on December 31,

1985. He can continue to receive royalties on all his work that was copyrighted in 1984 or earlier without diminishing his Social Security benefits in the slightest. Money from work that was copyrighted in 1985 (the year in which his sixty-fifth birthday occurred) or later will be subject to the "excess earnings" provision. If Penman works more than fifteen hours a month after that, his benefits may be reduced for each month in which he did the work.

The Social Security Administration has some complex regulations for figuring these things out; if you have any questions, you'd be best advised to get in touch with them. As we're writing this there has also been some talk that the government may raise the retirement age from sixty-five to sixty-eight in order to save money, and that would probably affect writers as well as everyone else.

Estimated Tax

The self-employed writer doesn't have anyone withholding money from his paycheck at regular intervals, which means the writer, not the government, has the use of that money until April 15 when income taxes are due. The government doesn't like this idea, so it has instituted the system of estimated tax payments, whereby self-employed people have to make a guess at how much income they'll receive in a given year and pay taxes on it in advance in quarterly payments.

Basically, if your final income-tax liability is more than $100 over what was withheld during the year, you were expected to pay estimated taxes on it, using Form 1040-ES. The four installments are due on or before April 15, June 15, September 15, and January 15 of each year. (If any of those dates is on a weekend, the deadline is extended until the next working day.) Failure to pay the estimated tax when it's due results in a penalty assessment, plus interest charged on the money between the time it's due and the time it's finally paid.

There are three exceptions that let you avoid the penalty. First, if the total of your prepayments is at least equal to your taxes for the previous year, you don't have to pay any penalty; that is, if your tax for last year was $1,000 and the amount you prepaid this year (through both withholding and estimated payments) came to $1,001, you wouldn't have to pay a penalty if your estimate was low. Second, there is no penalty if you based your estimated payments on last year's income adjusted for this year's rates and exemptions. (This is most useful if there is a large change in either the tax rates or the number of family members you have.) Third, you don't have to pay a penalty if the total amount you *did* prepay turns out to be at least 80 percent of the tax that's finally due. If your total tax is $1,000 and you prepaid at least $800, you won't have to pay a penalty.

Writing is one of the chanciest professions there is, and it's nearly impossible to predict how much you'll make during any given year. Your best strategy, if you're having trouble estimating your income, is to make prepayments totaling one dollar more than your tax for the previous year, which you *do* know. If it turns out, later in the year, that you'll be making far less money than you did the previous year, you can amend your estimated tax and pay less on the later installments—or you can keep on as you started and get a refund at the end of the year, like many other taxpayers. If it turns out that you made more money than the year before, you'll of course have to pay the difference between the amount you prepaid and the total due, but the first exception will spare you from having to pay a penalty and interest.

State and local governments may also insist on estimated tax payments. Check with the proper authorities in your area.

Keogh Plan

You've probably seen plenty of newspaper and TV ads by banks and other financial institutions describing the wonders of a Keogh retirement plan. These plans can provide a good benefit when you retire in addition to a sizable tax break while you're working. A Keogh plan is particularly helpful for the writer who also has a regular job.

Basically this is the way it works: You may set aside up to 15 percent of your self-employment net income or $7,500, whichever is less, in a special Keogh account each year. The amount you put aside is then deducted from your total income on Form 1040; the effect is to lower your adjusted gross income, which is the figure on which your income tax is based. The lower your adjusted gross income, the less tax you'll have to pay. (Again, this doesn't affect your *self-employment* tax; only deductions itemized on Schedule C can do that.)

The catch is that you have to let this money sit in your Keogh account until you retire or become disabled. There are strict penalties, too horrible to mention, if you withdraw any of the money early. You may start taking the money out when you reach age 59½, and you *must* start withdrawing it on a regular basis by the time you reach age 70½.

Between the time you deposit it and the time you withdraw it, the money is earning interest for you, depending on the type of account you have. You can put the money in a bank account and earn steady, solid—but low—interest, or you can take advantage of a "directed" Keogh account that some brokerage houses offer. These directed accounts give you a little more investment flexibility, and you may be able to earn higher interest than you could at a bank. A financial adviser can give you more details relevant to your own individual case. In any event, the interest you earn in your Keogh account is also tax free at the time you earn it.

When you start withdrawing the money from your account—presumably after you've retired—the money you take out is treated as income and is taxable again. The reasoning behind a Keogh plan is that, in your later years, you may be in a lower tax bracket—especially if you've retired from a regular job—and thus the Keogh money will be taxed at a lower rate than it would have been when you earned it. Of course, if you have a successful writing career, your earning power will be even higher in your later years as your reputation builds—but even if your tax bracket *isn't* lower than when you were younger, you'll at least have had the advantage of putting off the tax for a number of years. As any accountant will tell you, the longer you can legally postpone paying a tax, the better off you are.

Income Averaging

Another strategy for reducing your taxes is called "income averaging." This is only useful in special cases when your income is subject to wild fluctuations over a several-year stretch.

The way it generally happens is that a writer has been going along for years at a low income level and then suddenly hits it rich with a best-seller. Income for one year skyrockets, and the writer immediately leaps several tax brackets and winds up owing an embarrassingly high amount of money.

Incoming averaging, which you claim on Schedule G, allows you to spread this sudden wealth over the last four years as well as the present one. In effect, this raises the income level in those past years, meaning you'll have to pay more tax for those years—but you'll also lower your tax bracket for *this* year. If there's a big enough difference between your past and present incomes, this can represent a significant savings.

Incorporation

Many doctors and lawyers legally incorporate themselves to take advantage of certain tax breaks. We've heard of a few writers who have also done this. You must generally be successful and have a high annual income to make it worthwhile, but it's a possibility to keep in mind.

If you incorporate, your writing income is paid to the corporation rather than to you. The corporation then pays you an annual salary, which you declare on your income tax the way regular workers do. The corporation also must pay taxes on the money it makes. Your salary is, of course, deductible from the corporation's earnings, as are the normal deductions you would make yourself for business. In addition, a corporation can deduct certain expenses that you as an individual can't—such as a life insurance policy on you as a key executive, health insurance, and other employee benefits. There are some other nontax benefits, including limited liability for you and any other stockholders. This means that a judgment against the corporation must be paid out of the corporation's funds, not out of your personal account. Corporations also have continuity, and they can be transferred to new owners more easily. Corporations may also have an easier time getting business loans, and they pay taxes at a lower rate.

On the negative side, it can cost quite a bit of money in legal fees to establish a corporation (and also to dissolve it if it doesn't work). There's a lot more bookkeeping involved, and there are legal requirements like stockholders' meetings and financial reports. Incorporation is a serious step and should not be undertaken without competent and thorough legal advice.

Foreign Taxes

Some foreign publishers automatically withhold tax on any money paid to authors unless they're given a good reason not to. If you sell any of your work abroad, this could lead to a situation of double taxation; you pay tax in the foreign country and then again on your U.S. income tax.

To prevent this unfortunate occurrence, the United States

has entered into treaties with a number of other countries to avoid the problem of double taxation. When you sell something abroad, ask your agent (or your editor if you're unagented) whether the country has an agreement with the United States to avoid double taxation. If so, the foreign publisher should provide you with a form which you send to your local district director of the IRS. The IRS verifies on the form that you are indeed a taxpayer in this country. You return the form to your foreign publisher, who then will not withhold taxes from your payment. When his government questions him, he can show them the paper proving that you pay taxes here. This is a roundabout, time-consuming process, but it's better than paying taxes twice on the same money.

Sometimes you'll hear about foreign governments that don't tax writers on their writing income. Ireland is currently the best-known example of this, although we understand that Sri Lanka and Costa Rica have similar provisions. In order to take advantage of this offer, you must be a permanent resident of the country. We know of a number of authors who moved to Ireland to take advantage of this plan. (They don't have to stay in Ireland all the time; they can make periodic trips abroad, as long as their total time away isn't a substantial portion of the year.)

Before you start packing, however, consider this: A United States citizen must pay federal income tax anywhere in the world. Thus, even though Ireland wouldn't tax your writing income, the United States still would. There are a few tax deductions you might be allowed, such as a deduction for excess living expenses abroad, but on the whole, living in a tax haven like Ireland won't reduce your U.S. tax significantly.

If you become successful enough from your writing that state and local taxes grow larger than you like, *then* such a tax haven does offer a unique opportunity to save money. You could also consider giving up your U.S. citizenship—but that's a drastic step you shouldn't consider lightly.

Publicity

If this were the best of all possible worlds, your book would leap off the printing presses and immediately into the hands of a wildly eager public, but this sort of miracle isn't as common as writers would like. What most often happens is that your book comes out and promptly vanishes into a bottomless well of resounding apathy. Your mother has ten copies of it, you've got a copy or two on your brag shelf, and you've managed to talk some friends into buying it. Other than that, nothing. You had assumed your publisher was going to take out full-page advertisements in *Publishers Weekly,* in the *New York Times Book Review,* and in a number of prestigious journals; when this doesn't happen, you sit alone at your typewriter and wonder what went wrong.

The publishing industry fully expects the majority of its products to fail; in fact, something like 60 percent of the books published each year don't earn back their advances. The publishing industry survives on that other 40 percent. These are the best-sellers and the genre books—Westerns, mysteries, romances, science fiction, how-to books, Gothics, cookbooks—that are known to be steady sellers. If you don't fit one of those categories, chances are your book will simply vanish from the ken of man.

There are approximately 40,000 books published in the

United States each year, and yours is only one of them. With this number of books, publishers can't afford to spotlight every one—and even if they did, our minds would be so loaded with the overflow of information that we wouldn't remember anything. A publishing company must decide early on which of its books to spotlight and which will have to be left as orphans.

Creating a best-seller is a complex art, bearing a close relationship to horse racing, tarot cards, tea-leaf reading, and the use of the Ouija board. There are some books a publisher can almost guarantee will get noticed: self-help books covering a new diet, a new religion, a new exercise form—something the author can go on the *Today Show* and discuss in two or three minutes. There's also a very good market in this country for exploitative books which contain a mix of sex, scandal, descriptions of wealthy people, and a few thinly disguised celebrities. Stories about spooky houses or nasty children seem to sell pretty well these days too.

Giving a book a large advance generates its own publicity. When a writer like Mario Puzo, Judith Krantz, or Carl Sagan gets an advance in the millions of dollars, people read about it and think, Well, it must be good. I'd better get a copy.

If you haven't gotten a large advance, and if your book doesn't have some other highly attractive feature, you're likely to find yourself with the short end of the stick. If your book only received a $3,000 advance, the publisher isn't likely to spend upwards of $7,000 for a full-page ad in a major paper like the *New York Times;* it just isn't practical. Publishers invest their promotional energy on books they're sure will earn well. This leaves you with two alternatives: You can either sit in your ivory tower and trust to luck that the book will find its proper audience (and sometimes this does happen despite publishers' inertia), or you can go out and do some promotion for yourself.

Stephen Goldin has a belt buckle inscribed with the saying, "Success comes to those who hustle wisely." This should be the creed of the working writer. Not only must you hustle to sell your book to a publisher once it's written, but you must also hustle to sell your book—and yourself—to the general public after the book is published.

We live in an age when people have a wide choice of entertainment media. Your book is competing, not just with other books but with movies, nightclubs, cable TV, computer games, and all the other forms of recreation at our disposal. A consumer must have a *very* good reason to buy your book, considering all the other things there are to spend money on. You must provide that reason.

You can't allow yourself to coast in this business. Keep in mind the quantity of news the media gobble up and spit out; the star of today's newspaper will be wrapped around next week's garbage. If you're to have any effect at all, you must keep publicizing yourself, keep thinking up new and original ways to get your message across. In *How to Get Happily Published,* Judith Appelbaum and Nancy Evans tell the story of a man who wrote a book about vans. To publicize it, he put a flyer on the windshield of every van in his neighborhood so his natural audience—van owners—would be aware of his work.

You must realize from the very beginning that promotion is hard work. It only *looks* glamorous. It takes a lot of time and trouble to send out press releases, contact local newspapers, and set up speaking engagements. But all this is worth it. Every lecture, each personal appearance on a TV or radio interview show, while taking time away from your writing, is helping to further your career. You must consider it as part of your job. The days of sitting alone in an ivory tower—if they ever existed at all—are over.

Cooperating with the Publisher

A publishing house that hasn't invested much money in a book probably won't go to much effort to promote it. That doesn't mean they're *opposed* to publicizing it; they'd like each of their books to sell if there's a way to do it inexpensively. If you cooperate with them, there's still a chance you can mount some small scale campaign together.

One thing you have to realize is that when the book is published, the editor you've worked so hard to make friends with is no longer in control of it. The book is now in the hands of people in the subsidiary rights department, special sales department, and publicity department. The trick is that, long before the book reaches the final stages, you should have made friends with the people who'll be handling this end of the business. Do it with the same courtesy and politeness you showed to the editor.

Shortly after you turn your book in, you'll probably receive an author's questionnaire asking all about you, your family, your education, your work experience, your hobbies and interests, your professional, religious, and social affiliations, where you've lived, what your book is about, and whether there are any special groups that might be interested in what it has to say. You may also be asked whether there's anyone who might consider giving you a blurb—that is, a promotional quote to use on the cover or dust jacket—and whether you know of any special publications that might be interested in reviewing the book.

The publicity department doesn't send these questionnaires out on a whim, or because some publicist likes reading juicy gossip about the house's writers. This is a legitimate, if formalized, attempt to get a handle on you. Yet most writers fill these forms out grudgingly, if at all.

This is your first—and in some cases, your only—chance to show you care. Seize the opportunity. If there's anything newsworthy about yourself, point it out. If you belong to an organization, suggest that a mention in the group's newsletter might generate some extra sales. Consider carefully the target audience you want your book to reach and let the publicity department know. If there's anything controversial in what you say, by all means speak up; controversy makes news and sells books.

Even if your book is fiction, there are groups it may be slanted toward. If you have a strong female protagonist, perhaps feminists might be interested. If the action takes place in a steel mill, maybe steelworkers would like to see it. If the book takes place in your old home town, perhaps the local paper would play up the fact. (If the book treats the town in a complimentary way, the mayor may even declare a day in your honor.) Examine your work from all angles and see to whom it really appeals.

A strong quote praising your book is considered a good selling tool. If there are any recognized authorities in your field, suggest that the publicity department send them copies of the manuscript (even before the galley stage; the sooner you get your quotes, the better) to see if they'd be willing to give you a blurb. The worst they can do is say no.

The publicity department has lists of review publications that you probably never even heard of and will send copies of your book to them when it's published. But if your book is in a specialized category, you may know of some journals the publicity department doesn't; this includes local newspapers, club or church newsletters, etc. Submit a detailed list of possible review publications along with your questionnaire. The "Media" column of *Publishers Weekly* lists magazines, radio stations, and so forth that are willing to run reviews in various categories. Check also with *Literary Market Place, The Standard Periodical Directory,* and *The Editor and Publisher International Yearbook.* Some places don't do book reviews but might accept a press release about you; either annotate your review list to take this into account or do up a separate list of places that should receive press releases.

Your publisher's subsidiary rights department will try to make book-club and reprint sales. The person handling your book knows about the major book clubs—but again, if your book is aimed at a special market there may be a small book club serving that market. If so, bring it to the attention of the subsidiary rights department. Similarly, if you know of any other specialized markets for your work and the publisher owns the rights to exploit that market, make suggestions to the sub rights people. (Of course, if *you* own those rights, exploit them yourself.)

Most publishers these days have a special sales department. As you did for the publicity department, make up a list of the particular marketing group you think would be interested in your book and discuss the matter with special sales. The publisher might decide the market is big enough to engage in a direct-mail campaign on your behalf; if you've done a book on how to solve crossword puzzles, for instance, the publisher might decide to buy the mailing list of subscribers to crossword magazines and send out an offer through the mail. The special sales department may also think of a way to use your book as a premium for some other company; if you've done a book of chili recipes, perhaps the special sales department can arrange with a chili manufacturer to distribute copies of your book if people send in labels from chili cans. (The chili manufacturer would buy copies of the book from the publisher and arrange the distribution of them itself.)

Whenever you come up with a marketing idea, let your publishing house know. At best, they'll decide to do it and pay for the cost. If the decision is not to do it, ask if they have any objections to *your* doing it on your own. Usually they won't mind, but at least you gave them the chance to do it first. The worst thing you could do would be to barge ahead with something yourself and end up doing it badly, thereby ruining it for both you *and* the publisher.

Press Releases

Even if your publisher distributes review copies and press releases, that doesn't relieve you of the task of doing some publicity for yourself. The publisher's efforts will be toward selling this particular book, but you have a more long-range goal in mind. If you intend to have a career in writing, you'll want to get your name known as well. Only 10 percent of the books marketed each year sell because of the author's name; if you're going to be a success, you want to become part of that 10 percent.

The best tool you'll have going for you is the press release. The publishing house sends some out, and you can send out more on your own. Aside from the time it takes you to do it, the only expenses involved are duplication costs, envelopes, and postage. For this modest investment you can reap many rewards.

The press release is written in a particular format called "inverted pyramid style." This means you concentrate your most important information—who, what, why, where, when—in the first paragraph. Succeeding paragraphs enlarge on the information and add other details and background that are less important. The effect is that of a pyramid standing on its head; all the weight rests on that initial small paragraph, with subsequent layers getting broader and broader.

The reason for this is deadline pressure at newspapers. If the editor chooses to run your release when it comes in, there may not be time to rewrite it much. If there is only a small space for it, the editor will just use the first paragraph and cut the rest, so you want to make sure that opening paragraph contains the most important news. If there is more room, the editor will run more of your release, cutting off whatever doesn't fit. You want to make certain that anything getting cut is less important than the information preceding it.

Your press release should be typed and double-spaced, just like a manuscript, and either photocopied or mimeographed. It should have a release date mentioned prominently at the top, so a paper won't print it prematurely. If you send the release out before your book is published, you don't want people getting interested in it before they can buy copies;

their enthusiasm may have cooled by the time your book reaches the stands. If your press release is sent out after the publication date, you can just say "For immediate release." Your press release should also contain, at the end, your address, phone number, or some other way of getting in touch with you. If the editor is intrigued by your notice and wants to do a full story about you, you want to make it easy to contact you. Figure 6 shows a sample press release.

Once you've written your press release, you must send it to every place you can think of: local television shows, local radio shows, colleges, newspapers, magazines, libraries, bookstores, professional journals, alumni publications, club or church newsletters, and any magazines dealing with the topic of the book. You might even try press releases to places that don't generally publish news; if you've done a book on sports, for example, you might try asking local sporting goods stores to post the notice on a wall or bulletin board. If the store owner is amenable, you might even try for a window display of the book. Even though you've written the press release yourself, the mere fact of its being in print lends a certain weight of its own.

If a review or a press release of yours is published in some local publication, send a clipping to your publisher. Sometimes a show of publicity can garner more publicity; if the publicity department sees there's some outside interest in the book, it may capitalize on that and try to drum up more interest on its own. Besides, anything you can do to convince the publisher that your name is well known will work to your advantage when it's time to negotiate your next deal. Familiarity doesn't necessarily breed contempt in the publishing world; it breeds larger and larger book advances and publicity campaigns. The more notice you get from the buying public, the more value you have for the publisher.

Sometimes, sending out press releases can seem like a colossal waste of time. One writer familiar with advertising has

FOR IMMEDIATE RELEASE

Arthur Penman, a writer living in Freelance, California, has just had his first novel published by Obscurity Press. Entitled THE UNHAPPY YOUNG WRITER AND HOW HE GREW, it is a stirring rendition of the <u>angst</u>-torn life of a young writer dealing with the vicious world of publishing.

Mr. Penman's previous works were UNHAPPY, YOUNG, AND WRITING, a book of essays published by Local University Press, and "How to Write Your First Article," which appeared in <u>Unhappy Writers Review</u>. He has also edited <u>Young Writers Gazette</u>.

Mr. Penman is a member of the Unhappy Young Writers of America, Inc. (U.Y.W.A.), the Fraternal Order of Jabberwocks, and has a Bachelor's degree in Angst from Local University.

Mr. Penman is married to writer Susie Bodice-Ripper, author of the popular "Scarlet Petticoat" series printed by Hysterical Books. Mr. Penman and Ms. Bodice-Ripper will be teaching a seven-week course about "The Unhappy Writer and the Scarlet Bodice" on Wednesday nights at Local University Extension, beginning February 28.

> For more information contact:
> Arthur Penman
> 111 Literary Lane
> Freelance, CA
> (213) 555-1212
> or: Local University Extension Office

Figure 6. Sample homemade press release.

admitted that at least 80 percent of all advertising is totally useless—but you never know in advance *which* 80 percent it is, so you have to do it all. There are other times, though, when a simple press release can lead to vast unexpected rewards—and those times make the whole process worthwhile.

Case in point: We sent out a press release that led to a local newspaper doing a story about us in a Sunday edition. That story was seen by the dean at California State University, Northridge, who contacted us about teaching a class in science-fiction writing. That, in turn, led to our teaching a class on the business of writing—and *that* class led to our writing the book you're reading now.

The same newspaper story was noticed by a faculty member of a junior high school quite some distance from our home, and that led to Kathleen Sky's being asked to address a graduating class at the school. A different press release led to Kathleen's speaking at a local library—and the library itself put out a press release to publicize the event. The librarians even thought of contacting a publication we hadn't considered, the local auto club magazine; this publication was distributed over a wide area and helped generate further attention and interest. Writing a press release can be like dropping pebbles in a lake and watching the ripples spread out as they travel.

Another piece of publicity you can do for yourself is to have some publicity photos on hand. This is especially useful if you have a hardcover book being published, because the art department may want a picture of you for the dust jacket. Readers may be judging you and deciding whether or not to buy your book on the basis of that photo, so it should be something more than a snapshot your cousin took last Thanksgiving. You want it to make a statement about yourself. (You needn't be completely somber if you're subtle. One writer we know of had himself photographed wearing the standard tweed jacket with the elbow patches, seated by a fireplace with a dog stretched out beside him—but it was the dog, not the writer, who was smoking the traditional pipe.)

What you want is a series of black-and-white glossy prints; newspapers and magazines seldom appreciate color photos. If possible, try for shots of yourself in a variety of different poses and clothing styles, so you can pick a shot that's appropriate for different books. We like to go to local museums, historical houses, or botanical gardens to get interesting and distinguished backgrounds. We've found that getting prints in a 4-by-5 size is good because they can be mailed in an ordinary No. 10 legal envelope; you might also have some copies made 8-by-10 in case anyone specifically asks for that size.

If your spouse or a friend is a competent photographer, you can do the pictures yourself quite cheaply and turn the event into a pleasant afternoon's outing. If a local school teaches classes in photography, you might consider hiring a student to do your portfolio at a reasonable price. If you live in an area like Los Angeles or New York, with a high population of actors, you might look into the possibility of going to a studio that specializes in publicity photos; competition may be higher in these areas, which means lower prices. The most expensive option is to go to an ordinary commercial studio and have the photos done.

If you're being interviewed by a newspaper, the reporter may bring along a photographer, who will take pictures of you in various poses while the reporter is interviewing you. If you have your own publicity photos, handing one that you know looks good to the reporter may spare you from the embarrassment of having a possibly unflattering picture printed instead.

Business cards can also be a useful tool. Whenever you want to give someone—an editor, agent, bookstore owner, reporter, a person who might want you as a speaker—your address and phone number, it's much simpler to hand out a card than take time to search for a piece of paper and jot the information down. A local printer can probably supply you with basic cards for less than $20 per thousand; extras like special paper, embossed lettering, or distinctive logos can drive up the price considerably.

You should take care, however, not to hand out your cards indiscriminately. Giving your address and phone number to the wrong people may mean receiving a lot of unwanted attention. Unless you enjoy reading other people's manuscripts for free, never give your card to strangers who say they would like to be writers too, someday.

Professional Image

When you're meeting with an editor, agent, or publisher, you're trying to show that you're a competent professional and know what you're doing. When you're appearing before the general public, you're trying to convince the audience that you have something of interest to say and that they should listen to you. In both cases you're selling *yourself* just as much as your writing; you are as much a product as your work is. For this reason, you have to be concerned about the image you project to others.

Your behavior is an important part of that image. We know some writers who act eccentric, who say and do outrageous things and get a lot of attention that way. Some of them are very successful at it because they do it very well and it becomes second nature. These writers, however, are exceptions to the rule; most people who try to copy them merely end up looking silly. (These people sometimes get trapped inside their images too; we suspect a lot of them would like to get out and relax, but they can't.)

All through this book we've emphasized being polite to editors, publishers, agents, and anyone else who may have some influence on buying your work. You don't have to like these people, or even respect them, but you never know when you may have to deal with them. The old saying about catching more flies with honey than with vinegar is quite true. Making enemies is counterproductive, and you should avoid it.

You also must know how to behave before the general public. You have to tread an even line between modesty about your work and conceit that you're a published writer and they're not. You must be pleasant enough that people will like you and want to read your writing, yet just aloof enough that they won't try to impose on you. (Some of them will if you give them the chance. The worst part is that it's the boors who try to batten off you; the nice people you wouldn't mind doing favors for usually hang back shyly.)

This can be wearing at times. You'll wind up having to be nice to a great number of people who bore you silly, and doing a lot of things you'd rather not do. Just keep telling yourself it's part of your job. That boring person you talk to at an autographing party may someday offer you a large fee for speaking to his club; you can't discount the possibility. Your reputation does get around; if you're known as someone who is prompt, well organized, and pleasant, this will mean extra income and publicity somewhere down the line.

As you become more famous, you'll have to fight the tendency to slough off on this or to ignore the "little people" who helped you. We've known several writers who, after reaching a certain level of fame, became careless about making personal appearances. They would agree to appear at a certain event and then not show up, or even bother to inform the sponsors of the event that they couldn't make it.

This is extremly rude. If you're advertised as being someplace, people may have traveled some distance to see you; the least you can do is be there. If some emergency comes up— an illness, car failure, act of God, whatever—phone the people who arranged the event and tell them. Maybe they can make other arrangements to get you there, or maybe they can find a substitute for you. You might even be able to suggest another writer if you know someone who's available. (Maybe he'll return the favor for you someday.)

One of the most crucial factors in maintaining your image is your appearance. First impressions really do mean a lot. It's a sad fact that no matter how worthy you are, people will judge you first by your outward appearance because that's the most obvious thing about you. It's up to you to make that first impression a positive one.

Most of a writer's work time is spent alone in a room with a typewriter or other gadget which couldn't care less about appearances. Faded jeans and a sweat shirt, or an old bathrobe, or a bathing suit are all perfectly acceptable garments.

When you go out in public, though—either for a personal appearance or a meeting with an editor—you should take care that you look and smell presentable, that your hair is neatly cut and combed, and that your shoes are shined. Make sure your clothing is both comfortable and good looking whether you're sitting or standing, because you'll do a lot of both. Women should wear comfortable shoes; there's nothing worse than standing on your feet for an hour in tight, toe-pinching high heels.

Wear clothing that can be layered. Public buildings are frequently either overheated or overcooled compared to the outside temperature, and you may find yourself going from one extreme to another very quickly. If you're on a publicity tour, having items you can put on or take off at will can help you deal with changes of climate from city to city.

The overriding factor to keep in mind is good taste. You're trying to present yourself as a person of culture who is worth paying attention to. You can get attention by being loud, strident, and rude, but this is the sort of publicity you can do without. Don't present an image that will come back to haunt and embarrass you in the future.

Public Appearances

If your publisher decides your book is worth promoting, the publicity department may set up a series of bookstore autographing sessions and interviews on TV and radio. These can be quite hectic, on the order of twenty-one cities in eighteen days, when you wake up in the morning wondering where you are. If you prepare for the experience properly, you may survive with a minimum of damage. Take vitamins, eat wisely, avoid too much alcohol, dress for the climate, and get enough sleep each night.

There seems to be no middle ground for autographing sessions; they're either very good or they're awful. A celebrity author can generate a line going out of the bookstore and around the block. More commonly, however, you're stuck behind a table and ignored by customers who wander by; sometimes they ask who you are, and you have to explain self-consciously that you wrote a book. Sometimes bookstore clerks take pity on you and get you to autograph a stack of books for later sale. Sometimes, even more embarrassingly, the publisher's shipping department hasn't gotten copies of the book to the site of the autographing, and everyone stands around uncomfortably not knowing what to do. (You can avoid this problem by carrying with you a suitcase of your books, bought at your author's discount.)

Many people want a personal salutation added when you're autographing a book. In most cases, you can just ask the person the name they'd like the autograph inscribed to; you may choose to add a phrase like "Best wishes" or "I hope you enjoy this" to give the autograph a more personal touch. Stephen Goldin frequently dates his autographs and makes a notation of the event where the autograph occurred, which seems to please some readers.

One writer we know had some ballpoint pens imprinted

with her name and the titles of several of her recent books. (We're told that some stationery stores will make up such pens in quantity with three or four lines of printing for a reasonable rate.) When she makes a public appearance, she takes the pens with her. Every time she autographs a book, she gives the pen she used to the person who asked for the autograph. It's a very good way to make sure her fans remember her.

You may choose to carry a supply of felt-tip pens with you; they're easier on the hand and produce a very good signature. Practice your autograph until you have it down to a smooth, even line that you can do quickly. You'll see how important that is when you encounter a situation where you must autograph hundreds of copies of your book; it can hurt after a while.

If your publisher has arranged a series of radio and TV interviews, you should start your preparations far ahead of time. Check with the publicity director; usually a lot of the advance legwork will be done for you, and you don't want to confuse people by duplicating these efforts. If, for some reason, the publicity department has fallen down on the job, there are a few things you can do for yourself.

First, find out whether the shows are live or taped, so you can notify people of when your interview will be broadcast; the more people who know you're going to be on a program, the better.

Second, realize that talk-show hosts are busy people, and don't always have time to read your book. Send your interviewer a brief two- or three-sentence description of what your book is about; this will be appreciated, because it means you won't make the host look like a fool on the air. If your book contains any material that might spark a discussion or controversy, provide a list of pages on which this material can be found; this gives your host a chance to bone up quickly on your views and can lead to a stimulating discussion that may interest the audience in buying your book. Point out specific topics you'd like to discuss; you might even suggest questions for him to ask. (Hosts will usually go along with anything that makes them look knowledgeable on the air.)

Even if the publicity department was on the ball and took care of those things for you, you should still do some homework on your own. Read up on the city you're speaking in, its places of interest and local attractions. This way you can make a comment on an interview show about how you've heard of the excellent local museums, flower gardens, amusement parks, or whatever. This is a warm, friendly thing to do; it gives the impression you care about the city you're in.

If you're going to be on television, pay particular attention to your clothes; there are some problems over what photographs best. For a man, a bright white shirt or certain shades of blue may cause distortion; for a man or a woman, a vivid pattern or a loud color may shimmer and shift, making it uncomfortable to watch. It's best to be tidy and conservative; if the *only* thing the audience remembers afterward is how you were dressed, you haven't done it right.

Try to arrive a few minutes early. This gives you some time to meet the host and maybe discuss briefly what you're here to talk about. It also gives you time to relieve yourself. There's nothing worse than being trapped in front of an audience and trying to hurry through things because you have to get to a bathroom. You might ask if you can have a glass of water handy, too; it's amazing how dry your mouth can become when you have to do public speaking.

If your publisher doesn't line up a publicity tour for you, you can learn to do it for yourself; other writers have. Again, it's something that requires dedication and perseverance, but some people have reported it's exhilarating. If you don't want to do it yourself, you can think about hiring a publicity agent to arrange it for you; a good public relations person, though, can be very expensive.

Lectures are easier to arrange and can be a good supplementary source of income. Keep in mind the various groups that might be interested in your book, and find out whether they need speakers. Many groups are eager to have an expert come in and talk to them; it gives them something to do at their meetings.

Libraries are a good place to start; although they seldom have the budget to pay a speaker, they provide a good practice ground and can generate publicity that will lead to other offers. Make friends with your local librarians. This isn't too hard, since most of them are interested in books and pleased to meet a real author. Donating spare books to their libraries may also help the friendship.

The same rules apply for lectures as for interviews: Go to the bathroom beforehand and make sure you have some water with you on the lectern. It's also advisable to notify a speaking committee before your lecture if you have any particular allergies. Kathleen Sky is often presented with flowers when she speaks and has found it wise to tell committees that she's allergic to roses. If you're hired as a dinner speaker and you're a vegetarian, a diabetic/hypoglycemic, if you keep kosher or have any other dietary restrictions, settling such details ahead of time can save everyone a lot of embarrassment.

Many writers have found it profitable to bring copies of their own works when they appear as speakers. People like proof of having met a celebrity, and they'll frequently buy a copy of your book just to have it autographed. You can buy up remainder copies of your old books that go out of print, and some publishers allow you to use your author discount to buy copies at wholesale. It's a good idea to have someone *else* handle the actual book sales; it's very hard to talk to people and be professional while you're juggling money and books at the same time. Bring along your spouse or a friend, or ask a member of the speaking committee of the group to do the dirty work for you.

Publicity tours, lectures, and autograph parties can be fatiguing, but they can also be fun. Don't let yourself become too addicted to the glamour treatment; it can be a trap that will lure you away from the typewriter. You can find yourself wanting more and more ego caressing, and spending less and less time at the typewriter to earn it. Most writers agree that it's a great deal more fun to *have written* a book than to sit down and write a new one. Don't let your publicity become an excuse not to work.

14

Aid and Comfort

Writing can be one of the most exhilarating jobs in the world. The independence, the creative spark, the sheer rush of energy when you've finally gotten all the words exactly right—these are all ecstasies no drug can match. Your first fan letter, your first acceptance, the first time you see a total stranger buy something you've written, all add to the feeling of having contributed something, however slight, to the human saga.

But being a writer can, at times, also seem like one of the loneliest jobs in the world. During the main part of the creative process there's no one around to get between you and your work, no one to give you the reinforcement that you know will probably come later. It can be a time of great discouragement to some writers.

Take heart. There are indeed people and institutions who want to help. More often than not they take a little digging to track down, but think of it as yet another challenge. With determination and resourcefulness you can usually find the solutions to your problems.

Side Jobs

We've stressed the fact that you're much better off having a full-time job that pays a steady salary while you write part-time to express your creativity. Not everyone heeds that advice, however, and there come times when a full-time freelancer must earn some extra money. How can a writer make quick cash without resorting to the rigors of regular employment?

Many writers lecture. There are always groups in need of good speakers, and many of them are willing to pay. If you're bright, well-spoken, and interesting, you may find yourself making a substantial amount of money on the lecture circuit. If you write nonfiction, you have one or more topics in which you have some expertise; even fiction writers and poets, however, get their share of speaking income.

You can start small. Perhaps your local library would like you to give a talk, or perhaps you belong to some club that would like to hear from you. After you've gained a little experience, you can send a short résumé around to local organizations. As your speaking skills improve, you can widen the area to which you send your résumés and shoot for bigger groups. You might even consider signing up with a lecture agency if your business becomes so large you have trouble handling it yourself.

Poets and fiction writers can also give readings from their work. This is akin to lecturing, but the money usually isn't as good—if, in fact, there's any at all. Bookstores, universities, and cultural centers often have programs of inviting writers down to perform passages from their works. Sometimes you'll receive a small honorarium, sometimes just travel expenses, sometimes only a cup of coffee. If nothing else, you can look on it as more publicity for your work. If you're sharp, you'll bring along copies of your books for sale.

If you can't find anyone to lecture to, you might consider teaching. If you're a professional writer—even if you only have a couple of sales to your credit—you're way ahead of the vast majority of would-be writers. Depending on your level of experience, you might try for a class at a local night school, an experimental college, or a community college or university extension. Teaching is hard work, and it takes a lot of time away from your writing, but it can have some interesting rewards. It was our teaching an extension course, remember, that led to writing this book.

Some universities have a policy of establishing residencies for writers and will pay a salary for a writer to live on campus and teach. The salary might not be much by itself, but as a supplement to your writing income it might be enough to see you through tough times.

In the past few years a program known as Poets-in-the-Schools, or PITS, has sprung up nationwide. Details of the program vary from state to state, but the general purpose is to bring writers into the elementary and secondary schools to interact with students. The PITS program is funded jointly by the National Endowment for the Arts and the individual state arts councils and usually involves at least a small payment to the poet. If there is no PITS program in your locality, you might consider taking the initiative and asking your state arts council to help you start one—although, in these days of government cutbacks, funds for the arts are the first to be dropped from the budget.

Grants and Awards

There are some organizations that don't even insist you leave your typewriter to get money. These are the nice people who give grants, awards, prizes, and fellowships. Some are associated with the government, others are from foundations and private groups. Some go to veteran writers in honor of distinguished careers, others are given to promising newcomers to help them on their way.

The federal government gets involved through the National Endowment for the Arts. The most direct assistance given by the NEA has been a series of grants to writers. These have been awarded every other year throughout the 1970s to poets and fiction writers, the only criterion being that the NEA thought a sample of the writer's work deserved a grant. Erica Jong received one such grant, which helped her write *Fear of Flying*. When one congressman objected to government subsidies of "dirty books," it was pointed out to him that Ms. Jong had probably more than paid back that money to the government in the form of taxes on her best-seller.

The NEA has worked in other indirect ways to help writers, such as by co-sponsoring the PITS program and by giving grants to small, independent publishers of books and magazines who might not otherwise be able to make it on their own. The NEA also puts out a quarterly mailing to inform writers about arts-related bills in Congress.

Many states throughout the country have established arts councils of their own, each operating within a different set of rules. Some states do give prize money to native or resident authors; it can't hurt to ask whether your state is among them.

As we're writing this book the nation is entering a period of governmental budget cutting, and the arts are traditionally among the first to feel the sting. President Reagan has declared that the private sector should support the arts, and this bodes ill for many fine continuing programs. By the time you read this, those programs may have vanished altogether or mutated into something completely different from what we describe.

Some funds do come from the private sector. There are literary prizes for outstanding works in specific categories; these are often given by foundations or writers' organizations. Sometimes a committee gets together and makes nominations, but sometimes you can enter your own work in competition (or have your editor enter it for you). Sometimes even a publishing company will give an award to an outstanding work it published; the award may be a cash bonus, or a large advance against royalties, or a promise to spend a certain amount on promoting the work.

Private organizations also give grants or fellowships to enable a writer to finish a given work that he otherwise couldn't afford to do. There are even some organizations that give interest-free loans or outright grants to writers facing severe financial distress.

Listing all these financial programs is beyond the scope of this book—and they change so frequently that the information would be out of date before it could be printed. For up-to-the-minute information, contact either the P.E.N. American Center or Poets & Writers, Inc. (See Appendix C.)

Writers' Organizations

An individual writer is pretty helpless in the face of the monolithic publishing industry. Alone, you can't hope to challenge some of the more unsavory practices and clauses publishers try to get away with. There are so many people who *want* to be writers that a publisher can always tell you to go away if your demands become too strident; after all, there are plenty more where *you* came from. The individual writer must either give in or go the route of self-publishing and hope for a success.

To combat this helplessness, writers join together into groups for mutual protection. As a group they can exchange market information and let one another know which publishers are trying to force writers into signing iniquitous contracts. As a group they can put more pressure on publishers and educate one another on the practices of the industry. As a group they can lobby for legislation to protect writers' legal rights and win better tax treatment.

Of all the writers' groups we know, only one is an actual union: the Writers Guild of America, which covers the radio, TV, and movie industry. The Writers Guild fought long and hard to establish that position. Its members are considered employees and have deductions taken out of their paychecks. The Guild has a credit union, health and retirement plan, and other benefits that a regular union has. The Guild also has a right to strike to negotiate a better minimum contract for all its members. The Writers Guild is the strongest writers' organization in this country in terms of protecting its members' interests.

There is no organization with quite this much authority for writers who work in the print media. The one with the best credentials is the Authors League of America, which comprises upwards of 5,000 published writers in a voluntary association. The league itself is divided into two branches: the Dramatists Guild (for people who write for the theater) and the Authors Guild (for people who write books, articles, and stories). A member of either branch is automatically a member of the league as a whole. The Authors League can't tell its members to go out on strike against a given publisher; to do so would be in restraint of trade, because the league isn't a union. But the league and its component subgroups can do other things to improve the lot of its members.

The Authors Guild conducts periodic surveys of contracts its members have signed and then publishes the cumulative results. This gives individual writers a chance to see what is standard within the industry and ways in which they might ask for their next contract to be improved. The guild published a model contract, available to all its members, to further educate writers in matters of negotiation. The guild exerts pressure on the publishing industry to correct imbalances that individual writers have no chance of improving, such as more complete royalty statements and elimination of the "satisfactory manuscript" clause in publishers' contracts. The guild is one of the writer's best voices on Capitol Hill in matters regarding copyright, taxation, freedom of speech, and the upcoming fight over public lending rights. Although the guild doesn't act as a legal representative for any of its members, it will often file *amicus curiae* briefs in court cases where it feels an author's rights are being impinged upon.

The Authors Guild covers writers in general and has a large, diversified membership. Other groups, however, have organized themselves around more specific interests. Writers within a given field may have special problems that don't concern the writing community as a whole, and they need their own organization to address those problems.

For example, as science fiction writers we belong to the Science Fiction Writers of America. This organization keeps writers up to date on the state of the art within the genre. SFWA does what it can to publicize science fiction to the general public and presents "best of the year" awards called Nebulas. SFWA also has an effective grievance committee that intercedes in disputes between SFWA members and publishers.

There are similar organizations for writers in other fields: mystery writers, Western writers, children's book writers, journalists, and so forth. A partial list is given in Appendix C. In fact, writers' organizations have now proliferated to the point that an organization of the *organizations* is forming— the Council of Writers Organizations.

Some writers' organizations are little more than social clubs where people who share certain interests may congregate and swap stories; these groups can be very enjoyable for the lonely writer. Other groups are militant about protecting their members from abusive treatment. Each organization has its own rules for membership and admittance. If you see any on the list that are appropriate for you, write to them and find out more. (Be sure to include a SASE, of course.) You may end up meeting some interesting people and learning new things about your chosen profession.

Other Resources

Poets & Writers, Inc., is a publicly supported service organization which provides useful information to and about writers. It is funded by the National Endowment for the Arts, the New York State Council on the Arts, and private contributions. Although its specific intent is to help fiction writers and poets, even nonfiction writers can make use of its services.

Poets & Writers issues a number of publications for writers. One is *Coda,* a magazine published five times a year to which anyone may subscribe; not only does it carry up-to-the-minute news on awards and grants being offered and how to apply for them, but also listings of teaching positions open, small magazines looking for submissions, and other useful information. *Coda* has also run feature articles on marketing manuscripts, publicizing your work, taxes for writers, wills and estates, and a number of other subjects. Reprints of some of the best articles from *Coda* are available separately at reasonable prices.

In addition to *Coda,* Poets & Writers publishes very informative and detailed booklets on copyright, literary agents, organizations that give awards, organizations that sponsor readings, and other fascinating topics, as well as an annual directory of American fiction writers and poets so that people who want to reach them can do so. Any professionally published poet or fiction writer can get a free listing in the directory; call the organization (212-757-1766) for details on how you may qualify. (Writers who are listed in the directory get cheaper rates for buying some of the publications, including a reduced subscription rate on *Coda.* A few of the publications are even free for listed writers.)

P.E.N. American Center is a by-invitation-only association of writers of literary merit, plus distinguished editors and agents. In addition to holding literary events, P.E.N. publishes *The P.E.N. Newsletter,* to which nonmembers may subscribe, and *Grants and Awards Available to American Writers,* which is self-explanatory. P.E.N also issues awards of its own each year in nine different categories.

As we've indicated throughout this book, there are many occasions when a writer may need a lawyer to straighten out a tangled situation. We all know that lawyers are expensive, and a beginning writer without much money is at a disadvantage. Several groups of attorneys have banded together to offer their services to impoverished authors. Depending on which area of the country you live in, check with Volunteer Lawyers for the Arts, Lawyers for the Creative Arts, or Bay Area Lawyers for the Arts; their addresses are given in Appendix C. Volunteer Lawyers for the Arts has also published a booklet entitled "Fear of Filing" to help artists and writers cope with tax problems.

When the pressures of the outside world become too great, some writers feel they need to Get Away From It All in order to create more freely. There are places called writers' colonies designed specifically for that purpose. Most of them are located out in the country, away from city tensions, where writers can hole up in little bungalows and be alone with their thoughts and a typewriter. Some of these colonies are free, others charge a nominal sum for room and board. Many of these places have a long waiting list; check with Poets & Writers to find out where some likely writers' colonies are and how you can apply.

If you don't want to be lonely, you can sign up for a writers' conference. Dozens, if not hundreds, of them are held around the country each year, attended by scores of beginners and hopeful would-be writers. Established professionals come to share their knowledge and to answer pointed questions like "How do I submit a manuscript?", "How do I keep editors from stealing my ideas?", and the ever-popular "How do I get an agent?" We don't mean to make fun of these conferences; we've taught at several, and they do serve a useful purpose. After you've been to one, surrounded by people who all have a passionate urge to write, you become filled with energy and return home brimming over with concepts you *must* put down on paper. *Literary Market Place* lists some of the major conferences held each year; the writers' magazines and Poets & Writers can help you locate some others.

Most beginning writers are familiar with the magazines *Writer's Digest* and *The Writer.* Both magazines feature articles on how to write as well as market reports, news of the publishing world, and so on. Many libraries subscribe to them if you don't want to go to the expense yourself. Beware of the ads from vanity-press publishers and fee-charging agents.

We'd like to recommend a couple of magazines you're not likely to hear of because they're off the beaten track. Both of them are aimed at a very specialized audience, and for this reason they aren't carried by many libraries.

One is *The Bulletin of the Science Fiction Writers of America,* which is the official newsletter of the SFWA (and of which Stephen Goldin was once editor). It is, of course, directed primarily toward people who write science fiction, but it does carry articles that are helpful to all writers, regardless of genre. The fine explanatory booklet on the SFWA Model Paperback Contract was originally published as a series of articles in the *Bulletin.* Contact the Executive Secretary of SFWA for subscription information. (See Appendix C.)

The other publication is *Empire SF,* a small magazine also oriented specifically toward the would-be science-fiction writer—and again, it contains fine articles and information on freelance writing in general that many writers in other fields will find useful. The address is listed in Appendix C; write to them for subscription information.

Conclusion

Writing is the only art form that people think they can do without any practice or training. No one thinks he can be a sculptor just by taking a chisel to a piece of marble; no one becomes a ballet dancer just by donning a pair of tights. But writing is somehow different. After all, everyone had to write book reports and essays in school; what's so hard about that?

Beginning writers—and even some experienced ones who should know better—make mistakes. Some of these errors are laughable, some are pitiful, and some are truly tragic. There is a vast field of ignorance in which neophytes are constantly getting lost. No single work can obliterate that ignorance, but there *is* help out there if you know where to look for it. We hope our book will help you avoid some of the worst mistakes; if it does, then it was worth the writing.

Appendix A

When making changes in a manuscript, you only need to make the changes in the text itself. When correcting galley proofs, however, you should make two sets of marks. First, make the correction in the text itself; then make a notation in the margin beside the line in which a correction occurs to call attention to it.

IN MARGIN   **IN TEXT**

        delete letter/

        delete word ~~word~~

        delete and clo∮se space

        no sp⌢ace

        insert∧space

        insert period∧

        insert comma∧

        insert semicolon∧

IN MARGIN	IN TEXT
;	insert colon $_\wedge$
？	insert apostrophe
❝ / ❞	insert $_\wedge$ quotation marks $_\wedge$
=	insert hyphen
⊢/m	insert dash
e	insert lettr $_\wedge$
the	insert $_\wedge$ word
²⌄	insert superscript e=mc $_\wedge$
(spell)	spell out number ②‍
2	write number (two) as figure
lc/	SET in lowercase letters
cap/	set in capital letters
sc	set in small capitals
ital	set in italics
rom	set in (roman) type
bf	set in boldface type
lf	set in (lightface) type

IN MARGIN   IN TEXT

stet //   leeve as printed; do ~~not~~ make indicated cor-
             rection

tr   transpose lette(rs)

tr   \words\transpose '

             $\overrightarrow{\text{lines}}$
tr   (transpose

¶   ¶ make new paragraph

no ¶   no new paragraph

run in   run into last line

[[move left

]   ] move right

⌐ / ⌐   move ⌐ or $\underline{\text{down}}$
             up

(ɔ)   revers(e)

tr | # | *r* | o   tow or more corections per line

Appendix B

COPYRIGHT INFORMATION

Matters of copyright should be mailed to the Copyright Office at this address:

> Register of Copyrights
> Copyright Office
> Library of Congress
> Washington, DC 20559

If you wish to call about some business, use the following telephone numbers:

> Public Information Office: 202–287-8700
> Certifications and Documents Section: 202–287-6787
> Reference and Bibliography Section: 202–287-6850
> Licensing Division: 202–287-8130

If you want to visit in person, the Copyright Office is located in the James Madison Memorial Building on Independence Avenue between First and Second Streets SE in Washington, DC.

The Copyright Office will provide the following circulars and forms (each form with its instructions included) free of charge:

FORM TX: *Application for Copyright Registration for a Nondramatic Literary Work.* This is the basic application for registering works in the print media. (To register works in the performing arts, use Form PA; for works in the visual arts, Form VA; for sound recordings, Form SR.)

FORM GR/CP: *Adjunct Application for Copyright Registration for a Group of Contributions to a Periodical.* Use this form if you qualify to register a group of contributions all published within a twelve-month period; this form must be used together with a copy of Form TX, PA, or VA.

FORM CA: *Application for Supplementary Copyright Registration.* Use this form if you need to correct or amplify any information on a work that's already been registered.

FORM RE: *Application for Renewal Registration.* This is for renewing the registration on a work originally published between 1950 and 1978.

FORM IS: *Request for Issuance of an Import Statement.* Use this form if you own rights to a work that was printed abroad and you want to import it.

CIRCULAR R1: *Copyright Basics*

CIRCULAR R1E: *The Certification Space of the Application Form*

CIRCULAR R7B: *"Best Edition" of Published Copyrighted Works for the Collections of the Library of Congress*

CIRCULAR R8: *Supplementary Copyright Registration*

CIRCULAR R15: *Renewal of Copyright*

CIRCULAR R15A: *Duration of Copyright Under the New Law*

CIRCULAR R21: *Copyright and the Librarian*

CIRCULAR R22: *How to Investigate the Copyright Status of a Work*

CIRCULAR R31: *Ideas, Plans, Methods or Systems (What Can and Cannot Be Copyrighted)*

CIRCULAR R60A: *Registration for Periodicals on Form TX*
CIRCULAR R63: *Reproductions of Copyrighted Works for the Blind and Physically Handicapped*
CIRCULAR R99: *Highlights of the New Copyright Law*

TAX INFORMATION

Questions about taxes should be directed at your own financial adviser or your local District Director of the Internal Revenue Service. The following forms and publications of use to writers are available free from your District Director:

PUBLICATION 17: *Your Federal Income Tax*
PUBLICATION 54: *Tax Guide for U.S. Citizens Abroad*
PUBLICATION 334: *Tax Guide for Small Business*
PUBLICATION 463: *Travel, Entertainment, and Gift Expenses*
PUBLICATION 506: *Income Averaging*
PUBLICATION 533: *Self-Employment Tax*
PUBLICATION 534: *Depreciation*
PUBLICATION 545: *Interest Expense*
PUBLICATION 552: *Recordkeeping Requirements*
PUBLICATION 587: *Business Use of Your Home*
SCHEDULE C: for self-employment income and deductions
SCHEDULE G: for income averaging
SCHEDULE SE: for computing self-employment tax
FORM 1040-ES: for making estimated tax payments
FORM 2210: for use if you underpaid your estimated tax
FORM 3468: for computing investment credit if you bought equipment

Appendix C

ADDRESSES OF INTEREST
(subject to change without notice)

WRITERS' ORGANIZATIONS

The Academy of American Poets
 177 East 87th Street, New York, NY 10028
American Academy and Institute of Arts and Letters
 633 West 155th Street, New York, NY 10032
American Auto Racing Writers and Broadcasters Association
 922 North Pass Avenue, Burbank, CA 91505
The American Guild of Authors and Composers
 40 West 57th Street, New York, NY 10019
American Medical Writers Association
 5272 River Road, Suite 370, Bethesda, MD 20016
American Society of Composers, Authors, and Publishers (ASCAP)
 1 Lincoln Plaza, New York, NY 10023
American Society of Journalists and Authors, Inc.
 1501 Broadway, Room 1907, New York, NY 10036
The American Society of Writers
 890 National Press Building, Washington, DC 20045
American Translators Association
 P.O. Box 129, Croton-on-Hudson, NY 10520
Associated Business Writers of America, Inc.
 1450 South Havana Street, Aurora, CO 80012

The Authors League of America, Inc.
    234 West 44th Street, New York, NY 10036
    (includes Authors Guild and Dramatists Guild)
Aviation/Space Writers Association
    Cliffwood Road, Chester, NJ 07930
Boxing Writers Association
    270 Broadway, New York, NY 10007
Canadian Authors Association
    24 Ryerson Avenue, Toronto, ON M5T 2P3, Canada
Construction Writers Association
    202 Homer Building, Washington, DC 20005
Copywriter's Council of America
    Box 102 DMS, Middle Island, NY 11953
Council for the Advancement of Science Writing, Inc.
    Northwestern University, Evanston, IL 60201
Council of Writers Organizations
    c/o American Society of Journalists and Authors
    1501 Broadway, New York, NY 10036
Dog Writers' Association of America, Inc.
    3 Blythewood Road, Doylestown, PA 18901
Education Writers Association
    P.O. Box 281, Woodstown, NJ 08098
Feminist Writers' Guild
    P.O. Box 9396, Berkeley, CA 94709
The Football Writers Association of America
    P.O. Box 1022, Edmond, OK 73034
Garden Writers Association of America, Inc.
    680 Third Avenue, Troy, NY 12182
International Association of Business Communicators
    870 Market Street, Suite 469, San Francisco, CA
    94102
International Guild of Craft Journalists, Authors, and
    Photographers
    3632 Ashworth Street North, Seattle, WA 98103

The International Women's Writing Guild
    Caller Box 810, Gracie Station, New York, NY 10028
Music Critics Association, Inc.
    6201 Tuckerman Lane, Rockville, MD 20852
Mystery Writers of America, Inc.
    105 East 19th Street, New York, NY 10003
National Association of Gagwriters
    74 Pullman Avenue, Elberon, NJ 07740
National Association of Home and Workshop Writers
    27861 Natoma Road, Los Altos, CA 94022
National Association of Science Writers, Inc.
    P.O. Box 294, Greenlawn, NY 11740
The National Book Critics Circle, Inc.
    P.O. Box 6000, Radio City Station, New York, NY 10019
National Turf Writers Association
    Willco Building, Suite 317, 6000 Executive Boulevard, Rockville, MD 20852
The National Writers Club, Inc.
    1450 South Havana Street, Suite 620, Aurora, CO 80012
Newspaper Farm Editors of America
    4200 12th Street, Des Moines, IA 50313
Outdoor Writers Association of America, Inc.
    4141 West Bradley Road, Milwaukee, WI 53209
P.E.N. American Center
    47 Fifth Avenue, New York, NY 10003
Pen and Brush Club
    16 East Tenth Street, New York, NY 10003
The Poetry Society of America
    15 Gramercy Park, New York, NY 10003
Religion Newswriters Association
    1100 Broadway, Nashville, TN 37202

Rocky Mountain Outdoor Writers and Photographers
>   1111 Morningside Drive NE, Albuquerque, NM
>   87110

Science Fiction Writers of America, Inc.
>   68 Countryside Apartments, Hackettstown, NJ 07840

Society of American Social Scribes
>   c/o *The Plain Dealer,* 1801 Superior Avenue, Cleve-
>   land, OH 44114

Society of American Travel Writers
>   1120 Connecticut Avenue NW, Suite 940, Washing-
>   ton, DC 20036

Society of Children's Book Writers
>   P.O. Box 296, Mar Vista Station, Los Angeles, CA
>   90066

Teacher Author League of America
>   177 White Plains Road, Suite 60-F, Tarrytown, NY
>   10591

United States Harness Writers Association, Inc.
>   P.O. Box 10, Batavia, NY 14020

Washington Independent Writers Association, Inc.
>   1057 National Press Building, Washington, DC 20045

Western Writers of America, Inc.
>   Route 1, Box 35H, Victor, MT 59875

Writers Guild of America, Inc.
>   *East:* 555 West 57th Street, New York, NY 10019
>   *West:* 8955 Beverly Boulevard, Los Angeles, CA
>   90048

The Writers' Union of Canada
>   86 Bloor Street West, Suite 514, Toronto, ON M5S
>   1M5, Canada

OTHER ORGANIZATIONS

Bay Area Lawyers for the Arts
>   Fort Mason Center Building 310, San Francisco, CA
>   94123

R. R. Bowker Company
    1180 Avenue of the Americas, New York, NY 10036
Committee of Small Magazine Editors and Publishers
    (COSMEP)
    P.O. Box 703, San Francisco, CA 94101
Coordinating Council of Literary Magazines
    80 Eighth Avenue, New York, NY 10011
Dustbooks
    P.O. Box 1056, Paradise, CA 95969
Empire SF
    P.O. Box 967, New Haven, CT 06504
Independent Literary Agents Association
    c/o Elaine Markson Literary Agency, Inc., 44 Green-
    wich Avenue, New York, NY 10011
Lawyers for the Creative Arts
    111 North Wabash Avenue, Chicago, IL 60602
National Endowment for the Arts
    2401 E Street NW, Washington, DC 20506
Poets & Writers, Inc.
    201 West 54th Street, New York, NY 10019
Society of Authors' Representatives, Inc.
    P.O. Box 650, Old Chelsea, New York, NY 10113
Volunteer Lawyers for the Arts
    36 West 44th Street, New York, NY 10036

Bibliography

Appelbaum, Judith, and Nancy Evans. *How to Get Happily Published.* New York: Harper & Row, 1978. Especially good on marketing, self-publishing, promotion, and where to go for assistance.

Balkin, Richard. *A Writer's Guide to Book Publishing.* New York: E. P. Dutton/Hawthorn Books, 1977. How the publishing industry goes from manuscript to printed book, including sales and distribution.

Books in Print. New York: R. R. Bowker Co., published annually.

Burack, A. S., ed. *The Writer's Handbook.* Boston, MA 02116: The Writer, Inc. (8 Arlington Street). Published annually. Essays on writing, market reports, addresses.

Cassill, Kay. *The Complete Handbook for Freelance Writers.* Cincinnati, OH 45242: Writer's Digest Books (9933 Alliance Road), 1981.

Chickering, Robert B., and Susan Hartman. *How to Register a Copyright and Protect Your Creative Work.* New York: Charles Scribner's Sons, 1981.

Crawford, Tad. *The Writer's Legal Guide.* New York: E. P. Dutton/Hawthorn Books, 1977. Outstanding reference on legal aspects of writing: copyright, contracts, libel, taxes, wills.

de Camp, L. Sprague, and Catherine C. de Camp. *Science Fiction Handbook, Revised.* Philadelphia, PA 19101: Owlswick Press (Box 8243), 1975. Though mostly devoted to writing science fiction, it contains good practical advice on writing in general and an excellent record-keeping system.

Directory of Small Magazine/Press Editors and Publishers. Paradise, CA: Dustbooks, published annually.

The Editor and Publisher International Yearbook. New York, NY 10022: Editor and Publisher (575 Lexington Avenue), published annually.

Emerson, Connie. *Write on Target.* Cincinnati, OH 45242: Writer's Digest Books (9933 Alliance Road), 1981. Devoted specifically to strategies for marketing manuscripts.

"Fear of Filing." New York: Volunteer Lawyers for the Arts, 1978. Updated periodically; guide to income tax for writers and artists.

Greenfeld, Howard. *Books: From Writer to Reader.* New York: Crown Publishers, 1976. Step-by-step account of the printing process from manuscript to finished book.

Henderson, Bill, ed. *The Publish-It-Yourself Handbook: Literary Tradition and How-To.* New York: Harper & Row, 1980. Essays on how many different people have published their own books and magazines.

Herron, Caroline Rand. "How to Give an Unsolicited Manuscript Its Best Chance," *Coda: Poets & Writers Newsletter,* Vol. 6, No. 5 (June/July 1979). Manuscript preparation and marketing.

_____. "A Writer's Guide to Federal Income Taxes," *Coda: Poets & Writers Newsletter,* Vol. 7, No. 3 (February/March 1980).

How to Publish, Promote & Sell Your Book. Chicago, IL 60602: Adams Press (30 West Washington Street), 1971.

International Directory of Little Magazines and Small Presses. Paradise, CA: Dustbooks, published annually.

Literary Market Place. New York: R. R. Bowker Co., published annually.

MacCampbell, Donald. *The Writing Business.* New York: Crown Publishers, 1978.

A Manual of Style. Chicago: University of Chicago Press, frequent revisions. Considered one of the top style guides in publishing.

Mayer, Debby. "On Giving Readings—A Checklist for Writers," *Coda: Poets & Writers Newsletter,* Vol. 6, No. 1 (September/October 1978).

_____. "The Writer's Will," *Coda: Poets & Writers Newsletter,* Vol. 6, No. 4 (April/May 1979).

Meredith, Scott. *Writing to Sell.* Second revised edition. New York: Harper & Row, 1977.

Molloy, John T. *Dress for Success.* New York: Warner Books, 1977. A guide for men on dressing to improve image.

_____. *The Woman's Dress for Success Book.* New York: Warner Books, 1978. A guide for women on dressing to improve image.

Mueller, L. W. *How to Publish Your Own Book.* Detroit, MI 48203: Harlo Press (1672 Hamilton), 1976. A step-by-step guide to self-publishing.

Nicholson, Margaret. *A Practical Style Guide for Authors and Editors.* New York: Holt, Rinehart and Winston, 1967. Simple, no-nonsense style guide.

Poets & Writers, Inc. "Awards List." New York: Poets & Writers, 1978.

A list of grants, fellowships, and prizes offered to writers in the United States.

————. "Literary Agents: A Complete Guide." New York: Poets & Writers, 1978. Outstanding booklet about agents.

————. "The Quest for a Publisher—A Guide to Writers' Market References," *Coda: Poets & Writers Newsletter,* Vol. 6, No. 2 (November/December 1978). Analyzes reference volumes used for marketing.

————. *A Writer's Guide to Copyright.* New York: Poets & Writers, 1979. Good basic booklet on copyright.

Rees, Clair. *Profitable Part-Time/Full-Time Free-lancing.* Cincinnati: Writer's Digest Books, 1980.

Richardson, Nelson. "New Copyright Law Now in Effect," *Coda: Poets & Writers Newsletter,* Vol. 5, No. 3 (February/March 1978).

Sillen, Samuel. *The Standard Handbook of Style.* New York: Grosset & Dunlap, 1963.

Skillin, Marjorie E., and Robert M. Gay. *Words into Type,* third ed. Englewood Cliffs, NJ: Prentice-Hall, 1974. Outstanding style guide for manuscript preparation.

Small Press Record of Books in Print. Paradise, CA: Dustbooks, published annually.

Spinrad, Norman. *The SFWA Model Paperback Contract.* Hacketts-town, NJ: Science Fiction Writers of America, 1980. Outstanding analysis of a model contract.

The Standard Periodical Directory. New York, NY 10016: Oxbridge Communications (183 Madison Avenue), published annually.

Strunk, William, Jr., and E. B. White. *The Elements of Style.* New York: Macmillan, frequent revisions. The single most respected style guide in publishing.

Thomas, David St. John, and Hubert Bermont. *Getting Published.* New York: Harper & Row, 1973. Preparing and selling nonfiction books.

Writer's Market. Cincinnati: Writer's Digest Books, published annually. Contains many market reports, useful addresses.

Index